robinson jeffers: poet of inhumanism

robinson jeffers

1887-1962.

poet
of
inhumanism

arthur b. coffin

the university of wisconsin press
madison
milwaukee
london

Published 1971
The University of Wisconsin Press
Box 1379, Madison, Wisconsin 53701

The University of Wisconsin Press, Ltd.
27–29 Whitfield Street, London, W.1

First printing

Printed in the United States of America
George Banta Company, Inc., Menasha, Wisconsin

ISBN 0-299-05840-9; LC 74-121767

for
gertrude and cathleen,
who have waited

contents

preface

In the short poem *Theory of Truth,* Robinson Jeffers argues that "only tormented persons want truth." Only if the mind is powerful enough and if "tortured by some interior tension" leading to despair of happiness will it learn to disdain its "life-cage" and seek further for truth. I do not wish to suggest that Jeffers' was a tortured mind, but clearly he wrestled long and hard with truth.

Originally this book was to be a study of the patterns of ideas in the work of Robinson Jeffers, for I wanted to discover what ideologies contributed to the matrix of the poet's work—what philosophical concepts and postures of intellect influenced his poetic statements. I had no desire at the outset to analyze Jeffers' Inhumanism, which I thought had perhaps already been sufficiently studied, but as my work progressed I found that the patterns of ideas which I followed led me to a consideration of the genesis of his Inhumanism. This account of the ideological growth manifest in Jeffers' work should illuminate, I hope, some of the interior tensions—the dynamics of intellect—that lie within the poems, as well as the objectives which the poet pursued. I believe that there is much more to examine in the poet and his work, and I urge further study in such areas as religion and psychology. In the chronological listing immediately following, which gives the volumes of Jeffers' work and their contents (excluding those of *Flagons and Apples* and *Californians*), the reader will find the volume short titles which are used throughout the book. Quotations in the text from the long narrative poems—and from those short poems exceeding five pages—are accompanied by the appropriate volume short title and page reference in parentheses. The volumes in which the shorter poems appear can be determined by referring to the index. The reader should note, too, that the following poems were included in *The Selected Poetry of Robinson Jeffers,* but do not appear in the major volumes mentioned in the chronological list (as indicated, two of them also appear in the paperbound *Robinson Jeffers, Selected Poems* [1965]): *Apology for Bad Dreams (Poems), Ante Mortem, Post Mortem, Summer Holiday (Poems), Decaying Lambskins, Shiva, Now Returned Home,* and *Theory of Truth.* A final technical matter remains to be mentioned. Inevitably there are many instances of ellipsis in the quotations from Jeffers and other sources, and these have been acknowledged by the use of regular points of ellipsis. It is one of Jeffers' idiosyncrasies of style, however, to use occasionally three periods, where Poe or Emily Dickinson might have used a dash. In such cases, I have acknowledged this feature of his style by three close-set suspension points.

To the many critics of Jeffers before me, I owe a large debt, for I have gained much from their labors. I am grateful, too, for the labor on my behalf of the staffs of the Memorial Library at the University of Wisconsin, Occidental College Library, the New York Public Library, the San Francisco Public Library, the University of Washington Library, the University of Idaho Library, and the Holland Library at Washington State University. Among the people interested in the book who gave me assistance I want especially to mention Tyrus G. Harmsen, Donnan and Lee Jeffers, Ward Ritchie, and the editors of the *Robinson Jeffers Newsletter* (formerly Melba Berry Bennett and presently Robert J. Brophy). I am also indebted to Donnan Jeffers for permission to quote from his letter to me. To my colleague Don Ross, who read and criticized an early version of the book's first chapter, and to Katie Johnson and Edith Hilliard, who helped with part of the typing, I wish to express my appreciation.

This work was begun several years ago under the humane supervision and encouraging leadership of Walter B. Rideout; what my book and I owe this gentleman beggars summary. Another debt that cannot be summarized is noted in the dedication.

Arthur B. Coffin

February 1970

chronological list of the works of robinson jeffers

Short title and contents are indicated where appropriate.

1912
Flagons and Apples. Los Angeles: Grafton Publishing Co.

1916
Californians. New York: The Macmillan Co.

1925
Roan Stallion, Tamar and Other Poems. New York: Boni & Liveright. (*RS, T*)

Roan Stallion	People and a Heron
The Tower Beyond Tragedy	Haunted Country
Night	Autumn Evening
Birds	Shine, Perishing Republic
Fog	The Treasure
Boats in a Fog	Joy
Granite and Cypress	Practical People
Vices	Woodrow Wilson
Phenomena	Science

1927
The Women at Point Sur. New York: Boni & Liveright.
(*Women*)

1928
Cawdor and Other Poems. New York: Horace Liveright.
(*Cawdor*)

1929
Dear Judas and Other Poems. New York: Horace Liveright.
(*Judas*)

The Humanist's Tragedy   Hands
Evening Ebb   Hooded Night

1931
Descent to the Dead, Poems Written in Ireland and Great Britain. New York: Random House. (Included in *Give Your Heart to the Hawks.*)

1932
Thurso's Landing and Other Poems. New York: Liveright, Inc. (*Thurso*)

Thurso's Landing   The Bed by the Window
The Place for No Story   Edison
An Irish Headland   New Mexican Mountains
Fire on the Hills   Second-Best
November Surf   Margrave
Winged Rock

1933
Give Your Heart to the Hawks and Other Poems. New York: Random House. (*Heart*)

Give Your Heart to the Hawks   Antrim
The Stone Axe   No Resurrection
A Little Scraping   Delusion of Saints
Intellectuals   Iona: The Grave of the Kings
Triad   Shooting Season
Still the Mind Smiles   Ghosts in England
Crumbs or the Loaf   Inscription for a Gravestone
Descent to the Dead   Shakespeare's Grave
  Shane O'Neill's Cairn   The Dead to Clemenceau: No-
  Ossian's Grave   vember 1929
  The Low Sky   Subjected Earth
  The Broadstone   Resurrection
  The Giant's Ring   At the Fall of an Age
  In the Hill at New Grange

1935

Solstice and Other Poems. New York: Random House. (*Solstice*)

At the Birth of an Age	Praise Life
The Cruel Falcon	Northern Heather
Solstice	Distant Rainfall
Rock and Hawk	Red Mountain
Life from the Lifeless	Gray Weather
Rearmament	Love the Wild Swan
What Are Cities For?	Sign-Post
Ave Caesar	Where I?
Shine, Republic	Return
The Trap	Flight of Swans

1937

Such Counsels You Gave to Me and Other Poems. New York: Random House. (*Counsels*)

Such Counsels You Gave to Me	The Answer
Steelhead, Wild Pig, the Fungus	New Year's Eve
The Coast-Road	Hope Is Not for the Wise
Going to Horse Flats	Nova
The Wind-Struck Music	All the Little Hoof-Prints
Memoir	Self-Criticism in February
Give Your Wish Light	October Week-End
The Purse-Seine	Hellenistics
Air-Raid Rehearsals	Oh, Lovely Rock
The Great Sunset	The Beaks of Eagles
Blind Horses	Night Without Sleep
Thebaid	

1938

The Selected Poetry of Robinson Jeffers. New York: Random House.

1941

Be Angry at the Sun. New York: Random House. (*Angry*)

Mara
The Bowl of Blood
That Noble Flower
I Shall Laugh Purely
Prescription of Painful Ends
Faith
The Excesses of God
The Sirens
Birthday
My Dear Love
The House-Dog's Grave
Come, Little Birds
Contemplation of the Sword
Watch the Lights Fade

Nerves
The Soul's Desert
The Day Is a Poem
Great Men
Moon and Five Planets
Battle
The Stars Go Over the Lonely Ocean
For Una
Two Christmas-Cards
Drunken Charlie
Shine, Empire
The Bloody Sire
Be Angry at the Sun

1946
Medea: Freely Adapted from the "Medea" of Euripides. New York: Random House.

1948
The Double Axe and Other Poems. New York: Random House. *(Double Axe)*

The Double Axe
    I. The Love and the Hate
    II. The Inhumanist
Cassandra
Quia Absurdum
Advice to Pilgrims
Their Beauty Has More Meaning
Pearl Harbor
Ink-Sack
Fourth Act
Calm and Full the Ocean
The Eye
Eagle Valor, Chicken Mind
Teheran
Historical Choice

Invasion
So Many Blood-Lakes
The Neutrals
We Are Those People
Dawn
The King of Beasts
Moments of Glory
What Is Worthless?
Greater Grandeur
What of It?
Diagram
New Year's Dawn, 1947
Orca
Original Sin
The Inquisitors

1949
Poetry, Gongorism and a Thousand Years. Los Angeles: Ward Ritchie Press.

1954
Hungerfield and Other Poems. New York: Random House. *(Hungerfield)*

Hungerfield
The Cretan Woman
De Rerum Virtute
Local Legend
Carmel Point
Morro Bay
Ocean
Skunks
Fire

The Beauty of Things
Animals
The World's Wonders
Time of Disturbance
The Old Stonemason
To Death
The Deer Lay Down Their
  Bones

1963
The Beginning and the End and Other Poems. New York: Random House. *(Beginning)*

The Great Explosion
The Beginning and the End
The Great Wound
Passenger Pigeons
Ode to Hengist and Horsa
Star-Swirls
Unnatural Powers
End of the World
Do You Still Make War?
The Epic Stars
Monument
Prophets
To Kill in War Is Not Murder
How Beautiful It Is
Birth and Death
The Beautiful Captive
Let Them Alone
To the Story-Tellers

Eager to Be Praised
On an Anthology of Chinese
  Poems
Tear Life to Pieces
Believe History
Full Moon
The Dog in the Sky
Harder than Granite
The Monstrous Drought
Oysters
Savagely Individual
The Silent Shepherds
Storm Dance of the Sea Gulls
My Loved Subject
He Is All
Look, How Beautiful
Patronymic
Fierce Music

introduction

Robinson Jeffers' ideology and poetry are located in a contemporary intellectual milieu that included many serious artists who followed sometimes distinctly diverse paths to crucial and demanding goals. Very rarely, however, has Jeffers been treated as a member of the inquiring group that included Pound, Eliot, Hemingway, Faulkner, Sartre, and Camus, among others. Instead, he has usually been considered a twentieth-century classicist, or a spinner of morbidly sensational tales, or some sort of esoteric high priest of nature who presided at the altar of California's scenic splendors.

Yet Robinson Jeffers faced squarely the problem of human existence in a world which he felt was growing steadily more hostile toward the individual, his values, and his hopes of finding and preserving a satisfactory concept of self. With this hostility between the individual and the world in which he lived brought dramatically into focus by the cataclysmic events of World War I and the accelerated devaluation of long-cherished attitudes and venerated ab-

stractions, novelists, poets, and artists alike reviewed with a
sense of urgency the suddenly more meaningful ideological
speculations that had arisen during the latter half of the
nineteenth century. They saw the champions of individual
choice and of humanistic values locked in awesome conflict
with the advocates of empiricism, behaviorism, and naturalism, who sought to establish the "norm," the "laws" of
human behavior, and the rationale of an utterly deterministic universe.

To those who had "walked eye-deep in hell" and survived the war, Ezra Pound declared with characteristic emphasis in *Hugh Selwyn Mauberley* that theirs was "an old
bitch gone in the teeth . . . a botched civilization" which
had "made way for macerations," had seen Caliban cast
out Ariel, and had allowed the beautiful to be "decreed in
the marketplace." Culture was decaying, art had turned
frivolous, and religion, under secularizing influences, had
failed the people. Poets like T. S. Eliot turned to classicism
and to myth for the reassuring wholeness and the timeless
values they needed to reestablish the role of threatened
man. As the originators of Western thought, the Greeks
had first raised many of these humanistic questions about
the meaning of man's life, and, while Eliot worked out his
return to orthodoxy and to traditional religious postures,
Robinson Jeffers, taking with him modern theories of science and culture, also revisited the ancients to gather the
materials with which he could eventually construct his
doctrine of Inhumanism.

Comparisons between Eliot and Jeffers, however, should
not warrant agreement with the conclusions of many of
Jeffers' critics that the whole complex and sinewy ideological structure of his work represents simply a refusal to follow Eliot's path. Jeffers' poetry, which often appears to be
a monotonous litany of doom, reveals upon close study a

remarkably dynamic quest for satisfactory answers, and, regarded in the light of nineteenth-century philosophical inquiry and contemporary twentieth-century literary reaction to that thought, it assumes fresh significance and stature.

Consider the ideological matrix from which Jeffers' poetry emerged. To stall the advancing conformism of mass
society, modern philosophy and religion needed to throw
up new defenses around the severely damaged bastions of
the individual spirit. Already weakened by the fragile ri-
gidity of its institutions, religion temporarily gave way to
the greater vitality of philosophy, especially as it was
molded by Schopenhauer and Nietzsche. Schopenhauer
dismissed God as unknowable, and told mankind in *The
World as Will and Idea* that the existence of the world depended solely upon the existence of the individual and
upon the underlying force of the individual's insensate
and irrational will to live. But Nietzsche, who not only accepted the natural world as given, but also recognized the
validity of Schopenhauer's assertion that human behavior
is basically nonrational and instinctive, declared that the
task before man was to rise above the determinism of institutionalized society and to overcome a predacious world
through the Will to Power, which could raise for the
masses the Overman.

Where Nietzsche and Heidegger struggled to raise man
above banality to the level of authentic existence, Jeffers,
who preferred "the beauty of things," saw society as incapable of achieving and maintaining a sense of genuine
identity because it is doomed to be self-corrupting and dis-
appointingly inferior to the endless magnificence of nature. Jeffers, who saw man risen but lately from sea slime,
believed that man in society had failed nature. Where the
Romantic found himself eventually alienated from nature,

and the post-Romantic found himself alienated from his being or himself, Jeffers declared that modern man had proved unequal to his role in the universe and should, therefore, forfeit the miserable existence he had worked out for himself. Only certain superior individuals, nurtured on violence, yet attuned to nature's glorious beauty, could hope, according to Jeffers, to prove worthy of their existence. Like Emerson before him, but from a radically altered rationale, Jeffers undertook the task of discovering a satisfactory reconciliation of what Emerson a century earlier had called the Me and the Not-Me.

It may be hoped, then, that the following examination of ideas present in the work of Robinson Jeffers, which led to the development of his doctrine of Inhumanism, will produce information that will be useful in the final assessment of the poet's position in a period of widespread alienation of man from man and man from the world, and of searching for authentic existence.

robinson jeffers: poet of inhumanism

the poet and the poetry

In 1935, when Niven Busch observed that "detailed analysis of Jeffers's sonorous and macabre philosophy" would be dull work, he could not have foreseen how this philosophy was to develop into a significant ideological position which Jeffers was to call Inhumanism.[1] Actually for Jeffers, Inhumanism was a "philosophical attitude," rather than a genuine philosophy. An examination of the ideological patterns evident in Jeffers' work, however, will substantially facilitate a greater appreciation of his total artistic achievement. The matter of Jeffers' religion, which bulks large in his work, is only occasionally and then indirectly within the focus of this book; his religion should be the subject of another, perhaps complementary, study.

During the forty years in which the major poetry was produced—beginning with *Tamar and Other Poems* (1924) and concluding with the posthumous collection *The Beginning and the End and Other Poems* (1963)—Jeffers addressed warnings and admonitions to a world which heeded him more or less according to its changing moods.[2] With very few other writers has there been so much the air about each successive volume that the definitive statement would soon be forthcoming and that for the present the reader must be satisfied with the poet's latest pronouncement on the problem of living in this world. An attentive reading, however, of the successive volumes of poetry—especially the long, message-burdened narratives—clearly reveals Jeffers' desire to offer only tested conclusions. Hence not all the poems proceed to the same conclusion; some of them, like *Tamar* and *Give Your Heart to the Hawks,* might be characterized as calculated failures, which is to say that they are explorations of certain lines of action and that they honestly admit to having untenable conclusions.

In view of the undeniably oracular tone of most of his poetry and its obvious concern with the problems of living in what the poet considered to be an aging, therefore decadent, culture, Jeffers' verse sometimes emphasizes the idea at the expense of the poetry (as in the controversial *The Double Axe*). Thus, a study of the patterns of ideas in the poems, rather than the quality of the poems, shows ideas emerging as speculative propositions, generally derived from philosophical systems, and as attitudes toward and solutions to problems. As much as possible, this study steers clear of tracing possible nineteenth- and twentieth-century "literary influences." Jeffers knew the work of James Joyce, for example, but flirted only briefly with some of his devices and word-play. Among less recent literary influences, there is an indebtedness to the poetry of Rossetti and to the occasional sonorous sound of Swinburne in Jeffers' earlier lines, but rhyme was a technical device which he abandoned early in his career. In as early a poem as *Mal Paso Bridge,* Jeffers decided not to dally with rhyme and smooth meters, the "rhyme-tassels" as he called them. The system of ideas presented in the several works of Nietzsche, however, stands as one of the central concerns in this study of Jeffers' work. The appearance of Nietzschean ideas in Jeffers' verse coincides with the beginning of his major period; it lies like a keel to the subsequent work, to which several similar concepts are joined. But whatever Jeffers took from Nietzsche, he could not borrow the German's flashing wit or his aphoristic style.

Jeffers' Critics

Criticism dealing with Jeffers' verse is checkered with enthusiastic admiration and with self-righteous attacks. On the one hand, conservative and orthodox commentators have struck at Jeffers with considerable excitement and less precision, much as a pestered Sunday School teacher might swing at a picnic-disturbing wasp. (The ants could always be handled somehow.) His admirers, on the other hand, have always been free, if not careless, with their superlatives. For them, Jeffers is without parallel as the celebrator of the magnificent coastal region of California's Monterey County, where the meeting of the Pacific and the coastal mountain range presents a truly inspiring sight. Many of Jeffers' followers go with him only as far as inspiration, and then proceed on divergent paths, failing to recognize that the poet attributes the same grand significance to all of nature. In 1926, George Sterling, one of Jeffers' most enthusiastic admirers, presented his study, *Robinson Jeffers: The Man and the Artist*. Not much later, Lawrence Clark Powell wrote his doctoral dissertation, which appeared in 1932 as *An Introduction to Robinson Jeffers*. The book was revised in 1934, and again in 1940 as *Robinson Jeffers: The Man and His Work*. Powell's valuable book is the product of a long, personal acquaintance with the poet, his work, and the coastal settings of many of the poems.

In 1936, Rudolph Gilbert published *Shine, Perishing*

Republic: Robinson Jeffers and the Tragic Sense in Modern Poetry. In addition to its controlling interest in the tragic sense, this was the first study to deal largely with the ideas in Jeffers' work. With all but the last volume of Jeffers' work available to him, Radcliffe Squires wrote *The Loyalties of Robinson Jeffers,* which appeared in 1956.[3] "Almost alone," writes Squires of Jeffers, "he has believed that poetry can assimilate and reconstruct in a recognizably dramatic form the peculiar disunity and disloyalty of modern man."[4] Early in his study, Squires observes that "Jeffers' present reputation reflects a misapprehension of his philosophical and artistic position. I have accordingly sought to construct a cosmography from both his poetry and intellectual background."[5] In seeking to rehabilitate Jeffers' literary reputation by exploring his intellectual background, Squires is forced to shape his evidence to fit an a priori image of the poet. The result of this self-limiting design has inevitably affected the value judgments of some of the poetry; it is a sobering fact that, in addition to his good verse, Jeffers wrote much that was inferior. Squires also urges acceptance of the view that Schopenhauer, rather than Nietzschean idealist philosophy, is the stronger influence on Jeffers.

In 1962, the year of the poet's death, Frederic I. Carpenter's *Robinson Jeffers* was published in Twayne's United States Authors Series. Carpenter's earlier articles on Jeffers were sensitive interpretations.[6] The scholar and the poet had exchanged several letters, and it appears that Jeffers had permitted one of his rare disclosures of himself to Carpenter. Carpenter's well-ordered and thoroughgoing book is the best introduction to Jeffers.

His Career

Since Jeffers' production ran to something like seventeen

volumes, a sketch of the poet's career will help to remind the reader of the chronology of the major poems and their themes, and to indicate the kind of focus this book brings to the poetry. Many accounts of Jeffers' life have already drawn heavily upon such statements as those of George Sterling, who, having observed that appraising genius is "perilous business," wrote in 1926 that Jeffers "began to lisp in numbers at the early age of ten."[7] It is just this kind of vividness that may have attracted *Time* magazine's anonymous reviewer of Jeffers' *Thurso's Landing and Other Poems* (1932), who leaned on Sterling's account.[8] Or we might turn to Benjamin De Casseres' resounding tributes, which are supported by intimate glimpses into the life of the poet.[9]

Born on 10 January 1887, the first son of William Hamilton Jeffers, who was a minister and professor of Old Testament literature at Western Theological Seminary of Pittsburgh, Robinson Jeffers spent his early years under his father's tutelage and in boarding schools in Germany and Switzerland. When the family moved to Pasadena, California, for the sake of Dr. Jeffers' health, Robinson transferred from the University of Western Pennsylvania to Occidental College. As a student at Occidental, Jeffers was interested in literature—contributing to and editing college magazines—and he was an ardent hiker and explorer of California's wilderness areas, experiences that were, then and later, reflected in his verses.

After being graduated from Occidental College in 1905, Jeffers entered the graduate school of the University of Southern California, where he met and fell in love with another student of literature, Una Call Kuster, the vivacious and brilliant wife of a Los Angeles lawyer. During the troubled eight years that passed before Una was free to marry him, Jeffers visited Europe again, attended briefly the University of Zurich, returned to the University of

Southern California (this time as a student in the college
of medicine), changed to the school of forestry at the University of Washington, and finally married Una, 2 August
1913, in Tacoma, Washington. In 1912, his first volume of
poems, *Flagons and Apples,* had been published in Los Angeles, and, after discovering Carmel, California, and settling there with Una in 1914, he wrote poems which drew
on the region and which eventually appeared as *Californians,* in 1916, the year the couple's twin sons were born.
The years between *Californians* and *Tamar* embraced
World War I, which apparently stimulated Jeffers to self-
examination. It was a period in which both his thinking
and his craft matured and changed remarkably, as *Tamar*
revealed. Fortunately, today's student of Jeffers' life can
read about the man in Melba Berry Bennett's *The Stone
Mason of Tor House* (1966), which, obviously a labor of
love, is temperate and thorough.[10] From all reports, it is
clear that Jeffers was a quiet, calm-mannered man, resolute
and withdrawn, kind to the point that he was unable to
bring himself to exterminate ground squirrels on his property in Carmel. Sterling did that for him.[11] Yet in his major work, Jeffers left us some remarkable narratives of violence, sexual disorder, and apparent contempt for his fel-
low-man.

His Major Work

Jeffers' major work falls into three distinct periods. The
first is one of experimentation, in which Jeffers did some of
his thinking aloud and pondered various ideological possibilities without much concern about their practical success; he was prepared to reject a line of thought and action,
if it yielded unsatisfactory results. Beginning with *Tamar*
and ending with *Dear Judas,* this first period includes the

poetry of the twenties. Tamar Cauldwell represents Nietzschean ideas coarsely embodied in human action. Sensing
her entrapment in a household which is both decadent and
corrupt, Tamar struggles to alter her situation, to transcend the limitation imposed on her by life. As she learns
more about herself and her forebears, however, Tamar becomes increasingly bitter and eventually involves the
whole family, including her former suitor, in a fiery conclusion. In terms of what she tries to overcome, Tamar's
actions become insignificant as she proceeds. She fails to
comprehend all of the problem at the outset, yet chooses
drastic means to solve it, discovering later that both her
understanding of the problem of life and her particular solution have already been acted out by the previous generation, which had also failed. Her victimization by life was
actually greater than at first she could comprehend.

Tamar was an attempt to explore the problems of sterility and inwardness. Jeffers' solution was extremely radical
and the results described in the poem were catastrophic. As
we shall see, however, Tamar's fate is of a piece with that
of California in *Roan Stallion* and that of the Reverend
Arthur Barclay in *The Women at Point Sur*. Like Tamar,
California, in spite of her mystical union with the force
which the stallion represents, finds herself limited at the
time of crisis by a part of the same humanity to which her
despicable husband, Johnny, belongs. The crisis of her experience produces awareness but not material change, and
out of some obscure loyalty to humanity California shoots
the horse that has trampled her husband. Reverend Barclay of *The Women at Point Sur*, however, turns from a
life of orthodox religious views to one in which he desires
to transcend mundane life through an act of violence; in
the poem Jeffers clearly favors "old-fashioned morality," as
he told James Rorty in a letter:

Another intention, this time a primary one, was to show in action the danger of that "Roan Stallion" idea of "breaking out of humanity," misinterpreted in the mind of a fool or a lunatic. . . . just as Ibsen in the Wild Duck, made a warning against his own idea in the hands of a fool, so Point Sur was meant to be a warning; but at the same time a reassertion.[12]

Among other things *The Women at Point Sur* represented for Jeffers (as he went on to say in the letter) "an attempt to uncenter the human mind from itself." It was a "tragedy, that is an exhibition of essential elements by the burning away through pain and ruin of inertia and the unessential," and it was "a valid study in psychology; the study valid, the psychology morbid . . . a partial and fragmentary study of the origin of religions . . . [which] derive from a 'private impurity' of some kind in their originators . . . [as well as] a satire on human self-importance." *The Women at Point Sur,* along with other major poems of the first period, explores possibilities and posits solutions for the individual who is isolated by external forces or who isolates himself.

The second period of Jeffers' development is introduced by the transitional poem *Dear Judas,* which follows the now-familiar Nietzschean pattern in its rejection of traditional orthodox Christianity. It is unlike any other Jeffers poem in its forthright attack upon received Christian beliefs, but it should not be separated from *The Loving Shepherdess,* for the two poems together constitute a whole. As unconventional as she is, Clare Walker of the second poem represents a warm and outgoing love that contrasts with the selfishness of the previous poem. The second period—*Thurso's Landing* (1932) to *Be Angry at the Sun* (1941)—merges with the beginning of the third period; during this time Jeffers expanded his field of examination and turned from the individual to the more cred-

ible and genuinely involved life of the family. He stressed
the social implications of subjects treated in the previous
period, and violence and sexual license are always described with a sense of societal standards in the background. Unlike Tamar, to whom the idea of social justice
never occurs, Fayne Fraser, in *Give Your Heart to the
Hawks,* consciously opposes traditional social justice with a
strangely developed sense of personal responsibility. Helen
Thurso, in *Thurso's Landing,* is dissatisfied with her un-
eventful life at the Landing, and, when she seeks diversion
—perhaps romance—with Rick Armstrong, she is made to
return to her husband, Reave, and to bear the full effect of
the forces she has set in motion.

At the Birth of an Age, a two-part poem in the *Solstice*
volume, deals with the confrontation of Nietzschean individualism and decadent Christianity—a modern interpretation of the conflict of two cultures out of which Christianity emerged the victor. The title poem of the volume, however, is concerned with the Medea-like Madrone Bothwell,
who is caught between the conflicting demands of nature
and her sense of responsibility to society. In this poem, nature is beautifully, sometimes rather starkly, described. In
championing the rude forces of nature at the expense of
social responsibility, Jeffers foreshadows the theme of
alienation from society to be found in the poetry of the
third period.

Such Counsels You Gave to Me introduces Howard
Howren, who murders his niggardly father at his mother's
suggestion, but refuses to accept his mother's pressing invitation to possess her sexually. Within the context of the
poem, Howard commits a great crime, rejects a great temptation, and finally pledges to his doppelgänger, which has
been present throughout the poem, that he will stand trial
in spite of the image's protestation that Howard owes society nothing.

Jeffers closed the second period with the *Selected Poetry* volume of 1938. Most of the long poems, complete or in part, are included. Two passages from *Cawdor* appear, along with all of *Thurso's Landing*. *The Women at Point Sur*—"in spite of grave faults—the most inclusive, and poetically the most intense, of any of my poems"—was not included, Jeffers said in his foreword, because it was "the least understood and least liked, and because it . . . [was] longest." *Dear Judas* was also excluded because it "was not liked . . . though I think it has value, if any of these poems has." But a series of poems written in the British Isles, *Descent to the Dead* (1931), does appear in the *Selected Poetry*. Taken together, the inclusion of this series and the exclusion of *Dear Judas* may further illustrate the transitional character which I have attributed to *Dear Judas* and *The Loving Shepherdess*.

In leaving out *Dear Judas*, Jeffers apparently wished to avoid the adverse reaction that had followed his portrayal of a selfish and cruel Christ and of a loving Judas. The more popular poem *The Loving Shepherdess* was included presumably because its allegorical quality and severe criticism of Christianity are far less salient. Without *Dear Judas* to represent the closing of the first period of his production, Jeffers substituted the more varied and subtler statements of the *Descent to the Dead* series. Whereas the ideological explorations of the twenties had led, in accord with the logic of Nietzsche, to *Dear Judas* and the examination of Christianity and heroism, this series of elegiac poems reached back to the days of Celtic kings and heroes, and, with only a few exceptions, carried a merely implicit attack on Christianity as an exhausted institution. By making this change, Jeffers strengthened the argument propounded here that the poems of the twenties represented a single phase and those of the thirties a conscious reorientation in the light of the earlier experimental work.

When he commented on *Descent to the Dead* during readings at the Library of Congress and at Harvard in 1941, Jeffers observed:

> . . . I had several reasons for calling it "Descent to the Dead." First, I was tired, and wanted to indulge myself by playing dead for a few months. Foreign travel is like a pleasant temporary death; it relieves you of responsibilities and familiar scenes and duties. Then, the light and the life in those cloudy islands seem to be keyed so much lower than they are at home; everything appeared dim and soft, mournful and old; and the past, in that year of peace [1929], seemed to a foreigner much more present than the present. So it was easy to imagine myself a dead man in a country of the dead.[13]

Since these remarks were printed unchanged in *Themes in My Poems* (1956), we may conclude that Jeffers' view of the book and of its relationship to previous work supports to some degree the argument advanced here for the major divisions of his work.

The third period of Jeffers' career began with *Be Angry at the Sun and Other Poems* (1941), in which the poet sought to separate himself from the contemporary events of World War II, but found that he must not and could not do so. In *The Stars Go Over the Lonely Ocean,* the poet is "Unhappy about some far off things / That are not my affair," and, in the final stanza, an ill-disguised wild boar speaks:

> "Keep clear of the dupes that talk democracy
> And the dogs that talk revolution,
> Drunk with talk, liars and believers.
> I believe in my tusks.
> Long live freedom and damn the ideologies,"
> Said the gamey black-maned wild boar
> Tusking the turf on Mal Paso Mountain.

"Poetry is not private monologue," Jeffers wrote in the

Note to the volume, "but I think it is not public speech either; and in general it is the worse for being timely." This problem of the public character of poetry, further complicated by topicality, went unsolved, and reached a crisis of sorts in *The Double Axe and Other Poems* (1948), where it became a sore issue. Jeffers felt that the collapse of a civilization was at hand: it was not "the world's end, / But only the fall of a civilization," he wrote in *I Shall Laugh Purely*. He expected another age to follow the total destruction of war, for, as he explained in the same poem, "all that pain was mainly a shift in power . . . 'Oh Christian era, / Make a good end.' " I-told-you-so echoes stridently through the poems of this period. For years, he had predicted, in the light of his reading of Spengler, Vico, and Petrie, that the current cycle of civilization was coming to a close; war would be the best way to eradicate vicious humanity, as the poet saw it, for the world must be cleansed of the stain it had received from mankind. Events of the day seemed to fulfill Jeffers' predictions; the day of doom was indeed at hand.

Poems of this period have themes of withdrawal, isolation, and resignation. Some of Jeffers' poorest poetry is loaded with dismal freight, but an exception to the rule in this period is his "free adaptation" of Euripides' *Medea,* which was generally very well received, though some reviews pointedly emphasized Judith Anderson's performance in the title role. In his changes from the original, Jeffers gave rein again to his continued preoccupation with the theme of power. His Medea is a heroine of courage and action, equipped with the poet's own view of the world, and beset by problems that are characteristic of both ancient Greece and modern America.

Two years after he wrote *Medea, The Double Axe and Other Poems* came out, bearing the marks of differences of opinion between the publisher and the poet. "Its burden," Jeffers wrote of the title poem, "as of some previous work of mine, is to present a certain philosophical attitude, which might be called Inhumanism, a shifting of emphasis and significance from man to not-man; the rejection of human solipsism and recognition of the transhuman magnificence." It is this philosophical attitude of Inhumanism, which had been announced as early as *Roan Stallion,* that provides the continuum against which the three periods of Jeffers' production must be compared. Jeffers' longstanding preference for the "not-man" part of the world and his awareness of the shortcomings of human nature were examined and variously tested in the first period, in the light of Nietzschean doctrine, modern science, and constraining religious orthodoxy. What could be used from the first period of trial he carried into the second period for application and verification in a broader social context, and the poet's more or less pessimistic hypotheses were borne out. In the final phase, as a result of the second period of inquiry and of concurrent historical developments, Jeffers expressed confidence in his theories and resigned himself to the position of an unheeded Cassandra in a stubborn world.

The death of Una Jeffers in 1950 was a severe blow to the poet, for theirs had been a long and satisfying relationship, involving unashamed dependency of the poet upon his wife, as Jeffers was always ready to acknowledge.[14] The title poem of *Hungerfield and Other Poems* (1954) is about Hawl Hungerfield, a war veteran who believes he once out-faced Death in a French hospital, and who successfully grapples with Death and wins, when it comes to take Hungerfield's sick mother. This is an unfair simplification of Jeffers' poem, but it gives an idea of the narrative which is enclosed in a frame formed by the poet's address to his dead wife, whom he called "faithful and a lion heart like this rough hero Hungerfield" (p. 23). In *The Cretan Woman,* another poem from this volume, Jeffers again took up Euripides' Hippolytus story. There are other poems over which the funereal presence of death hangs; in these the poet reiterated his preference for the beauty of things, the message that "It is easy to know the beauty of inhuman things" (*The World's Wonders*), and, in *The Deer Lay Down Their Bones,* the conclusion that

>   I am bound by my own thirty-
> year-old decision: who drinks the wine
> Should take the dregs; even in the bitter lees and sediment
> New discovery may lie.

The last volume, *The Beginning and the End and Other Poems* (1963), brought no new discovery, save that the complaints were brought up to date by considering such issues as the cold war and the arms race. The poet was an old man, who was prepared for death and who had taken his poems as far as he could; phrases and images from earlier poems began to reappear. At the end, one marks time.[15]

His Poetics

Robinson Jeffers' theories of poetry and of the function of the poet remained pretty much unchanged after he first decided, between the appearance of *Californians* and *Tamar,* to chart his own poetic course. By 1948, in *The Double Axe,* the next to the last volume of verse published during the poet's lifetime, we are not surprised to hear Jeffers say, in *Cassandra,*

>   Poor bitch, be wise.
> No: you'll still mumble in a corner a crust of truth, to men
> And gods disgusting.—You and I, Cassandra.

This, Jeffers said in a book that bore an unusual Publishers' Note, which announced that Random House felt "compelled to go on record with its disagreement over some of the political views pronounced by the poet in this volume." The Cassandra of the poem *The Tower Beyond Tragedy* (1925) had predicted such a war as the readers of *The Double Axe* volume had just come through. Furthermore, Jeffers had preached throughout the thirties that such war was inevitable, unless the United States changed its course of action in world affairs, and in *Such Counsels You Gave to Me* (1937) and in *Be Angry at the Sun* (1941) he foretold events that history was yet to record.

Jeffers' remark to Cassandra (in the later poem) came at perhaps the most trying time in his career: the principles to which he steadfastly clung had apparently been proved by the events of history, as he saw them, but there seemed to be no one listening. What was more, he had to endure, with "cheerful consent," as he generously put it, the singular treatment from his publisher.[16] He was right from his point of view, but, when he needed the emotional support, very few of his readers gave him credit for his perspicacity.

Yet, in 1946 he wrote an adaptation of Euripides' *Medea* which, when produced in 1948 with Judith Anderson as Medea, was a popular success. Ironically, in the same year, his poems in *The Double Axe* were poorly received, but the success of *Medea* resulted in Jeffers' being invited to write an article for the magazine section of the *New York Times,* which appeared as "Poetry, Gongorism, and a Thousand Years" (18 Jan. 1948).[17] In it he spoke about the nature of poetry and the character of a "hypothetical great poet." As a poet who had "an insuperable will," Yeats came closest to filling this niche of greatness, Jeffers claimed. Yeats was born of the right moment, of the right people—just "in that magic time when a country becomes a nation, it was Ireland's good fortune that there was a great poet in Ireland." There is considerable special pleading in the article, of course, for the very kind of poet Jeffers believed himself to be, and for the poetry he had written. From Shelley, whom he read and admired, and of whom his wife, Una, was a lifelong student, Jeffers apparently drew the earliest support for the conception of poets as seers and prophets, "the unacknowledged legislators of the world."[18] In this role, the poet should concern himself only with the future and with permanent things, as Jeffers said in the important foreword to *The Selected Poetry of Robinson Jeffers* (1938). There he wrote, "poetry is bound to concern itself chiefly with permanent things and the permanent aspects of life," for whereas "prose can discuss matters of the moment; poetry must deal with things that a reader two thousand years away could understand and be moved by."[19] In his foreword to D. H. Lawrence's *Fire and Other Poems* (1940), Jeffers remarked, after chastising Lawrence for adding a "humanistic tag" at the end of a revised poem and for substituting "excitement for intensity":

> We have lost the way, and we know it at last. We must just live as well as we can, and listen to the Sibyls muttering—the inspired persons: Lawrence is one of them—finding in their obscurity and confusion many bright flashes, and sometimes a little guidance.[20]

Jeffers had already said in the foreword to *Selected Poetry* that he had decided "Long ago . . . that poetry—if it was to survive at all—must reclaim some of the power and reality that it was so hastily surrendering to prose." Because poetry "was becoming slight and fantastic, abstract, unreal, eccentric; and was not even saving its soul," the poet must do whatever he can to help it "reclaim substance and sense, and physical and psychological reality."[21] Responding to the inquiry of Graham Bickley, a student at the University of California, Jeffers said of poetry:

> The thought is more primitive and less specialized. . . . Poetry appeals rather to the emotions than to the intelligence and especially to the aesthetic emotion. It appeals more eagerly than prose does to the imagination and to the bodily senses. It deals with the more permanent aspects of man and nature. It tends to be farther removed from quotidian life in order to be nearer to natural, unspecialized and passionate life.[22]

What "physical and psychological reality" meant for Jeffers is a large and complicated subject, discussed below, involving the theories of Nietzsche, Spengler, and Vico, as well as the thought of Lucretius. At any rate, it was this wish to reclaim the old freedom of poetry and to deal afresh with reality that led Jeffers to narrative poetry and to the desire "to draw subjects from contemporary life . . . to attempt the expression of philosophic and scientific ideas in verse."[23] Fortunately for Jeffers, as he readily admitted, he married Una Call Kuster, who "excited and focused" his "cold and undiscriminating" nature and "gave it eyes and nerves and sympathies."[24] A second bit of good fortune brought the couple to the Monterey coastal mountains where the poet found "contemporary life that was also permanent life; and not shut from the modern world but conscious of it and related to it; capable of expressing its spirit, but unencumbered by the mass of poetically irrelevant details and complexities that make a civilization."[25]

Not unexpectedly, Jeffers took the stand that the "worthy audience" of a thousand years hence would endow a poet like himself with a posthumous reputation which his works of art would perpetuate.[26] And so to a hypothetical young poet, who aspires to be the "hypothetical great poet," Jeffers advised in the *New York Times* article, "posthumous reputation could do you no harm at all, and is really the only kind worth considering." He was not, however, without occasional misgivings about the merits of making verses. In the poem *Second-Best,* the poet compares himself to his forefathers, Celt, Briton, "Gaelic chiefling" (all men of action and adventure); and then to himself he says, "And you are a maker of verses. The pallid / Pursuit of the world's beauty on paper."

That Jeffers was a conscientious artist, devoted to his craft and possessed of unshakable integrity, has never been questioned, I believe, and in the following lines from the sonnet *Love the Wild Swan* these qualities are strikingly affirmed:

> "I hate my verses, every line, every word.
> Oh pale and brittle pencils ever to try
> One grass-blade's curve, or the throat of one bird
> That clings to twig, ruffled against white sky.
> Oh cracked and twilight mirrors ever to catch
> One color, one glinting flash, of the splendor of things.
> Unlucky hunter, Oh bullets of wax,
> The lion beauty, the wild-swan wings, the storm of the wings."

There are recognizable overtones here of a certain "hypothetical great poet," and it is normal to find a poet complaining about elusive goals. But it is interesting that in a later book Jeffers should take the attitude expressed in this passage and relate it obviously to his own background. For Jeffers, his father presumably represented unquestioned orthodoxy, though the poet noted in a letter to H. H. Waggoner that his father "was a clergyman but also intelligent, and he brought me up to timely ideas about origin of species, descent of man, astronomy, geology, etc."[27] In *Come, Little Birds,* Jeffers addresses his elderly father, who has appeared to him from the realm of death at the summons of an old woman whom the poet, disregarding ministerial propriety, has paid to sacrifice a calf in order to call forth the dead: "Forgive me. I dishonored and wasted all your hopes of me, one by one; yet I loved you well."[28]

Carrying the mood of self-examination still further in *For Una*, Jeffers wrote:

> Tomorrow I will take up that heavy poem again
> About Ferguson, deceived and jealous man
> Who bawled for the truth, the truth, and failed to endure
> Its first least gleam. That poem bores me, and I hope will
>   bore
> Any sweet soul that reads it, being some ways
> My very self but mostly my antipodes;
> But having waved the heavy artillery to fire
> I must hammer on to an end.

Ferguson is the hypocritical hero of *Mara*, and Jeffers' estimate of him and of the poem is just, for Jeffers felt obliged to hammer home the message in *Mara*, even though, as he suspects in *For Una*, one will not hear the poetry for the hammering.

Jeffers' well-known poem *Self-Criticism in February* is a dialogue between the two sides of the poet's intellect, between the conventional, rational voice of orthodox self-reproach and that of the intuitional, truth-seeking artist. Against the charge that he has "loved the beauty of storm disproportionately," the poet defends himself by answering that he did not write in a "pastoral" time, and that the violence in the poems was not "Perversity but need that perceives the storm-beauty." But the worst fault, charges the poet's other voice in the poem, is:

> *you have never mistaken*
> *Demon nor passion nor idealism for the real God.*
> Then what is most disliked in those verses

Remains most true. *Unfortunately. If only you could sing
That God is love, or perhaps that social
Justice will soon prevail.* I can tell lies in prose.

Though there is much crucial matter here for a discussion
of Jeffers, we are concerned, for the moment, with only the
last sentence, "I can tell lies in prose." Jeffers developed
this point in the following year in his foreword to the *Selected Poetry*.[29] Describing the formative principles that
guided him, Jeffers mentioned Nietzsche's line: "The poets? The poets lie too much." After pondering this statement for some years, Jeffers concluded, "I decided not to
tell lies in verse. Not to feign any emotion that I did not
feel; not to pretend to believe in optimism or pessimism,
or unreversible progress; not to say anything because it was
popular, or generally accepted, or fashionable in intellectual circles, unless I myself believed it; and not to believe
easily." In order for the poet to reclaim the old freedom in
his verse, he would write narratives with subjects drawn
from contemporary life, which presented aspects of life
generally avoided in modern poetry, and which attempted
to express philosophic and scientific ideas.

Speaking in the *Times* article of the effect of poetry, Jeffers referred to the *Medea* of Euripides (and indirectly to
his own version of it), the *Oresteia*, and *Oedipus Rex*, and
declared that tragedy is *not* "a moral agent," as it has been
regarded since Aristotle, "a purifier of the mind and emotions." All these dramas "tell primitive horror-stories," but
"what makes them noble," according to Jeffers, "is the poetry; the poetry, and the beautiful shapes of the plays, and
the extreme violence born of extreme passion."[30] To Professor Camille McCole's query, Jeffers responded that he
thought "the difference between poetry and unpoetic verse
lies in the appeal of poetry to the aesthetic emotion. . . . the
quality that I most value in poetry is of imaginative power

activated by powerful emotion, so that the imagination is not displayed idly for a show but as if of necessity and in earnest, under emotional compulsion."[31] And, as noted in his statement to Graham Bickley, Jeffers still believed that the power of poetry lay in its appeal to emotions, especially to the aesthetic emotion, rather than to the intelligence.[32] In an undated note among Jeffers' papers, there is the further indication that he expected an appeal to aesthetic emotions in a modernized poetry that was abreast of the latest scientific theories. He wrote, "I do not think I am wrong in using even in verse some of the fruits of contemporary psychoanalytic study. Poetry has been called a flower of all knowledge; this is only an ideal desire, but we have to live by the gospel that 'beauty is the effulgence of truth.' "[33]

Jeffers had some moving and interesting thoughts about the capacity of poetry to engender passionate response. At least twice he turned to the example of Milton for inspiration, once in his foreword, written in October 1933, to Powell's study on Jeffers, and once in some notes on a theory of poetry, written in Ireland in 1937. In the first instance, he said:

> Poetry, by Milton's definition, must be "impassioned;" poetical speech has little value and no likelihood unless it is born of passionate feeling. The lyrical poet finds the feeling in himself; the maker of narrative or dramatic poetry must cause the persons of his imagination to feel passionately.... Most often he chooses a tragic story, because pain, being more intense than pleasure, produces stronger emotions. The story may deal with war, like the Iliad, or religion, like the Divine Comedy; but in times of high civilization war becomes too specialized and inhuman, and religion too vague or incredible, for poetry to fix its roots in. Other sources of emotion must be tapped; and, when poetry has remained vigorous in civilized times, the poets have turned with singu-

lar unanimity to one source in particular, to the family and its relationships. . . . These relationships are always unhappy and often vicious, not because the poets prefer vice and sorrow, but because happiness makes no story, and but calm emotion.[34]

In the later comment, Jeffers contemplates the possibility of formulating a theory of poetry, as well as the distinctions one must make between poetic prose and poetry:

> I have ideas on the subject of poetry but really no theory. To develop the ideas would require a big book—Milton's specifications for good poetry, "simple, sensuous, impassioned" are the best statement on the subject so far as they go, with exceptions (Milton's own example is not exactly simple!). And poetic prose can fulfill all these specifications yet not be poetry! Therefore something should be added about metrical or at least rhythmical lines and parses; for poetry is poetic expression in verse and something should be added about beauty and sound, assonance, alliteration, etc., and all that more subtle music that distinguishes poetic verse from verse that is metrical but not poetic.[35]

In these two passages, we find not only Jeffers' customary emphasis on passion as a requisite of good poetry, but also suggestions about the sources of strong emotion and observations about maintaining the necessary distinction between poetry and poetic prose. Moreover, in his long narrative poems, Jeffers, like the Greek tragedians, customarily exploits the powerful internal tensions of family conflicts.

These remarks about passion notwithstanding, Jeffers warned that, "The story that heaps emotions or complexities and makes no thoroughfare is a weakening story and so I should think an immoral story; but the story that through whatever passes attains significant release will influence its readers in the same sense, and this is good for him, it is moral."³⁶ The questions of catharsis and the morality of tragedy are before us again, for in "Poetry, Gongorism, and a Thousand Years," Jeffers explicitly rejected the notion, handed down from Aristotle, that tragedy is a moral agent. Furthermore, a cultivated people, Jeffers believed, should not be expected to react to Greek tragedies in any other way than they would react to a story "about a criminal adventurer and his gun-moll," as he characterized *Medea*. It is apparent from these two statements that at one time Jeffers tacitly accepted the Aristotelian definition of tragedy with the same emphasis that Aristotle placed upon a "medicinal" catharsis; it is also apparent that by 1948, after Jeffers had "read more attentively the *Medea* of Euripides," he reversed his position and continued henceforth to believe in it, at least until 1954 when the 1948 essay appeared again, unchanged, as "Poetry and Survival." Two considerations, then, come to mind. All but one of the long narrative poems, which are about violent tensions and deeds within families, had been written by 1948 when a close examination of the *Medea,* a notorious disrupter of many Aristotelian conclusions about the nature of tragedy, caused Jeffers to change his mind publicly—if he had not already done so privately. The other consideration involves the morality of art, which derives its moral nature from the morality of the original creative act. If this is actually an operative principle in Jeffers' theory of art, and it can be fairly well defended as such, it is another strong echo of the Miltonic credo.

Although Jeffers believed that poetry was supposed to appeal powerfully to the aesthetic emotion, he doubted that rhyme would contribute to the effect. In the early *Mal Paso Bridge,* he says that, though verse is "a light weapon, that leaves / In the wound seeds of live fire," he swears that henceforth he will "shear the rhyme-tassels from

verse." In actual practice, however, he had not yet finished
with occasional uncomfortable experiments in rhyme. In
another instance, the Sweeper in *At the Birth of an Age*
grumbles,

> I forget the rhyme, I cannot help it.
> At every new era we have to
> learn a new set of verses,
> but damn this tinkle-tankle.
>
> *(Solstice,* p. 48)

Later still in the poet's career, one of the maskers in *The
Bowl of Blood* lists a catalog of destroyed cities and pauses
to ask, "how do you rhyme these things?" *(Angry,* p. 88).
Because he considered rhyme an artificiality of poetry, Jeffers questioned how it could be used sincerely in tolling
destruction. As early as the year of *The Women at Point
Sur,* he repudiated the formal conventions of traditional
poetry. In a memorial issue devoted to George Sterling, the
Overland Monthly included *A Few Memories* by Jeffers.
Defending the work of Sterling, but, as was often the case,
defending his own as well, Jeffers said, "fashion is no
doubt the most contemptible of the critical yardsticks applied to poetry."[37] A year later, in 1928, Jeffers expanded
upon his objectives in this area:

> I want it rhythmic and not rhymed, moulded more closely
> to the subject than older English poetry is, but as formed as
> alcaics if that were possible too. The event is of course a
> compromise but I like to avoid arbitrary form and capri-
> cious lack or disruption of form. My feeling is for the num-
> ber of beats to the line. There is a quantitive [*sic*] element
> too in which the unstressed syllables have part. The rhythm
> comes from many sources—physics, biology, beat of blood,
> the tidal environments of life, desire for singing emphasis
> that prose does not have.[38]

It is not necessary here to take up the complex matters of Jeffers' metrics, but it is apparent that he felt unrestrained by conventional practices, and that such mechanical artificialities of verse as neat rhymes and precise rhythms were subordinated to concepts of form more closely aligned with organic principles and long periods of time. We may reasonably conclude, moreover, from both Jeffers' criticism and his poetry, that he favored an organic form which was suited to his view of the tides of civilization and all other forms of life in an eternal universe.[39]

In a review of Mark Van Doren's *Now the Sky and Other Poems* (1928), Jeffers acknowledged, "The war between a poet and his genius is one of the most interesting of shows. It is a war of collaboration, and it ought to be a war without victory; for whether the man triumphs after a while, as in Wordsworth's work, or the bright spirit, as in Blake's, the collaboration ends, and the work ceases to be significant."[40] This sense of division within the poet is frequently apparent in the poems and in their characters. For example, *The Loving Shepherdess* was intended to balance *Dear Judas*, which it followed; and a number of the long narratives are divided into sharply contrasting halves: *At the Birth of an Age*, *The Double Axe*, *The Tower Beyond Tragedy*, and, more elaborately, *Hungerfield*. There are several examples of doppelgänger, the ghostly counterpart of a living character—Arthur Barclay in *The Women at Point Sur*, Onorio Vasquez in *The Loving Shepherdess*, Howard Howren in *Such Counsels You Gave to Me*, Bruce Ferguson in *Mara*. Clearly, Jeffers subscribed to his own theories when he used the tension between opposing structural parts of a poem, and "divided" personalities to communicate the content of the poem.[41]

Benjamin Miller, in a 1939 article on religious philosophy of the theatre, defined "*sensuous mysticism* as sense-ex-

perience of appreciative relations with the sustaining processes of reality which we call God."[42] Possibly because he
recognized in Jeffers the likelihood of intellectual endorsement, Miller had approached the poet on the subject; Jeffers' reply (February 1938) contributes to the set of principles under discussion here:

> I did not in my verses intend a distinction between aesthetic
> experience and what you call sensual [sic] mysticism. The in-
> tention in poetry is not primarily analytical; in my experi-
> ence the two feelings were wound together, and so I ex-
> pressed them. I think there *is* a distinction, and that the
> beauty of things may be felt without any mystical recogni-
> tion. But in that case it seems to me to be felt incompletely,
> however keenly. It seems to me that the mystical experience
> grows out of the aesthetic experience, naturally, almost logi-
> cally.[43]

A. W. von Schlegel, Coleridge, and Poe had each examined at length the possibilities of reversing the synthesizing
process of art in order to analyze the distinctive roles of the
contributing elements, and apparently Jeffers, too, pondered these problems. Unlike his predecessors, however, he
left no detailed record of his exploration of the subject,
but he was evidently aware of the operative principle and
presumably felt that it was enough to acknowledge the capacity of art to organize experience and synthesize a superior truth, much as Shelley, in *A Defence of Poetry*, said
imagination and poetry should function. But Jeffers did
speak of his desire to permit the meaning of his poems to
emerge naturally from the tension of opposing structures
or ideological positions. Yet there is almost always the
overbearing presence in a Jeffers poem of the intellectual
statement to be made—simply the existence of which contradicts his aesthetic theory and occasionally threatens the
success of the work itself.[44] The accusation has often been

made that the characters in Jeffers' long narrative poems
are not full, round, and credible, but rather mere vehicles
for abstract ideas, which are skeletal, flat, and lifeless.
There are other readers, of course, who find the same characters quite vivid, but I am inclined to believe that these
readers have been overwhelmed by the actions which Jeffers gave to his characters and that they have never gone
beyond the actions themselves to discover the sometimes
astonishing vacuity of the individual characters. Furthermore, it is just this confusion of objectives within Jeffers
that impeded the growth of his aesthetic theory and possibly a comparable artistic fulfillment of its tenets. Consider
for a moment Voltaire's *Candide,* in which the characters
represent ideological abstractions. They are abstractions
presented in one of the best examples of the genre of the
conte philosophique, or Menippean satire, which was intended to deal solely with ideas; but the indomitable Dr.
Pangloss, the much-tried Cunegonde, and the searching
Candide have endured remarkably their respective abstractions. In other words, Voltaire gave them life and the capacity to impress the reader lastingly with their individuality.

A final aspect of the poetry remains to be discussed. In
the poem *The Beginning and the End,* from the posthumous volume, Jeffers presents a summary of his world
view. He observes that

> The human race is one of God's
> sense-organs,
> Immoderately alerted to feel good and evil
> And pain and pleasure.
>
> (*Beginning,* pp. 9–10)

The mission of man, the poet asserts, is "To find and feel,"
to register sense impressions of God's world. Men stand in
relationship to God, he believes, as poems do to men.

As Titan-mooded Lear or Prometheus reveal to their
    audience
Extremes of pain and passion they will never find
In their own lives but through the poems as sense-organs
They feel and know them: so the exultations and agonies of
    beasts and men
Are sense-organs of God.

                                              (*Beginning,* p. 10)

Modern man has come to suspect sensory data experi-
enced under certain circumstances and to realize that interesting changes can occur between the object as it really
is and the object as he apprehends it. This deceptive nature of sense experience is implicit in the analogy between
sense organs and such poems as *The Great Wound,* in
which Jeffers says, "The poet also / Has his mythology"—
that Troy was burned for Helen, for example, or that the
moon arose "Out of the Pacific basin." But the poets are
not alone, continues Jeffers:

The mathematicians and physics men
Have their mythology; they work alongside the truth,
Never touching it; their equations are false
But the things *work.*

                                              (*Beginning,* p. 11)

Undoubtedly, Jeffers would have approved equally of the
poets' hypothesis that Venus contributes to mortal love
and of the physicists' hypothesis that the flow of electricity
from positive to negative poles in circuits is due to the
movement of electrons. Neither explanation, of course, is
completely demonstrable, but for the moment they will
serve. "Oh happy Homer," Jeffers says in *The Epic Stars,*
"taking the stars and the gods for granted." If the mytholo-
gies of the poet and the scientist seemed to share equal authority in *The Great Wound,* the superiority of the poet's,

as we should have anticipated, is established in *Let Them Alone:* "If God has been good enough to give you a poet / Then listen to him." The poet, then, partakes of the "divine" in Jeffers' view, a view resembling that of Shelley, who affirmed in *A Defence of Poetry,* "Poetry is indeed something divine.... it is that ... to which all science must be referred." In *Let Them Alone* Jeffers adds, "A poet is one who listens / To nature and his own heart," and this sentiment, as romantic and commonplace as it may be, serves Jeffers admirably. The poet's poems are sense organs reporting the universe of God to the people. Whatever data are transmitted, however, are reduced to order in the alembic of the poet's craft. Not only is he supersensitive to the world about him, but the poet, because of his office, assumes an interpretive role.

In his *Defence,* Shelley declared that the poet is both legislator and prophet, and "participates in the eternal, the infinite, and the one," adding that it is the poet who apprehends the relation between existence and perception, perception and expression. To some extent, Nietzsche also shared this view of the poet-philosopher when he said, "Genuine philosophers, however, are ... legislators."[45] With these sentiments Jeffers agreed, as when, in *The Silent Shepherds,* he acknowledged the necessity of an extraordinary intermediary figure between the people and the truth. "Science and mathematics / Run parallel to reality," he observed; "they symbolize it, they squint at it, / They never touch it." In the last paragraph of *Themes in My Poems,* Jeffers declared that poetry is "a means of discovery, as well as a means of expression." The superiority of poetry is obvious as he goes on: "Science usually takes things to pieces in order to discover them; it dissects and analyzes; poetry puts things together, producing equally valid discovery, and actual creation. Something new is found out, something that the author himself did not know before he wrote it; and something new is made."

With the exception of the moral effect of tragedy, Jeffers was extraordinarily consistent from the beginning of his major production onward with respect to the role of the poet in society and to the function of poetry. The poet is a superior being—a mixture of Plato's divinely inspired Tynnichus and Shelley's "hierophants of an unapprehended inspiration, the mirrors of the gigantic shadows which futurity casts upon the present." He is the prophet who knows a higher truth because of his greater range of vision; unlike other men, he is able to free himself to a greater degree from the limitations of contemporary details in order to view the broader vistas of the future. He must deal with everyday life, as Jeffers apologetically admitted in the Note to *Be Angry at the Sun,* but the seer's natural concern is with the future—"great poetry is pointed at the future," he said in "Poetry, Gongorism, and a Thousand Years." Thus he dealt with universal themes and eternity, and he addressed himself to a worthy audience who would read him a thousand years hence. For a poet to be great in his own time required the sort of accident—the right man in the right place at the right time—that befell Yeats.

Jeffers regarded poetry as the rightful vehicle of truth, but, with Nietzsche, also believed that "poets lie too much." Thus a resuscitation of poetry was required in which the artificialities of form such as rhyme, meter, and intricate stanzaic arrangement would be scrapped in favor of more truly organic structure related to the living forms it was meant to describe. Furthermore, though Jeffers held that the truth of poetry is superior to that of prose, mathematics, and science in general, the poet must use the analogy of myth in representing the truth he has seen. Consistent with this aspect of Jeffers' theories is the notion that human beings are the sense organs of God and the implied parallel that poems are likewise the sense organs of the people. It is characteristic of Jeffers' special interest in science that this latter aspect of his theories preserved the element of physiological error or psychological distortion, which can be represented in nonpoetic terms, for example, by the "burning" touch of ice or the "unfelt" (at first) amputation.

In his poems, Jeffers meant to provide the images and ideas from which the reader could derive his message. He meant the reader to receive the commentary of the poem through a sort of Hegelian synthesis of opposed images, ideas, and structures. Finally, Jeffers believed that poetry should synthesize and focus the experience of man.

2

jeffers and schopenhauer

From the beginning of Jeffers' major work—with the publication of *Tamar and Other Poems*—critics have commented variously on the influence of Schopenhauer's and Nietzsche's thought on the poems. Some writers discounted altogether the influence of Nietzsche, some referred only obliquely to the Nietzschean character of the work, and some tried to provide a specific analysis of the Nietzscheanism which they detected.[1] Other critics, however, believed they found greater support for the influence of Schopenhauer, the most recent and thorough advocate for this position being Radcliffe Squires in *The Loyalties of Robinson Jeffers*.[2]

"It is to Schopenhauer that Jeffers bears a resemblance, and not, as critics for the past twenty years have been insisting, to Nietzsche," contends Squires. The difference between Jeffers and Nietzsche, as Squires sees it, is equal to that between Nietzsche and Schopenhauer.[3] Squires does not cite external evidence to support his argument for the primacy of Schopenhauer's influence, and regrettably the case he builds from internal evidence is inconclusive. From a letter by the poet's son, we now know, however, that "most of the works of Nietzsche and of Schopenhauer ... [were] in [his] father's library."[4] As we shall see, Jeffers' poetry clearly does not reflect the influence of Schopenhauer; this argument is only strengthened by the knowledge that the poet had in his library and presumably read Schopenhauer's works, and we may conclude that Jeffers simply did not find in Schopenhauer a congenial source for the ideas in his poems.[5]

When Squires states that "the essential concern in Schopenhauer, the relation of matter and idea, is an essential concern in Jeffers," and that Schopenhauer and Jeffers come to the same conclusion, i.e., "that there exists a superior reality behind appearance, a reality which is discoverable, though not easily so," he merely points to an epistemological problem which has occupied the minds of most Western thinkers since the time of Plato.[6] It is true that Jeffers' preoccupation with these matters could have derived from Schopenhauer, but it might as easily have come from him via Nietzsche, or from his study of Shelley, or, especially since Jeffers was a student of the classics, from Plato himself, or from Lucretius.

In order to meet the pro-Nietzschean argument upon which he says "critics for the past twenty years have been insisting,"[7] Mr. Squires cites the example of the old man in *The Double Axe*, who addresses the universe:

> Dear love. You are so beautiful.
> Even this side the stars and below the moon. How can you be
> ... all this ... and me also?
> Be human also? The yellow puma, the flighty mourning-
> dove and flecked hawk, yes, and the rattlesnake
> Are in the nature of things; they are noble and beautiful
> As the rocks and the grass—not this grim ape,

> Although it loves you.—Yet two or three times in my life my
>   walls have fallen—beyond love—no room for love—
> I have been you.
>
> (Double Axe, p. 89)

This passage, however, cannot be used as evidence that the
old man held the Schopenhauerian view of the universe
because the declaration insists explicitly upon an existing
dualism of self and nature that Schopenhauer's whole argument in *The World as Will and Idea* labors to refute.
For Schopenhauer, the phenomenal world exists for an individual only insofar as he can make it real through the
exercise of the will. In another instance, Squires, referring
to the problematical dramatic poem *The Tower Beyond
Tragedy,* notes that Jeffers' Orestes "almost too perfectly
realizes Schopenhauer's concept [i.e., the noblest men surrender life]. . . . Orestes in effect excises the Dionysian element which Nietzsche insisted on in his definition of tragedy."[8] Two items here demand consideration. Orestes,
noble man or not, has not surrendered life; rather, the
poem rings with the affirmation of life. The other point is
that the Dionysian element is *not* excised, but, instead, subjected to Apollonian control, an absolutely necessary
union of the two components of what Nietzsche called the
Will to Power. In *The Birth of Tragedy,* Nietzsche enunciated the dualism of Apollo and Dionysus, but the dualism
modulated subsequently to a monism absorbed within the
concept of the Will to Power.[9]

In order to respond to Squires' conclusion that "it
would seem in the final analysis that Jeffers and Nietzsche
represent two opposed responses to the Schopenhauerian
concept,"[10] it will be necessary to review some of the basic
principles in Schopenhauer's thought and to restudy relevant passages in Jeffers' work; for, though we shall find Jeffers and Schopenhauer fundamentally opposed, there are,
in fact, some interesting resemblances.

The Will

Let us examine three aspects of Schopenhauer's thought: (1) the will, its character and function, (2) Nature, and (3) death. Such a scheme is destined to leave things unsaid and certain of Schopenhauer's ideas unconsidered, but my method is dictated by the relevance of the material to the central subject matter.

"The world is my idea," claimed Schopenhauer by way of summing up his position that knowledge of objects is necessarily confined to the sphere of "ideas," or representations of a perceiving subject. The world exists as "idea" as a result of, and coincidentally with, the perceiving will of the subject, i.e., an individual being. But the awareness that an individual has of his own body as an expression of will, and of his own movements as acts of will do not constitute a dualism. Schopenhauer explains in *The World as Will and Idea*:

> The act of will and the movement of the body are not two different things objectively known, which the bond of causality unites; they do not stand in the relation of cause and effect; they are one and the same, but they are given in entirely different ways,—immediately, and again in perception for the understanding. The action of the body is nothing but the act of will objectified, *i.e.,* passed into perception. ... the whole body is nothing but objectified will, *i.e.,* will become idea. ... Thus in a certain sense we may also say that will is the knowledge *a priori* of the body, and the body is the knowledge *a posteriori* of the will.[11]

Having begun in the middle of things, let us go back to discover what Schopenhauer means by the will, for it appears at first to be similar to Nietzsche's Will to Power. But it is a serious error to confuse them, for such an error could lead to misunderstanding Jeffers' design. Schopenhauer's concept of will is:

... not merely willing and purposing in the narrowest sense, but also all striving, wishing, shunning, hoping, fearing, loving, hating, in short, all that directly constitutes our own weal and woe, desire and aversion, is clearly only affection of the will, is a moving, a modification, of willing and non-willing, is just that which, if it takes outward effect, exhibits itself as an act of will proper. (2:412)

When the individual, striving, wishing will realizes its objectification as idea (mind the Schopenhauerian distinction that *idea* equals *object*), the individual participates in the principle of individuation (*principium individuationis*). The individual is then able to recognize his phenomenal self as the physical manifestation of the objectified will, and this phenomenal existence is distinct from the "thing-in-itself," as Schopenhauer termed it—the noumenon.

The concept of good "is essentially relative," according to Schopenhauer, "and signifies *the conformity of an object to any definite effort of the will*" (1:465). The bad man is he who, in asserting his own will to live, insists on denying the will of another as it appears in that other person's body. The good man, realizing that all individuals are truly one (i.e., individuations of a common noumenon), asserts his will in such a way as not to deny that of others. The "veil of Maya" is a figure that Schopenhauer uses to represent the principle of individuation. A bad man, we may say, is enmeshed in the veil of Maya and has no awareness of individuality other than his own; a just man penetrates the veil to the extent that he refuses to assert himself egoistically and thus injure others, whom he places on a level with himself; but the good and virtuous man realizes that individuality is illusion, for he has penetrated the veil of Maya and sees himself truly, when he can say in reference to all other individuals, *Tat tvam asi* ("This thou art").[12] The extremes of good and bad are not likely to be actually occupied by men, and the greatest number of people fall somewhere in between, simply exhibiting an individual tendency toward one or the other extreme.

Why, then, do not the operation of the will to live through the principle of individuation and the implicit morality involved account completely for the natures of Jeffers' Tamar, Fayne Fraser (*Give Your Heart to the Hawks*), Madrone Bothwell (*Solstice*), Hungerfield and his mother, Alcmena (*Hungerfield*), Medea, and even Clare Walker (*The Loving Shepherdess*)? Such an explanation is attractive, indeed, until we recognize that in each case—with the exception of Clare Walker (whose special function is mentioned above)—the struggle of the individual concerned is not simply with "striving, wishing, shunning, hoping, fearing, loving, hating," but with the achieving of power, or the failure to achieve it, through the mastery of one's surroundings and of oneself, i.e., the Nietzschean doctrine of Overcoming founded in the lively opposition of Dionysian and Apollonian impulses within the individual.

In his recent study, Patrick Gardiner deals at length with the striking correspondence between the notions of Schopenhauer and Freud regarding the operation of the censoring function of the mind.[13] When Schopenhauer described the role of the sexual impulse and its satisfaction, he anticipated Freudian doctrine. The "focus of the will, *i.e.,* its concentration and highest expression," according to Schopenhauer, "is the sexual impulse and its satisfaction. . . . The assertion of the will to live . . . has its centre in the act of generation" (3:380). The sexual impulse is important in dramatic literature and novels, Schopenhauer observes, as well as "in the real world, where next to the love of life, it shows itself the strongest and most powerful of motives"

(3:339). Schopenhauer declares that the satisfaction of the sexual impulse—which may appear to an individual as simply the fulfillment of his urgent desires by psychologically heightened pleasure (i.e., the search for and union with an "ideal" mate)—is "short-sighted" and merely private; the true character of the act is procreative with the aim of continuing the species. In other words, the individual's egoistic pursuit of satisfaction is guilefully designed by nature to preserve the species (3:346–49). In this connection, Schopenhauer makes the interesting observation that to attain satisfaction of the sexual impulse, a man "often sacrifices his own happiness in life, contrary to all reason, by a foolish marriage, by love affairs which cost him wealth, honour, and life, even by crimes such as adultery or rape, all merely in order to serve the species in the most efficient way, although at the cost of the individual, in accordance with the will of nature which is everywhere sovereign" (3:347–48).

There, cries the advocate of Schopenhauer's influence on Jeffers, is just the answer intended in the conclusion of *Give Your Heart to the Hawks,* in which Fayne Fraser, after burying her suicide husband under rocks at the foot of a cliff, declares that her husband's unborn child will change the world. One might at first agree with the advocate's assertion, but, in the light of other Nietzschean aspects of the poem, Jeffers' ending may be explained as an instance of the principle of Eternal Recurrence. But consider the case of Jeffers' Tamar, who had her desire, as he says in *Apology for Bad Dreams (Selected Poetry).* Procreation and survival of the species have no place in her vision of life. When she becomes pregnant, the sin of her incestuous desires is made substantial and her plans are thwarted until a spontaneous abortion clears her way. When, from the sick bed, she turns her physical charms on her hypocritical father, Tamar not only scores a triumph of mind over matter in the person of her foolish father, but she makes it emphatically clear that she is employing the sex impulse to achieve a private end—personal satisfaction *and* power—survival of the species be damned.

In his portrayals of Tamar, Reverend Barclay (*The Women at Point Sur*), and Fera Martial (*Cawdor*), Jeffers drew characters who sought to alter their situation or condition in life by gaining power and by exercising this power, without consideration for others. They exemplify Nietzsche's Will to Power. It is not clear whether Nietzsche intended that an individual who employed the Will to Power to overcome himself (as Zarathustra preached) would significantly change his ethical constitution; overcoming oneself and thus transcending mediocrity apparently was to Nietzsche a necessarily reckless and careless procedure, which, incidentally, admits a ruthlessness that Jeffers clearly repudiated in the course of his examination of Nietzsche's system. Schopenhauer, however, is clear on this item. Pangs of conscience, he says, or anguish of conscience are simply pain at the knowledge of oneself in one's inmost nature and the disturbing realization that this nature is unalterable. Ethical characteristics, whether virtuous or vicious, are "innate and ineradicable." In his book *On the Foundation of Morality* (sec. 20), Schopenhauer explains: "the wicked man is born with his wickedness as the snake is born with its poison fangs and its sac of venom, and the one can as little change his nature as the other."[14]

Like Nietzsche, who followed him, Schopenhauer was largely negative in his treatment of ethical matters, for he was concerned with clearing away the presuppositions which support traditional moral philosophy, but, unlike Nietzsche, as Gardiner explains, he sought to suppress "especially the conception of the moral agent as a being capable of moulding his own character and manner of life by acts of free rational choice and conscious volition."[15] It is possible to see an apparent freedom of will in the actions of men compared with those of animals, Schopenhauer asserted in *The World as Will and Idea,* because in "the case of the brute there can only be a choice between perceptible motives presented to it, so that the choice is limited to the narrow sphere of its present sensuous perception" (1: 384). To the spectator the motives of the brute are thus observable; "while in the case of man the motives are almost always abstract ideas, which are not communicated to the spectator, and even for the actor himself the necessity of their effect is hidden behind their conflict" (1:384). Thus in the choice a man makes there is an *apparent* freedom of will, but Schopenhauer is quite firm in stressing that in actuality a man's choices tend to reveal his personality. Such expression, Schopenhauer averred, "is by no means to be regarded as freedom of the particular volition, i.e., independence of the law of causality, the necessity of which extends to man as to every other phenomenon" (1: 388). The phenomenon of the human will, however, is denied other animals by definition, and it is just this phenomenon that permits a man knowledge of ideas through the *principium individuationis.*

At this stage, there is an "actual appearance of the real freedom of the will as a thing-in-itself . . . by which the phenomenon comes into a sort of contradiction with itself, as indicated by the word self-renunciation," and the "in-itself of its nature suppresses itself" (1:388–89). In this reconciliation of determinism and freedom of the will, there is an interesting parallel between Schopenhauer's arguments and those of Jonathan Edwards' famous defense of freedom of will within the confines of Calvinistic determinism. Schopenhauer maneuvered within a deterministic framework to preserve a nevertheless restricted freedom of will, but his objectives clearly contrast with those of Nietzsche and such Nietzschean characters in Jeffers' poems as Tamar Cauldwell, Fera Martial, Fayne Fraser, Walter Margrave, Helen Thurso, Howard Howren, and Hungerfield, who all valiantly fought violent battles with those external forces often regarded as deterministic. For many years it has been customary among Jeffers' critics, epitomized by H. H. Waggoner, to note the determinism in the long narrative poems, especially *Tamar* and *Cawdor*. Waggoner sees a similarity between Jeffers' position and that of the behaviorist John B. Watson, who said, "We need nothing to explain behavior but the ordinary laws of physics and chemistry."[16] Waggoner's estimate is not without its truth, of course, but it fails to recognize that, although the rationale of Jeffers' poems, like the rationale which Nietzsche used as a point of departure for his philosophy, is often deterministic, the chief concern of Jeffers' heroines and heroes is the possibility of their transcending these imposed hereditary and environmental limitations. That their attempts regularly follow the Nietzschean formulas is evident to the reader who is prepared to recognize them.

We only come to know ourselves a posteriori through our experiences, according to Schopenhauer, and our deeds thus become the expression of our determined character. In these acts, the expression of our character, "the mirror of the will" (as he calls it), we see and recognize our inmost self; therefore, he says, "it behoves us to strive and fight in time, in order that the picture we produce by our deeds may be such that the contemplation of it may calm us as much as possible, instead of harassing us" (1: 390). Such contemplation leads the individual to the awareness of himself and his possibilities, that is, he contemplates what Schopenhauer called the acquired character. Acquired character is "nothing but the most perfect

knowledge possible of our own individuality," or, put
more negatively, a fulfilling of our given limitations (1:
393). We are what we are, and Schopenhauer insists that
"since the whole man is only the phenomenon of his will,
nothing can be more perverse than to try, by means of reflection, to become something else than one is, for this is a
direct contradiction of the will itself" (1:395).

Individual men, therefore, are "free" to fulfill predeter-
mined images of their distinct capabilities, and they cannot expect to develop in a fashion that contradicts these
images. Yet it is possible to escape from the constant series
of willings that define one's life by entering a "state of
pure contemplation," which may be attained through "aesthetic pleasure in the beautiful" (1:504). It follows, therefore, that since pleasure is derived from the cessation of
willing during the contemplation of the beautiful, continued bliss may be maintained by silencing the will as much
as, and as long as, possible. If a man can conquer his will,
"nothing can trouble him more, nothing can move him,
for he has cut all the thousand cords of will which hold us
bound to the world, and, as desire, fear, envy, anger, drag
us hither and thither in constant pain" (1:504–5). In
such a state, man sees "life and its forms" as fleeting illusions which evaporate like mists and reveal to him true reality. As we have already seen, Schopenhauer's ideas are analogous to the Upanishadic doctrine that the veil of Maya
represents phenomenal reality behind which exists true reality; man seeks to identify with this permanent reality in
accord with the Upanishadic formula, *Tat tvam asi* ("This
thou art"), i.e., the inner identity of the individual with
the world as a whole.[17] And though he has expressly con-
nected his doctrine of the denial of the will with the Buddhist conception, Schopenhauer does not relinquish the
tenet which asserts that, "denial, abolition, conversion

[turning] of the will, is also the abolition and the vanishing of the world, its mirror," since the world is no more than "the self-knowledge of the will" (1:529–30).

Nature

It is abundantly evident in Jeffers' poetry that he seeks identity with a Nature that represents reality, peace, and permanence. When, in *Rock and Hawk,* Jeffers seeks to unite the symbols of "bright power" (the hawk) and "dark peace" (the rock)—"Fierce consciousness joined with final / Disinterestedness"—he reveals vividly the quest that directs so many of his poems. But the stone will endure; that is why, Jeffers says in *Tor House,* he made his house of stone to permit one to "look for this place after a handful of lifetimes."

> My ghost you needn't look for; it is probably
> Here, but a dark one, deep in the granite, not dancing on
>   wind
> With the mad wings and the day moon.

These sentiments are thoroughly representative of Jeffers' entire production; his problem was to find a manner of living that would lead to this sort of reconciliation with a permanent universe. Repeatedly, Jeffers emphasizes the questionable merit of man's life which transpires within a lasting, yet often unappreciated, terrestrial environment made beautiful by Nature and despoiled by man. And clearly, the world to which Jeffers addresses his hymns of praise does not depend for its existence upon the poet's creating will. His house will be there "a handful of lifetimes" from now. In *Hooded Night,* the poet looks about him, "at night, toward dawn," and sees the world huddled in a sea fog and "the heavy granite bodies of the rocks of the head-

land" which were there "before the first man." Comparing
the vast beauty of such surroundings with inconsequential
human life, he says,

> Here is reality.
> The other is a spectral episode: after the inquisitive animal's
> Amusements are quiet: the dark glory.

If the phenomenal world also represents a physical manifestation of a more real mystical identity analogous to the
Buddhist conception of the veil of Maya, it does not, for
Jeffers, depend upon any individual will for its objectification, as it must according to Schopenhauer's doctrine of
the world as "self-knowledge of the will." This doctrine, if
it were operative in the case of Jeffers, would be an impossible intellectual foundation for nearly all of his poetry.
Schopenhauer's main tenet denies the possibility of Jeffers'
main objective.

What has already been said about the will and about the
phenomenal world as the objectification of the "tireless"
will serves as a convenient background in an examination
of Schopenhauer's ideas on Nature and their possible relevance to Jeffers' poetry; for without the will, as Schopenhauer describes it, there could be no Nature to discuss.
Schopenhauer's summary of the relationship of man to
world is quite clear:

> Every one is thus himself in a double aspect the whole world,
> the microcosm; finds both sides whole and complete in him-
> self. And what he thus recognizes as his own real being also
> exhausts the being of the whole world—the macrocosm; thus
> the world, like man, is through and through *will,* and
> through and through *idea,* and nothing more than this.
> (1:212)

In the light of the foregoing discussion of the denial of will
and of the phenomenal world as each individual's willing

objectification of a commonly accessible noumenon, the possibility that Jeffers had a similar view of Nature is obviously ruled out. Furthermore, the enduring Nature with which Jeffers dealt was created by a Supreme Being, whom the poet variously described as his work and thinking developed.

Throughout his career, Jeffers repeated substantially what he said in the early poem *Divinely Superfluous Beauty* that he longs for "divinely superfluous beauty" as an ardent lover longs for union: "O let our loves too / Be joined...." Properly seen, the world of Nature is a world of excessive beauty divinely given. *Oh, Lovely Rock* is a paean to the lasting beauty of the world in which the poet finds himself. Jeffers ponders the inevitability of his own death and the deaths of his sons, who are camping with him in a "pathless gorge of Ventana Creek"; the wolves will howl again "in the snow around a new Bethelehem"; but, the poet says of the "lovely rock,"

> the energies
> That are its atoms will still be bearing the whole mountain
> above: and I, many packed centuries ago,
> Felt its intense reality with love and wonder, this lonely rock.

Jeffers says,

> it is deep peace and
> final joy
> To know that the great world lives, whether man dies or
> not. The beauty of things is not harnessed to human
> Eyes and the little active minds: it is absolute.
> (*Double Axe,* p. 113)

After this observation, there can be no doubt that Jeffers' conception of the world cannot be reconciled with Schopenhauer's doctrine of the world as will and idea. Jeffers is pleased to discover that the existence of the beauty of Na-

ture is independent of man's intellect or imagination, and
it is comforting for him to realize that his own low regard
for humanity will not in turn reflect upon God's world.
The poet does not always hold men entirely responsible
for their shortcomings; they are largely to blame, but not
entirely; for in *De Rerum Virtute,* the poet admits,

> I believe that man too is beautiful,
> But it is hard to see, and wrapped up in falsehoods.
> Michelangelo and the Greek sculptors—
> How they flattered the race! Homer and Shakespeare—
> How they flattered the race!

Difficult to discover and often misrepresented is the beauty
of man, but

> One light is left us: the beauty of things, not men;
> The immense beauty of the world, not the human world.
> Look—and without imagination, desire nor dream—directly
> At the mountains and sea.

Jeffers concludes his poem:

> The beauty of things means virtue and value in them.
> It is in the beholder's eye, not the world? Certainly.
> It is the human mind's translation of the transhuman
> Intrinsic glory. It means that the world is sound,
> Whatever the sick microbe [i.e., man] does. But he too is
>   part of it.

Here Jeffers presents the reverse of Schopenhauer's argument for the moral nature of the world, and for the very
reasons that Schopenhauer rejects pantheism. The objects
of Nature are beautiful for Jeffers and should be accepted
as the unexplained and unwarranted gifts of an inscrutable
deity who creates and appears to forget. So it is clear, for a
number of reasons, that Schopenhauer's doctrines are not
operative in this instance.

In his study of Schopenhauer, Father Copleston concludes: "The philosophy of Arthur Schopenhauer cannot provide a metaphysical basis for natural beauty: it is impossible to see how natural beauty can be in any manner the manifestation of a senseless, empty striving, the metaphysical Will."[18] As if in reply to such a charge against him, Schopenhauer wrote in an essay: "The chief objection I have to Pantheism is that it says nothing. To call the world 'God' is not to explain it; it is only to enrich our language with a superfluous synonym for the word 'world'." Schopenhauer rejects pantheism because, instead of starting with God and explaining Him in terms of the world, it begins with "what is really given, that is to say, from the world, and say[s], 'the world is God,' [thus] it is clear you say nothing, or at least you are explaining what is unknown by what is more unknown." And if logic alone is unconvincing, Schopenhauer offers the opinion that "it must be a very ill-advised god who knows no better way of diverting himself than by turning into such a world as ours. . . ."[19] One of Schopenhauer's main tenets holds that the world depends on the will of the individual, who is obliged to fulfill himself as well and as completely as he can, thereby exercising moral choice. Although both Schopenhauer and Jeffers acknowledge the moral meaning of the world, it would be erroneous to attribute to Jeffers Schopenhauer's insistent and very diverse interpretation of that moral meaning.

Consider, moreover, the following lines from Jeffers' poem *Sign-Post*. The poet advises us to let the "doll" of humanity lie and to "love things, not men." With obvious Biblical overtones, he continues,

> Consider if you like how the lilies grow,
> Lean on the silent rock until you feel its divinity
> Make your veins cold, look at the silent stars,

. . . .

> Things are the God, you will love God, and not in vain,
> For what we love, we grow to it, we share its nature.
> .   .   .   .
>   but now you are free, even to become human,
> But born of the rock and the air, not of woman.

To Schopenhauer, such sentiments would have been ob-
noxious—especially if they were alleged to derive from his
philosophical doctrines. Nor does it seem reasonable to believe that Jeffers would have insisted on an obvious contradiction between his pantheism, a doctrine specifically rejected by Schopenhauer, and Schopenhauer's atheism.

Death

Schopenhauer's ideas about death are frequently misunderstood and falsely used. Too often the pat generalization
is made that Schopenhauer's view of death (and the pre-
sumed advantages of suicide) is roughly equivalent to any
one of the several varieties of death wish. In fact, however,
Schopenhauer says that to seek death, to consider suicide,
for example, is to misunderstand life itself, for such striving can solve nothing for the individual. Suicide differs
most widely, says Schopenhauer, from the denial of the
will to live, which arises "only if suffering assumes the
form of pure knowledge, and this, acting as a *quieter of the
will,* brings about resignation" (1:513). Suicide is "the actual doing away with the individual manifestation of will,"
and "far from being denial of the will, suicide is a phenomenon of strong assertion of will" (1:514). The individual who chooses suicide shuns the joys of life, not its
sorrows, says Schopenhauer; therefore, "the suicide wills
life, and is only dissatisfied with the conditions under
which it has presented itself to him" (1:515). Not only is
Schopenhauer's argument unlikely to alter the intentions

of an individual who is predisposed to suicide, but, in effect, the philosopher reveals a soft underbelly in his thinking vulnerable to attack by theologians.

Death, Schopenhauer explains, means the loss of nothing to the individual who, according to the nature of his will, merely returns from existence as an individual phenomenon to the thing-in-itself from which his individuality originally derived. And Schopenhauer concludes: "Thus the will to live appears just as much in suicide (Siva) as in the satisfaction of self-preservation (Vishnu) and in the sensual pleasure of procreation (Brahma). . . . The suicide denies only the individual, not the species" (1:515). Schopenhauer specifically rejects the idea that death is annihilation, and in a familiar passage he says:

> whoever is oppressed with the burden of life, whoever desires life and affirms it, but abhors its torments, and especially can no longer endure the hard lot that has fallen to himself, such a man has no deliverance to hope for from death, and cannot right himself by suicide. The cool shades of Orcus allure him only with the false appearance of a haven of rest. The earth rolls from day into night, the individual dies, but the sun itself shines without intermission, an eternal noon. (1:362)

The subject of death in Jeffers' poetry involves some problems, for there are situations in his poems where Jeffers comes rather close to Schopenhauer's attitude toward death and suicide. Whereas some of the poet's late work— *My Burial Place, To Death, The Deer Lay Down Their Bones, Hungerfield,* poems written by an old man who had lost his wife and was himself ready for death—appears to reflect Schopenhauer's thinking, an understanding of Schopenhauer and a closer reading of Jeffers' poems preclude a genuine Schopenhauerian influence.

Some of Jeffers' characters clearly reject suicide as a

means of escaping the troubled present. *Thurso's Landing* is a full-scale narrative which touches repeatedly on the subjects of death, suicide, and the afterlife. Thurso's Landing is the site of an exhausted limeworks on the Pacific Coast, where two generations of Thursoes have lived. Old man Thurso, for whom the location is named, chose suicide as an escape from the overwhelming problems of his life. At the time of the narrative, the present generation includes Reave Thurso, Helen, his wife, and his brother Mark, who was wounded while in France with Reave during the war. Reave's mother, who has "the alienation and tamelessness and sullied splendor / Of a crippled hawk in a cage" (p. 23), is also present. *Thurso's Landing* may appear to have no single protagonist; it is the tale of a troubled family in a particular area—exemplifying Jeffers' theory that tragedy should deal with families.[20] Jeffers is content to give his characters some violent action and the freedom to discuss death and suicide, ostensibly to show, as he notes at the end of the poem, that "our nature," as bad as it may be, can "at stricken moments . . . shine terribly against the dark magnificence of things" (p. 123). Nevertheless, the fact that Helen has just cut her crippled husband's throat while kissing him, and that she in turn dies horribly after gulping contraceptive pills as Reave's mother looks on and refuses to give Helen the quick death for which she begs as the pills begin to take effect weakens the poet's closing message that occasionally human nature is "More shining than that of the other animals" (p. 123).

The chief motivating force in the actions of Helen and Reave Thurso and the chief conflict in the entire poem is the relationship of these individuals and their generation to their fathers. Early in the poem, Helen and Reave make pointed comparisons with their fathers. Like Fera Martial's father in *Cawdor,* for whom Fera made great sacrifices to support his weakness, Helen's father was weak and lacked the ability to succeed. Helen feels, on the one hand, that her father did not possess essential courage, for he "died crying" after living as long as he could on the wages Helen made while working in a laundry and later crating fruit. On the other hand, old man Thurso also lacked courage, Reave and Helen agree, for when the lime kilns failed he could not redirect his holdings to another kind of production. Accepting his first setback as defeat, old Thurso killed himself, leaving his wife and young sons to fend for themselves. They manage to get back on their feet by turning to farming, but the family is convinced that the specter of old Thurso returns regularly to survey his property, the supervision from the past being symbolized by the cable and skip that still spans the canyon in which the family lives.

Both Helen and Reave reject their fathers, and each seeks to compensate in himself for the character of the parent. Like Tamar and Fera and Fayne Fraser, Helen follows a strong-willed course of action, but her characterization is often self-contradictory and plainly subordinated to that of Reave; Helen says of him, as he is about to sever the cable and thus his relationship to the past (specifically to his father), "That's the man we're measured against" (p. 76).

If Reave at that point represents a very high standard of moral fortitude, as it may be called in the context of the poem, he immediately becomes a still more exacting model, for the cable, parting, smashes him down like the lizard that he killed in the desert and leaves him pain-wracked and impotent, but determined to endure every minute of his suffering. "I'll never ease myself out by hand" (p. 83), Reave tells Helen. (Early in the poem, however, Helen sharply criticizes Reave for shooting Bones, the aged dog, and he answers simply that he saved pain, which apparently he feels is without value to nonhumans.) Reave's determination sounds like Schopenhauer, but so does another incident. Just before the cable-cutting, Mark, the maimed and much less dynamic brother, receives a message from the father's ghost:

> "Life's all a dream," it said,
> "And death is a better more vivid immortal dream,
> But love is real; both are made out of love,
> That's never perfect in life, and the voids in it
> Are the pains of life. . . ."
>
> (*Thurso,* pp. 72–73)

Although these comments are recognizably reminiscent of Schopenhauer in their attitude toward life and death, they do not constitute a justification of suicide, and it is significant that the poet interrupts the narrative at this point to declare these pronouncements of the ghost to be the singing of "the false prophet."

Just after Reave declares that he will never ease himself out by hand, the poet returns again in his own voice to deliver the following opinion:

> No life
> Ought to be thought important in the weave of the world,
> whatever it may show of courage or endured pain;
> It owns no other manner of shining, in the broad gray eye
> of the ocean, at the foot of the beauty of the mountains
> And skies, but to bear pain; for pleasure is too little, our
> inhuman God is too great, thought is too lost.
>
> (*Thurso,* p. 84)

Even if this conception of life as pain were derived from Schopenhauer's philosophy, the insistence here upon God —even this unorthodox conception of Him—and upon the obvious dualism of man and Nature, or more precisely Nature's independence of man, nullifies further argument in favor of the positive influence of Schopenhauer.

It is Mark, maimed and passive, who first yields to the advice of the paternal ghost and to suicide. When Reave brings Helen home from her amorous year of escape with Rick Armstrong, she finds an opportunity to turn her seductive ways upon the mild Mark, but he fails to respond, and Helen does not repeat her invitation. On the eve before Mark is found hanging from a sycamore, he maladroitly offers to join Helen in the act of love, but Helen, now otherwise occupied, rejects his fumblings. Ineffectual and weak-willed, Mark cannot come to terms with life and withdraws to where "this room is purer," as he says in his suicide note.

In spite of Reave's firm stand that "there's nothing a man can't bear" (p. 91), Helen believes that she is obliged to deliver him from his suffering after the accident with the cable. Whether or not her solicitude for Reave's suffering actually obscures a revenge motive is insufficiently clear, but revenge is certainly a possibility in a character like Helen. Reave's mother frustrates Helen's plan by warning her son of his wife's intentions. Yet high on the brow of a hill, on a platform overlooking Thurso's Landing, Helen succeeds at last. She cuts her husband's throat as she kisses him:

He heard her crying

She'd done it for love, he formed his lips to say "Bitch,"
But breath and the light failed.

. . . .

Then all was perfect

 No-pain.

(*Thurso*, pp. 119–20)

Helen kills herself ironically with contraceptive pills, and Reave's mother, the remaining representative of the willingness to suffer what is required to live, refuses to shorten Helen's agony. Not only has Helen killed Reave and ended his suffering, but she has also eliminated the man against

whom the characters of the poem are measured. In the ago-
nizing death which she chooses, Helen finds that she cannot "shine terribly" like her husband, and she begs Reave's
mother to hasten the end to relieve her suffering.

Fera Martial, who mourned her father's weaknesses and
who married Cawdor for the power he represented, also attempted suicide. She is revived, however, and saved by her
husband from a moment of weakness. Again suicide is
ruled out by the dominant forces in the poem, but Jeffers
describes old Martial's death earlier in the poem in terms
that invite comparison with Schopenhauer's ideas. As
death invades the body of Fera's father, his dreams of
death are fulfilled:

> Out of time, undistracted by the nudging pulse-beat,
>   perfectly real to itself being insulated
> From all touch of reality the dream triumphed, building
>   from past experience present paradise
> More intense as the decay quickened, but ever more
>   primitive as it proceeded, until the ecstasy
> Soared through a flighty carnival of wines and women to the
>   simple delight of eating flesh, and tended
> Even higher, to an unconditional delight.
>
> (*Cawdor*, p. 50)

The "unconditional delight" toward which ecstasy soared
is not explicitly specified and quickly diffuses the concentration of images and idea at the beginning of the passage,
but the terminology at the beginning also admits the possibility of Schopenhauer's influence. Man's individuality as
a phenomenon of the will depends, said Schopenhauer, on
temporality, which in turn involves spatialization. Thus, to
Schopenhauer, death, the return to the thing-in-itself, is a
freeing from time, a return to a state of timelessness; but
the dream, as an extension of the noumenon, has less actual reality as phenomenon than it has as idea. In other

words, the progress in Schopenhauer from less reality to greater reality is the reverse of the presentation given in the above passage. Upon close analysis, what appears to be sound Schopenhauer doctrine turns out to be otherwise.

This conclusion is supported by other evidence taken from the same section of the poem. Jeffers describes the death of old Martial and that of the caged eagle later in the poem in terms that are predominantly physiological. For Jeffers, who had had training as a medical student, life was a sort of glowing, an incandescense which transformed inanimate material into living organism. Life is a beautifully complex system of chemical, metabolic, and synaptic processes that do not click off in an instant of death, but that fade out and deteriorate until all the processes of the chemistry of life have run down. As a medical student especially interested in the physiology of the cell, Howard Howren, in *Such Counsels You Gave to Me,* is Jeffers' most articulate spokesman of these theories.

Therefore it is possible for Jeffers, in the lines just preceding those quoted above, to say, "gently the dead man's brain / Glowing by itself made and enjoyed its dream." After the ascent of the ecstasy to unconditional delight, Jeffers says,

> But then the
> interconnections between the groups of the brain
> Failing, the dreamer and the dream split into multitude.
> Soon the altered cells became unfit to express
> Any human or at all describable form of consciousness.
> (*Cawdor,* p. 50)

Here Jeffers' emphasis is materialistic.

An early poem, *Suicide's Stone,* is written from the point of view of a man in the grave who chose premature death. "Peace is the heir of dead desire," the man says, "Peace is the ashes of that fire." This suicide found peace

through his act—"This last and best and goal"—yet he
counsels the living,

> you shall not reach a finger
> To pluck it unripe and before dark
> Creep to cover.

Apologetically, the dead man tells us that "life broke ten
whipstocks / Over [his] back, broke faith, stole hope," before he "denounced the covenant of courage." Characteristically, Jeffers endorses courage in the face of whatever
life brings, and man's value is measured in terms of what
he can endure. The dead man in the poem tries to qualify
his failure to accept adversity, but he admits that he now
enjoys peace. Schopenhauer asserted that true peace and
calm are attainable only by denial of the will to live (arising
only "if suffering assumed the form of pure knowledge")
and that suicide is the "actual doing away with the individual manifestation of will," thus "far from being denial
of the will, suicide is a phenomenon of strong assertion of
will" (1:514).

In *The Beginning and the End*, the title poem of his last
volume, Jeffers "speak[s] of the life [which grew] . . . from
that chemical energy," and he wonders how "pleasure and
pain, wonder, love, adoration, hatred and terror . . . grow /
From a chemical reaction" (p. 7). Evidently, Jeffers still
held the materialistic views that would separate him from
Schopenhauer. Another poem, *Momument*, from the same
volume, reveals an inclination toward a monistic view of
life but still a view unlike that of Schopenhauer: "It is all
truly one life, red blood and tree-sap, / Animal, mineral,
sidereal, one stream, one organism, one God" (p. 25). In
this instance, Schopenhauer's essay on pantheism is sufficient refutation of the argument that he influenced the
poet.

In *The Shears,* one of the Three Uncollected Poems in the appendix to his last volume, Jeffers watches his "little flower-greedy daughter-in-law" snip off a rose and take it indoors, where the rose "is part of the life she watched" through the window. Jeffers concludes that so at death "we become part of the living earth / And wind and water whom we so loved. We are they." From the beginning to the end of his career, Jeffers attempted the reconciliation of a materialistic view of the world, modern science, and a modified theology. At some points, his handling of these subjects seems at first to resemble the views of Schopenhauer; but these instances are rare and always turn out on closer examination to differ from Schopenhauer's views. For all practical purposes, Jeffers' handling of death and suicide is free of Schopenhauer's influence.

Under three main topics in Schopenhauer's philosophical system—the will, Nature, and death—there are significant ideas that Jeffers could have shared, but the evidence presented shows that the two men are plainly opposed in their fundamental conceptions. Although occasional teasing similarities can be discovered, they are generally contingent upon a foundational agreement between the systems which cannot be admitted in the light of this examination of Schopenhauer and Jeffers.

jeffers and nietzsche, the beginning

Jeffers' thinking, we have seen, is fundamentally unlike that of Schopenhauer, and the assertion that Schopenhauer influenced the poet's work appears to be very dubious. In the consideration of Nietzsche's influence, however, we find quite another situation. With some assurance, we can claim that Jeffers not only knew the major works and ideas of Nietzsche, but also experimentally adopted Nietzschean principles in various poems as he gave expression to his poetic vision.

There is no doubt that Jeffers was familiar with the work of Nietzsche. Powell points out that, when Jeffers was a student (between twelve and fifteen years of age) at various boarding schools in Geneva, Lausanne, Zurich, and Leipzig, he "was greatly excited by two books which came into his hands: *Also Sprach Zarathustra* and Rossetti's *Poems.*"[1] Jeffers, whose familiarity with German is easy to substantiate, apparently read *Zarathustra* in the original language; moreover, a recent inventory of the poet's remaining library disclosed English translations of Nietzsche's *Beyond Good and Evil* and *Thus Spoke Zarathustra.*[2]

Alberts' *Bibliography* bore a prefatory statement by Jeffers, who observed that Alberts' persistent thoroughness made him think "sadly that this young man, though himself a poet, seemed infected with the spirit of the conscientious person in *Also Sprach Zarathustra,* the man who is determined to know all about the leech ... but simply all ... or, if that is too wide a subject, the brain of the leech."[3] Included in the Alberts *Bibliography* was a letter which Jeffers wrote to James Rorty sometime after the appearance of Mark Van Doren's review of *The Women at Point Sur.* Referring to his title poem, Jeffers wrote, "It is a matter of 'trans-valuing values,' to use the phrase of somebody that local people accuse me quite falsely of deriving from," and Alberts quite reasonably identified "somebody" as Nietzsche. The subject matter of the poem is accurately described as the "trans-valuing of values," and I suspect from the context that Jeffers' disavowal was meant ironically. Nevertheless, Nietzsche came to mind again when Jeffers wrote the foreword for his *Selected Poetry.* In the course of discussing the development of his verse, Jeffers acknowledged, "Another formative principle came to me from a phrase of Nietzsche's: 'The poets? The poets lie too much.'" The quotation is from *Thus Spoke Zarathustra;* Jeffers goes on, "I was nineteen when the phrase stuck in my mind; a dozen years passed before it worked effectively, and I decided not to tell lies in verse." In other words, Nietzsche was an active factor in a decision Jeffers made midway between the appearance of *Californians* (1916) and *Tamar* (1924). This decision is almost certainly the thirty-year-old promise mentioned in *The Old Stonemason, The Deer Lay Down Their Bones,* and *But I Am Growing Old and Indolent.*

Obviously, then, *Thus Spoke Zarathustra* occupied a prominent place in Jeffers' thinking for years. As a youthful reader, at ease with the German language, Jeffers was attracted to the book, and, looking back as a mature poet, he credited it with playing an important role in his decision to write the kind of poetry that began with *Tamar* and earned him an international reputation as a major poet.

In the following discussion of Nietzsche's main ideas I have drawn most heavily on *Zarathustra* because it is obvious that Jeffers knew the book, and knew it well. Furthermore, his familiarity with German permitted him to respond to the subtleties of the text in a way that Nietzsche's translators until only recently have failed to do. I have emphasized *Zarathustra* with good reason, but I have also felt free to draw from Nietzsche's other works, for they often amplify or support the ideas set forth in *Zarathustra*. From the internal evidence of the poems, we may infer that Jeffers knew *The Birth of Tragedy, The Antichrist,* and *The Will to Power;* moreover, both *Beyond Good and Evil* and *Thus Spoke Zarathustra* were among the remaining books in his library. In any event, the "germs" of these books (and nearly all that Nietzsche wrote) were present in *Zarathustra,* with the exception, of course, of *The Birth of Tragedy.* But most of what Nietzsche believed was important in *The Birth of Tragedy* was restated in *Zarathustra.*

Nietzschean Background

Perhaps Nietzsche is most widely known for his announcement to the world that "God is dead." His statement has undoubtedly won him both friends and enemies—sometimes for the wrong reasons. What Nietzsche meant was that modern man's religious conception of, or emotional response to God had died, and not that God as a divine power beyond man had actually ceased to be. The philosophical task, which Nietzsche accepted with incredible vigor, may be seen as an attempt to justify his statement for men from the facts of their lives and to prepare them to live accordingly. In his brief, but revolutionary, *The Birth of Tragedy* (1872), Nietzsche began his assault by advancing his conception of tragedy and of the tragic implications of life, as a constant striving for equipoise between the two forces called Dionysus (i.e., frenzied, destructive fury) and Apollo ("the god of all plastic energies, is at the same time the soothsaying god").[4] From this initial insight into the nature of man's being, Nietzsche went on to formulate the concepts of the Will to Power, the Overman, Eternal Recurrence, Antichrist, and the necessity of Revaluation of Values.

In order to escape nihilism, which he believed was the chief philosophical problem of his day and upon which he felt Schopenhauer, Schelling, and Hegel had spent themselves, Nietzsche experimented with the possibility of putting "in place of our 'moral values' only *naturalistic values*," i.e., of establishing values that are not based on supernatural authority, or, as Walter Kaufmann puts it, agreeing "not to invoke God to cut short discussion."[5] The Revaluation of Values was to be "an act of supreme self-examination on the part of humanity," Nietzsche said in *Ecce Homo* (*BWN*, p. 782). He meant it to be a contradiction or destruction of received values, and not necessarily the institution of new values in their places. In *Beyond Good and Evil*, for example, he said that Christianity was the "revaluation of all the values of antiquity," and as a result of his examination he condemned the so-called goodness of modern man as not virtuous and his religion as not religious. Men who are already truly powerful and rich will always act with kindness and generosity, and instinctively practice virtue, Nietzsche felt, but the weak man will insist on conformity to old standards which prove a convenient mask for his "petty wickedness."[6]

The Will to Power functions as a method of revaluation, but to understand it we must first consider the forces of Dionysus and Apollo, which Nietzsche described in *The Birth of Tragedy*. The capacity of the Apollonian force within the individual to create harmonious and measured beauty and to shape one's character is always pitted against and must control the conflicting Dionysian impulse to destroy all forms and codes. For Nietzsche, Apollo is "the glorious divine image of the *principium individuationis*," described by Schopenhauer in *The World as Will and Idea* (*BWN*, p. 36). Unlike Schopenhauer's will to live, which is monistic, the Nietzschean Apollo cannot be properly understood except in conjunction with the counterimpulse of Dionysus. Out of this vital oppositon of dynamic forces, Nietzsche contends, tragedy arose.

The dualism of Apollo and Dionysus presented Nietzsche with difficult and all but disruptive philosophical problems, until he introduced the Will to Power (first announced in *Zarathustra*), by means of which he was able to reconcile Dionysus and Apollo, nature and value, wastefulness and purpose. The Will to Power developed out of his investigation of the psychological phenomena of fear (negative) and the will to power (positive). Fear he soon denominated as the negative aspect of our will to power, and he thereby reduced the dualism to a monism. Moreover, because he revised his thinking as he came to realize the ruling concern with power in Greek culture, Nietzsche began again with the problem of the origin of tragedy and substituted the concept of the Will to Power for the dualism of Apollo and Dionysus. When the Will to Power was first announced in *Zarathustra*, Nietzsche equated the principle with the overcoming of oneself: "A tablet of the good hangs over every people. Behold, it is the tablet of their overcomings; behold, it is the voice of their will to power."[7]

To the degree that one can overcome the struggle of opposed forces within himself and achieve balance, that individual exercises his Will to Power. Unlike Schopenhauer's,
Nietzsche's analysis remains consistently psychological. But
how are these conflicting impulses overcome, and what
kind of control is possible? Anticipating Freud, Nietzsche
developed the principle of sublimation. According to
Nietzsche, "Sexual stimulation in the ascent involves a tension which releases itself in the feeling of power: the will
to rule—a mark of the most sensual men; the waning pro-
pensity of the sex impulse shows itself in the relenting of
the thirst for power."[8] In *Beyond Good and Evil,* he wrote:
"The degree and kind of a man's sexuality reach up into
the ultimate pinnacle of his spirit," but by this statement
Nietzsche did not intend to reduce the Will to Power to
sexual libido (*BWN,* p. 271). Sexuality was only a manifestation of the more basic drive, the Will to Power, and
should not be considered the essence of the drive, for
through the mechanism of sublimation, sexuality was canceled. In effect, sex, through sublimation, was a means to
an end, not to sexual fulfillment but to the Will to Power.

In *Zarathustra,* Nietzsche developed two points in discussing the Will to Power. First, the Will to Power is
mainly the struggle toward personal transcendence and the
perfection of oneself. Clearly differentiating between his
position and that of Schopenhauer, he wrote:

> And life itself confided this secret to me: "Behold," it said,
> "I am *that which must always overcome itself.* Indeed, you
> call it a will to procreate or a drive to an end, to something
> higher, farther, more manifold: but all this is one. . . .
>
> Rather would I perish than foreswear this; and verily,
> where there is perishing . . . there life sacrifices itself—for
> [more] power. . . .
>
> Whatever I create and however much I love it—soon I
> must oppose it and my love; . . . 'will to existence': that will

does not exist. . . . not will to life but . . . will to power.

There is much that life esteems more highly than life itself; but out of the esteeming itself speaks the will to power." (*PN*, pp. 227–28)

Second, the powerful man will be creative, but he is not apt to be restricted by previously established rules. Self-mastery is the highest degree of power, and, in *The Twilight of the Idols,* for example, Nietzsche cites Goethe as one who "disciplined himself into wholeness, . . . [who] *created* himself" (*PN*, p. 554).

The Will to Power, which leads to self-mastery, calls forth in turn the idea of the Overman. In his prologue, Zarathustra introduces the important theme of Overcoming, "*I teach you the overman.* Man is something that should be overcome. What have you done to overcome him?" (*PN*, p. 124). Just as Nietzsche sought to break with tradition in order to realize his own unique individuality, he urged the Overman to fulfill himself completely by repudiating conformity and by overcoming the obstacles of mediocrity and stagnation.

Frequently, interpreters of Nietzsche have found in the Overman the basis for a Superman concept—for example, the perversion of Nietzsche's philosophy by Alfred Bäumler (author of *Nietzsche, der Philosoph und Poliker* [1931]), whom the Nazis called to Berlin to "interpret" Nietzsche so as to give the impression that his ideas supported their program. Nietzsche would have contemned this development as a gross distortion of his principle. In *Ecce Homo,* he mentions the matter:

> The word "overman," as the designation of a type of supreme achievement, as opposed to "modern" men, to "good" men, to Christians and other nihilists—a word that in the mouth of a Zarathustra, the annihilator of morality, becomes a very pensive word—has been understood almost

everywhere with the utmost innocence in the sense of those very values whose opposite Zarathustra was meant to represent—that is, as an "idealistic" type of a higher kind of man, half "saint," half "genius."

Other scholarly oxen have suspected me of Darwinism on that account. Even the "hero worship" of that unconscious and involuntary counterfeiter, Carlyle, which I have repudiated so maliciously, has been read into it. (*BWN*, p. 717)

Nietzsche's conception differs from Carlyle's hero-worship in this respect: As a historian, Carlyle believed that a stable society, free of anarchy, depended on hero-worship, i.e., the worship of the great men who made history. For Nietzsche, as Kaufmann points out, "the overman does not have instrumental value for the maintenance of society: he is valuable in himself because he embodies the state of being for which all of us long; he has the only ultimate value there is; and society is censured insofar as it insists on conformity and impedes his development."[9] Again, unlike Schopenhauer, Nietzsche put less emphasis on the preservation of the species than he did on the preservation of the best of the species.

Although Nietzsche reversed his position at least twice during his career on the doctrine of Eternal Recurrence, by the time he wrote late in life the following passage in *The Twilight of the Idols,* the matter had been resolved: "And herewith I again touch that point from which I once went forth: *The Birth of Tragedy* was my first revaluation of values. Herewith I again stand on the soil out of which my intention, my *ability* grows—I, the last disciple of the philosopher Dionysus—I, the teacher of the eternal recurrence" (*PN,* p. 563). But, since in this context *Zarathustra* is a key document, it is particularly significant that in that work Nietzsche wrote, "O Zarathustra . . . behold, *you are the teacher of the eternal recurrence*—that is your

destiny!" and "[Zarathustra] come[s] back eternally to this
same, selfsame life, in what is greatest as in what is small-
est, to teach again the eternal recurrence of all things"
(*PN*, pp. 332–33). As Hegel apparently did, Nietzsche concluded that the idea of infinite progress was the Bad Infinite, and rejected it in favor of Eternal Recurrence.

Antichrist, the last of the principles to be discussed here,
was the original revaluation of values, leading always to a
continuing reassessment of Christianity, to clearing away
the dead wood, as Nietzsche saw it, of orthodox Christianity with its traditional forms and postures. Nietzsche wrote
an illuminating preface for the 1886 edition of *The Birth
of Tragedy* in which he reflected that he had written several times "that the existence of the world is *justified* only
as an aesthetic phenomenon." Furthermore, he wrote,

> Indeed, the whole book knows only an artistic meaning and
> crypto-meaning behind all events—a "god," if you please, but
> certainly only an entirely reckless and amoral artist-god
> who wants to experience, whether he is building or destroy-
> ing, in the good and in the bad, his own joy and glory—one
> who, creating worlds, frees himself from the *distress* of full-
> ness and *overfullness* and from the *affliction* of the contradic-
> tions compressed in his soul. The world—at every moment the
> *attained* salvation of God, as the eternally changing, eter-
> nally new vision of the most deeply afflicted, discordant, and
> contradictory being who can find salvation only in *appear-
> ance*. (*BWN*, p. 22)

For Nietzsche, Christianity as a movement or system was
repugnant; it obscured its own good and protected its
weaknesses. He censured Christianity for its emphasis
upon "another" world and a "better" life:

> Hatred of "the world," condemnations of the passions, fear
> of beauty and sensuality, a beyond invented the better to
> slander this life, at bottom a craving for the nothing, for the
> end, for respite, for "the sabbath of sabbaths"—all this al-

ways struck me, no less than the unconditional will of Christianity to recognize *only* moral values, as the most dangerous and uncanny form of all possible forms of a "will to decline"—at the very least a sign of abysmal sickness, weariness, discouragement, exhaustion, and the impoverishment of life. (*BWN*, p. 23)

In spite of the lack of specific external evidence to confirm the supposition that Jeffers ever read *The Birth of Tragedy*, we know that he owned "most of the works of Nietzsche," and it seems reasonable to assume that a poet who was interested in tragedy and in classical literature should turn to this book, once he had found intellectual stimulation in *Zarathustra*.[10] But in this instance, too, Jeffers had available to him in *Zarathustra* Nietzsche's general attitude toward Christianity, that is, a sincere respect for Jesus and severe criticism of Christianity as an institution begun by Paul, the disciple.

In everything he wrote, Nietzsche maintained the distinction between Jesus of Nazareth and the Christ of the creed; one was a superior man in whom an individual could take pride and encouragement, the other was a fabrication advanced by opportunists and weaklings. In *The Antichrist*, which was to form the first part of the planned *Revaluation of Values*, he said he would tell the "*genuine* history of Christianity":

> The very word "Christianity" is a misunderstanding: in truth, there was only *one* Christian, and he died on the cross. The "evangel" *died* on the cross. What has been called "evangel" from that moment was actually the opposite of that which *he* had lived: "*ill* tidings," a *dysangel*. It is false to the point of nonsense to find the mark of the Christian in a "faith," for instance, in the faith in redemption through Christ: only Christian *practice,* a life such as he *lived* who died on the cross, is Christian. (*PN*, p. 612)

Jesus died "too early," Nietzsche argued; he had not seen

enough of life and people. "He himself would have re-
canted his teaching had he reached my age. Noble enough
was he to recant," declared Zarathustra (*PN,* p. 185). As
the "bringer of glad tidings," Nietzsche emphasized, Jesus
"died as he had lived, as he had taught—*not* to 'redeem
men' but to show how one must live. This practice is his
legacy to mankind" (*PN,* pp. 608–9).

In *The Dawn,* Nietzsche said that Paul was "the first
Christian"; and later in *The Antichrist* he wrote that in
Paul "was embodied the opposite type to that of the
'bringer of glad tidings': the genius in hatred, in the vision
of hatred, in the inexorable logic of hatred" (*PN,* p. 617).
The great danger in the teachings of Paul was the risk of
discrediting the possibilities of this life. According to
Nietzsche, Paul took over the image of Jesus' good example and preached salvation through faith in Christ rather
than salvation through good works and Christ-like living.
Nor did Nietzsche fail to note, to their disadvantage, the
emphasis by Luther and Calvin on faith rather than on
works. (Both Nietzsche and Jeffers, incidentally, were sons
of Protestant ministers.) For Paul, Nietzsche reserved the
severest criticism:

> From now on there enters into the type of the Redeemer,
> step by step: the doctrine of judgment and return, the doc-
> trine of death as sacrificial death, the doctrine of the *resur-
> rection* with which the whole concept of "blessedness," the
> whole and only actuality of the evangel, is conjured away—
> in favor of a state *after* death! (*PN,* p. 616)

Nietzsche inveighed against Christian morality because
he saw it to be founded by the weak for the weak, i.e., for
those who lacked the power to act according to their own
personalities in pursuit of their own objectives. Christian
morality frustrated the power of an individual to realize
his potential, he believed, and, in *The Dawn,* he wrote of

such moral fashions: "These greatest wonders of a classical morality—Epictetus, for example—did not know anything of the now customary glorification of thinking of others and living for others."[11]

In the chapter entitled "On the Tarantulas," in *Zarathustra*, Jeffers must have found the same ideas. Nietzsche there characterizes "Christians" as tarantulas, "poisonous spiders, with their backs turned on life, . . . [who] speak in favor of life, but only because they wish to hurt" (*PN*, p. 213). Zarathustra warns against the "preachers of *equality*," and he advises his friends:

> Mistrust all in whom the impulse to punish is powerful. They are people of a low sort and stock; the hangman and the bloodhound look out of their faces. Mistrust all who talk much of their justice! Verily, their souls lack more than honey. And when they call themselves the good and the just, do not forget that they would be pharisees, if only they had—power. (*PN*, p. 212)

Among similar statements later in *Zarathustra*, Jeffers must also have read:

> When power becomes gracious and descends into the visible—such descent I call beauty.
>
> And there is nobody from whom I want beauty as much as from you who are powerful: let your kindness be your final self-conquest.
>
> Of all evil I deem you capable: therefore I want the good from you.
>
> Verily, I have often laughed at the weaklings who thought themselves good because they had no claws. (*PN*, p. 230)

We have seen how Nietzsche began with the idea that tragedy was born of the uneasy union of Apollo and Dionysus, which dualism was later absorbed by the encompassing monism called the Will to Power. The Will to Power (including the principle of sublimation) solved the prob-

lem of the dichotomy of the Apollonian versus the Dionysian by uniting them, but it did so without surrendering
the original energy and aesthetic consciousness of the original conception. The Will to Power became embodied in
the idea (and type) of the Overman, who functioned in accord with the doctrine of the Eternal Recurrence. Having
arrived at the doctrines of the Overman and of Eternal Recurrence, Nietzsche was able to join his view of human psychology (fear, power, sublimation) and his "supra-historical" view of history. These ideas, the accompanying
changes, and the concept of Antichrist are all evident in
Thus Spoke Zarathustra.

With this admittedly brief and schematic summary in
mind, we can pursue more easily the discussion of "Nietzscheanism" in Jeffers' poetry. In the following discussion of
Nietzsche's influence in the poetry, all of the long narrative poems and appropriate shorter poems are considered
chronologically (within the three periods defined in Chapter 1). The remaining short poems are discussed in other
chapters.

Nietzsche's Influence

Tamar

When Radcliffe Squires contends that *Tamar* and *Roan
Stallion,* the first two poems of any stature, "reveal the
double potential" in the poet, he makes a very useful observation. Certainly, they embody "the saga formula and
the classical, the diffuse and the unified," as do *The Women
at Point Sur* and *Cawdor.*[12] It may be hazardous to suggest
that the poetic production of six to eight years convincingly
demonstrates the interaction of the forces of Apollo and
Dionysus, but I find the parallels recognizable and inviting.
The Tower Beyond Tragedy, essentially dramatic in form,

presents a similar Nietzschean aspect, but let us begin with *Tamar*.

Tamar is a bold poem about a young girl who recklessly sets about the task of discovering life and making changes in it to suit herself. She is the first of Jeffers' characters to attempt revaluation of values by an implicit attack on conventional Christian morality. She seeks power and exercises it within her circumscribed world in a brash attempt to overcome herself and her surroundings. She is thwarted, it appears, by the eternal recurrence of events.

The characters in the poem exist midway between tragic human figures and abstract allegorical masks. Tamar's father, David Cauldwell, is waiting out his days in Bible-leafing resignation on his Pacific Coast farm. Lee, Tamar's brother of about the same age, has been recently chastened by a drunken plunge down a sea cliff with his pony and by the advent of his being drafted for military service in Europe during World War I. Accordingly, Lee gives up his alleged life of sin which has flourished in Monterey, when a succession of events at home makes the trip to town an extravagance. Stella Moreland (David's sister-in-law) and the "idiot Jinny" (his sister) disturb the homelife of the Cauldwells with their nocturnal rantings, seances, and evil intimations about the past. David, who always has his Bible in hand and who represents hypocritical orthodoxy, is haunted by the memory of his incestuous love for his now dead sister, Helen. Lee represents wild youth sobered by the sudden awareness of the seriousness of life, and Tamar is the rebellious spirit who discourages her brothers's reform. Stella and Jinny, of course, are choric witnesses from the past.

One may understandably sympathize with Tamar when she registers her discontent with life at home, for her surroundings are not encouraging, and she has considerable justification for feeling "trapped" by life. "What are we for?" she asks Lee as they ride together, "to want and want and not dare know it" (p. 111). Of their home, she says, "The withered house / Of an old man and a withered woman and an idiot woman. / No wonder if we go mad, no wonder" (p. 111). Despising the lack of vitality and the emotional emptiness of her present life, Tamar attempts to alter her prospects by offering herself to her brother on the bank of a mountain pool with such urgency that he abandons his waning resolve to reform his moral life. With the only power she has, Tamar seeks to change the status quo with an act that is at once loving and violent; "I chose my teacher," she says after giving herself to her brother, "Mine, it was my doing" (p. 113). But later when Stella and Jinny reveal to Tamar her father's love for Helen, Tamar observes, "It makes me nothing, / My darling sin a shadow and me a doll on wires" (p. 116). "Poor little Tamar," the incredible ghost of Helen says during a seance, "a trap so baited / Was laid to catch you when the world began" (pp. 116–17). Although critics like Gates have noted "an atmosphere of predeterminism" in *Tamar* (perhaps in part because the title recalls a similar event in 2 Samuel 13), the obvious emphasis in the narrative of the poem is on the cyclical recurrence of events, not on foreordination.[13]

To provide an alibi for the pregnancy that has developed during the fifth month of her rebellion, Tamar sets the same trap (with slightly greater bait now) for another youth from Monterey, who actually has had honorable intentions toward Tamar. Stunned by this unexpected reversal in his hitherto coolly received suit for Tamar's hand, Will Andrews falls in the same way that Lee fell, in virtually the same place, with the same verbal responses, even in the same physical attitudes on the bank of the pool. In the description of Tamar's "seduction," Horace Gregory recognized the clear ring of Ovid's touch, but it seems to me that one must not fail to distinguish between the seduction of a pregnant woman and that of an adventuresome virgin.[14] Again the emphasis in this scene, through the repetition of situation and details, is on the recurrence of events.

In order to talk with the dead Helen, Tamar calls upon Aunt Stella, who helps her "talk to the dead" in a seaside cave. Before Tamar communicates with Helen, she is commanded by masculine voices to strip herself naked and dance wantonly along the tide line, where she soon collapses in ecstatic abandon and submits to the repeated ghostly ravishments of "half a dozen savages, / Dead, and dressed up for Gods" (p. 131). The practical advantage of this otherwise gratuitous episode is that, thanks to the exertion of her spectral unions in the cave, Tamar aborts spontaneously, solving at least one of her problems. When she finally talks to Helen, Tamar discusses the power she has, and Helen tries unsuccessfully to discourage her plan. After her conversation with Helen, Tamar says to Stella, the medium:

> I have so passed nature
> That God himself, who's dead or all these devils
> Would never have broken hell, might speak out of you
> Last season thunder and not scare me.
>
> (*RS, T,* p. 133)

In addition to the statement that God is dead, the "passing" (that is, going beyond) of nature is pertinent to the Nietzschean theme; the same phrase occurs later in one of the speeches of Aegisthus in *The Tower Beyond Tragedy*.

While Tamar lies ill in an upper bedroom, recovering from her communion with the dead, David Cauldwell visits her, Bible in hand, hoping to find solace for her in the

good book. Instead they have a bitter exchange about their
respective incestuous loves, after which Tamar performs a
tour de force from her sick bed: she seduces the old man—
and down he falls, bristling beard, bad breath, Bible and
all. Repeatedly, Tamar claims that she, not the old man,
will have power in the household: "You cannot think what
freedom and what pleasure live in having abjured laws, in
having / Annulled hope, I am now at peace" (p. 145).
There is no peace, however, but God's, says her father,
"He never forgives, He never forgives, evil punishes evil"
(p. 145).

Still intent on possessing power, yet bothered by the possibility that her sin will appear to the world as simply the
pale copy of the sin of her father and Helen, Tamar directs
the old man's thinking in this comparison:

> Is the echo louder
> than the voice, I have surpassed her,
> Yours was the echo, time stands still old man, you'll learn
> when you have lived at the muddy root
> Under the rock of things; all times are now, to-day plays on
> last year and the inch of our future
> Made the first morning of the world. You named me for the
> monument in a desolate graveyard,
> Fool, and I say you were deceived, it was out of me that fire
> lit you and your Helen, your body
> Joined with your sister's
> Only because I was to be named Tamar and to love my
> brother and my father,
> I am the fountain.
>
> (*RS, T,* pp. 145–46)

The poem concludes with a violent confrontation in Tamar's bedroom. Tamar, Lee, Will Andrews, and David
Cauldwell face each other in confusion and hatred. Tamar
alone feels that she has control of the situation, for she has

gathered her lovers about her. Old Jinny, who is momentarily neglected downstairs, manages at last to embrace a candle (throughout the poem she has been fascinated by flame) and ignites herself and the house, exclaiming, "Why I'm like God" (p. 167). Fire consumes the household, and Tamar prevents the escape of her lovers by barring a window with her body.

The Nietzschean ideas in the poem are fairly obvious. The Will to Power is sexually sublimated in Tamar—she has no other means of asserting her will. Eternal Recurrence is brought home to Tamar when she discovers that her "darling sin" makes her nothing. In a nearly classic fulfillment of Nietzsche's doctrine of the transvaluation of values, she repudiates the laws to which her hypocritical father still clings. David Cauldwell, the weak man seeking shelter at last in orthodoxy and the old laws, remains false. And feeble-minded Jinny, feeling ironically like God, brings the whole adventure to nothing. Both the outworn traditions and Tamar's mode of rebellion are canceled: the Nietzschean solutions are explored and found to be partly unsatisfactory.

Of Jeffers' interest in Tamar's problem—her entrapment between a dull world and a decaying moral structure—there can be no doubt; the poem is the evidence. Whatever may be said for life and the Will to Power as represented by Tamar, her course of action is reckless to the point of self-destruction. In the end she is humbled before decrepit orthodoxy which, in spite of its patent corruption in the person of David Cauldwell, manages to retain an undeniable and perhaps disappointing superiority. In a letter he wrote (5 August 1927) to James Rorty, Jeffers says, "Tamar seemed to my later thought to have a tendency to romanticize unmoral freedom, and it was evident that a good many people took it that way. That way lies destruction of course, often for the individual but always for the social organism."[15]

The Coast-Range Christ

In poems of the *Tamar* volume, dreams figure prominently in foreshadowing the events of the narratives. In *Tamar*, there is an interesting opposition of dreams and events. At the end of Section 1, Tamar dreams that "a wild white horse / Came out of the wave and trampled her with his hooves" (p. 108). At the end of Section 2, Lee, who survived a fall into the sea with his pony at the beginning of the poem, dreams that he is an aviator dueling with a German: "he fired his gun and mounted / In steady rhythm" (p. 110). And in the next section, Lee and Tamar commence their incestuous relationship. In her second of two dreams in Section 5, Tamar sees "Will Andrews curiously wounded in the face [who] came saying . . . 'I will take care of you' " (p. 121). In the final scene of the poem, Lee, trying to stab Andrews' throat,

> opened the right cheek,
> The knife scraping on bone and teeth, then Tamar
> In a sea-gull voice, "I dreamed it in his face,
> I dreamed a T cut in his face——."
>
> (*RS, T,* p. 166)

For modern readers accustomed to more sophisticated use of the dream device, Jeffers' technique is obvious, but in *The Coast-Range Christ,* which continues the examination of Nietzschean themes, the technique is noticeably more complex and symbolical.

Peace O'Farrell is married to Jamie O'Farrell, who is much older than she and who exerts himself far more in a search for the silver rumored to be hidden on his land than he does in his attentions to his young wife. Lonely and all but unnoticed, Peace O'Farrell asks herself, "What is

youth for but to spill it with joy at the altar-foot of life?"
(p. 175). To put this observation into action, Peace turns
affectionate eyes upon her neighbor, "Christian David"
Carrow (as she calls him), who resists her seductive de-
signs because as a "Dreamer of mystical brotherhood he
had built to music a mountain of faith / Over desperate
Golgotha rock and found a star to follow to death" (p.
176). He is also a conscientious objector, sought after by
Sherman Hicks ("the sheriff's man") as a World War I
draft dodger. Having lost in her bid to join forces with
Christian David, Peace recognizes an opportunity to revenge David's indifference to her by cooperating with
Hicks in his efforts to ferret out the mystical draft dodger.

There are some resemblances in technique between this
poem and Strindberg's *The Dream Play*. Jeffers' poem is
filled with dreams; and in it we may recognize some of the
symbols of Strindberg's play. Jamie lives in a dream, always pursuing the fugitive silver. Of his wife, we are told:

> Peace also
> had singular dreams,
> Swam in a pool of darting serpents, or played in a novelist's
> chariot-games,
> Under thousands of men's eyes round the high stone altars
> and theater-courses,
> Scaled with plates of blazing silver, guiding a galloping hur-
> ricane of horses.
>
> (*RS, T*, p. 179)

The underlying eroticism of these revelations of the unconscious is self-evident.

The symbols of the star-window and the wonderfully tu-
mescent tower which bursts into a flower in *The Dream
Play* are suggested in a passage which describes how, having made a pact with Hicks, "Peace dreamed marvelously
all night" (p. 180). She finds herself in the Carmel Mission church, which has grown larger and more resplendent

in her dream, crowded now most obviously by "Soldiers too, thousands of soldiers, bayonet-carriers, beautiful killers" (p. 181). The scene of the chapel is striking and forceful in its presentation of the psychological conflict of the poem:

> First the worshipers adored the small star-window over the door,
> While the door moved eagerly wide for the entrance of multitudes more and more.
> Then the sweet silver and terrible bells rang out wild welcome and swayed the domed steeple,
> While the sucking wings of the doorway pulsed and quivered for the entrance of people.
> Next the multitude adored the crucifix over the high stone altar,
> There a serpent for Christ was hanging, the whole crowd worshiped and did not falter.
>
> (*RS, T,* p. 181)

The scene pulses with erotic suggestion, and, when she is called for by "Sepulchered saints beneath the altar," Peace feels unworthy, for "her vestment silks were torn and she would be ashamed before them all" (p. 181). She is embarrassed by her unreadiness for the call to a religious life, but David appears and says, " 'Come with me Peace, we will see Christ.' / Though her body was naked he did not see nor mind" (p. 181).

Through the dream of Peace, Jeffers reveals a possible resolution of the conflict between the given personalities. In a more favorable situation, Peace and David would ideally complement each other. The balance of the poem, however, deals with what actually happened: The mystical David is hounded out of existence by the forces of both good (his overzealous father) and evil (Peace and Hicks); Christians are shown to be the inadequate and self-destructive victims of life; and dreamers like Jamie O'Farrell are doomed to suffer disillusionment. In this poem, Jeffers' examination of the Nietzschean Will to Power is subtle and perhaps deceptive. It is the tale one might expect of Strindberg (who was a self-admitted follower of Nietzsche), if he were to write a wild-west story, yet the poem concludes in choruses and antichoruses which suggest classical influence as well as intended parallels with an Easter sunrise service. In Peace O'Farrell, Jeffers has embodied elements of the Will to Power. Like Tamar, she is restless and yearns for more from life than she has so far received—"What is youth for," she wonders. She despises weakness, and because she thinks him weak at the beginning of the poem, Peace makes the first move and collars David with a "hot soft kiss" that is meant to make him more compliant. He runs from temptation, however, and, when she discovers that he is a draft dodger, Peace thinks even less of David and contrives to assist in his apprehension. "Sanctified young puppy," Peace says of David, "that yellow streak is certain to show" (p. 180). Weakness and piety are identified in Peace's mind, for she fails to recognize the magnitude of David's own rebellion against convention. David's mother is the soul of Christian charity, whose kindness and generosity Peace rejects emphatically. His father is also a Christian, yet severe and watchful. Like Theseus in *Hippolytus,* David's father is too ready to believe the worst of David, his own flesh.

Peace represents the Will to Power, metaphorically described in her sexual ambitions (what Nietzsche calls sublimation, although the relationship that might have developed between Peace and David is normal from one point of view), and her attitude toward David's spiritualism and his mother's "Christianity" approximates the antireligionist point of view of Nietzsche's philosophy. What is peculiarly Jeffersian in the poem is represented in Jamie O'Farrell, whose thematic statement depends for its defini-

tion upon the Nietzscheanism of the poem. As Jamie
plowed his land in days gone by, he turned over the bones
of the converts of the priests of St. Francis; then he heard
that their silver hoard was also buried on his land. Jamie
has violated nature by marrying the much younger Peace,
whose own vitality is thereby canceled; he further violates
nature by abandoning his farming in order to dig through
the earth uselessly looking for the legendary silver. The
mole images which describe his digging and the dark, fu-
tile tunnels that he carves out of the earth symbolize Jamie's blindness to everything else around him. The images, which represent the earth he digs as the breast of nature and the tunnel he lies in as the womb, also support
the theme of violation. In the end, Jeffers has the sharpest
censure for Jamie. David, the pure coast-range Christ, is
freed to meet his God by his father's bullet, which represents the blind, retributive justice of patriarchal Christianity, the good of this world; Sherman Hicks and Peace
O'Farrell, who represent the bestiality in man, embrace in
the background; while Jamie with his horse-hair hacka-
more hoists himself by the neck into a pine tree, thus greet-
ing the dawn with his ultimate violation of nature. Again,
the Nietzschean elements in Peace O'Farrell (chiefly an errant Will to Power) are inadequate and dangerous when
divorced from a sense of individual responsibility. Nietzsche knew that his doctrines could succeed only in the
minds of exceptional people, and Jeffers, in poem after
poem, dramatizes the proof of the philosopher's conclusions.

Roan Stallion

First published in 1925, *Roan Stallion* proved that Jeffers could produce an artistically unified narrative of un-
doubted power; it also introduced the Inhumanism that

was to become the central doctrine of Jeffers' philosophy. With its obvious theme of zooerastia the poem both won and lost followers for Jeffers.[16] Nevertheless, after the tumultuous episodes of violence and ugliness of *Tamar* and *The Coast-Range Christ,* came *Roan Stallion;* after Dionysus rampant came a poem that exhibited Apollonian control in its craftsmanship.

California, "a nobly formed woman; erect and strong as a new tower" (p. 11) and one-quarter Indian, is married to Johnny, a dissolute, drunken gambler, whose depravity is seldom rivaled elsewhere in literature. Johnny is an "outcast Hollander," and their child Christine has "inherited from his race blue eyes, from his life a wizened forehead" (p. 12). Two days before Christmas, Johnny returns home from the valley with a roan stallion which he has won, but he has forgotten to bring gifts for the child. "Don't tell Christine it's Christmas," he says simply (p. 12). The next day, however, California goes to the village with the wagon to get the gifts, but the unexpectedly amorous Johnny, his thoughts running on the stallion, delays her departure an hour. The delay means that on the way home California must ford a rain-swollen stream in the dark. In the utter simplicity of her faith, she appeals to Jesus for light—and He appears, a "child afloat on radiance." Safely at home, California ponders at length the "shining and the power" of God, who can perform such miracles.

About Easter, Johnny returns to the valley with a man who has come up for the roan stallion as stud to his mare. Johnny leaves with a promise (as much for the man's benefit as for California's) of deeds comparable to the stallion's when he returns the next night. At this point, the poet intrudes for the first time in his own voice:

> Humanity is the
> start of the race; I say

Humanity is the mold to break away from, the crust to break
through, the coal to break into fire,
The atom to be split.

(RS, T, pp. 19–20)

While Johnny is absent, California goes down to the corral
and looks at the stallion. Within her mind, she easily identifies the horse with God, herself with the Virgin Mary.
Once begun, this chain of associations encourages her to
lead the horse out of the corral and up onto a height:
"Here is solitude, here on the calvary, nothing conscious /
But the possible God and the cropped grass" (p. 23). Up
to this point, California has dwelt on the "shining and the
power" of God the Father (she repeatedly tells Christine
about the vision at the fording of the stream), and she has
moved steadily toward an identification of the stallion with
God (in retelling her adventure to Christine, she finds herself habitually substituting the words "roan stallion" for
"God"), and she thinks of herself as a fit vessel, like Mary,
for the power of God. Moreover, experience has taught
California that sex is a power which *she* has.

Addressing herself to the majestic scenery about her,
California says,

O God I am not good enough, O fear, O strength, I am
draggled.
Johnny and other men have had me, O clean power!
Here am I.

(RS, T, p. 23)

Whether or not California put on the stallion's knowledge
with his power, the brute invasion makes her "more incredibly conjugate / With the other extreme and greatness; passionately perceptive of identity" (p. 24). "Out of
the fire in the small round stone," as the poet describes
California's head between the forehooves, rise images:

> The fire threw up figures
> And symbols meanwhile, racial myths formed and dissolved
>   in it, the phantom rulers of humanity
> That without being are yet more real than what they are
>   born of, and without shape, shape that which makes
>   them:
> The nerves and the flesh go by shadowlike, the limbs and
>   the lives shadowlike, these shadows remain, these shad-
>   ows
> To whom temples, to whom churches, to whom labors and
>   wars, visions and dreams are dedicate:
> Out of the fire in the small round stone that black moss
>   covered, a crucified man writhed up in anguish.
>
> <div align="right">(<i>RS, T,</i> p. 24)</div>

When Johnny does come home, he finds a less compliant California. She successfully thwarts his advances, and he becomes sodden with the red wine which he has brought home to ease the bolt. He spills part of the wine and asks, "Who stuck the pig?" and adds, "here's blood, here's blood" (p. 25). Thus begins the sacrificial theme which develops to the end of the poem. California slips out the door during Johnny's confusion, and he, regarding her elusiveness as a coy embellishment of the routine of their sexual play, pursues her to the corral, where he finds her standing unafraid beside the stallion. The opposition of values represented in this scene is unmistakable.

Christine awakens to follow her parents to the corral in time to see Johnny injured by the horse, to see California shoot their dog when it momentarily stalled the horse's attack upon the man, and to see the stallion renew its attack —"hooves left nothing alive but teeth tore up the remnant" (p. 27). Having done its work, the roan stallion appears to express "obscene disgust" for the smear of man that is left on the ground, and the poem concludes:

                             then California moved by
    some obscure human fidelity
Lifted the rifle. Each separate nerve-cell of her brain flaming
    the stars fell from their places
Crying in her mind: she fired three times before the
    haunches crumpled sidewise, the forelegs stiffening,
And the beautiful strength settled to earth: she turned then
    on her little daughter the mask of a woman
Who has killed God. The night-wind veering, the smell of
    the spilt wine drifted down hill from the house.

                                       (*RS, T*, p. 28)

Undoubtedly *Roan Stallion* is one of Jeffers' most mem-
orable poems; it is moving poetry, but critics have said curious things about it. Monjian, in her *Robinson Jeffers*,
compares the misanthropy of Jeffers' tragic vein and that
of Swift's satire. "The resemblance is especially notable in
'Roan Stallion,' " she observes. "Like Gulliver, who finds
paradise with the Houyhnhnms, the horses that are the embodiment of reason and good, California finds her ideal in
a magnificent roan stallion, the opposite of her weak, corrupt husband."[17] Though there may be something to rec-
ommend this approach to the poem, its critical rationale
also permits, on the same grounds, consideration of such
works as *Black Beauty*. In Gilbert's *Shine, Perishing Republic,* we are told that Indians had "a phallic stallion,
Mamoji, to touch which caused maidens to bear children."
But menstruating women were kept away for fear of con-
taminating and weakening the animal. In *Roan Stallion,*
Gilbert contends, "a menstruating woman is involved,
hence the tragic conflict"; and then, as if to prove his
point, he quotes the three lines in which California shoots
the horse![18]

    In one of the first international acknowledgments of Jef-
fers' acceptance as a literary figure, Cestre, with character-

istic urbanity, discusses *Roan Stallion*. He finds the germ
of the poem in the association in California's mind of God
the savior (from the vision at the ford) and male passion
(the demands of Johnny to be satisfied before she was free
to leave in the morning). She is disgusted by Johnny's
claims as a husband, argues Cestre, "mais il monte en elle,
des profondeurs du subconscient, le désir primitif de se
sentir dominée par la force unie à la beauté, et de con-
naître dans l'amour la joie ineffable des extases célestes."
Cestre's comment is valuable because it brings sophistica-
tion to the poem without obscuring its essential primitiv-
ism. He underlines my theory that at this point Jeffers was
concerned with the individual rather than with society, for
he says of the poet, "Ce n'est pas un réformateur social: c'est
un disciple émancipé d'Emerson, qui s'est mis à l'école de
Nietzsche, et qui dresse la *self-reliance* contre les nuées
pour escalader le ciel."[19]

Roan Stallion makes its statement through symbols.
Primitive sex and religion and human aspiration are
brought into conjunction without sacrificing any of the
validity of an individual symbol; in other words, a plurality
of meanings is preserved. California aspires, with the most
pure of motives, to the shining and power that she recognizes in the eminence of God, and within her psychology
she associates the sexual force of the stallion with the power
of divinity. By reducing the mysteries of metaphysics to the
level of sex, California reaches terms with which she is
familiar and which she can use. As California moves toward
the godhead, she leaves behind her the contemptible
Johnny and his associates: "Humanity is the mold to break
away from, the crust to break through" (p. 20).

The theme of sacrifice is insistent and cannot be discounted, for the poem that began at Christmas ends at
Easter when California led the stallion to a summit: "Here

is solitude, here on the calvary" (p. 23). The last scene in
the cabin is a grotesque, fragmented parody of the Last
Supper in the style of Luis Buñuel. We remember that when
Johnny spills his wine on the table he declares, "here's
blood, here's blood." The trampling of Johnny in the corral
may be regarded as a sacrifice to the stallion god over which
California presides, having lured her victim to the horse
and having cut short the dog's interference. "Some obscure
human fidelity" moves California to pump three shots (the
three betrayals?) into the stallion. Furthermore, it is not a
woman, but the mask of a woman, "who has killed God,"
which turns to little Christine. To emphasize the ritualistic
significance of this episode, the poem concludes by noting
that down through the trees to California came the smell
of spilled wine from the house.

Whatever may have been the possible value of California's rebellion against the life represented by Johnny
and, though unwittingly to be sure, against orthodox institutionalized Christianity, her overcoming is reduced to
nothing by that same "mold" or "crust" of humanity
against which the poet warned earlier in the poem. It is
the same restraining humanity, as the poet suggests by
"mold" and "crust" and "mask," that provides the "obscure human fidelity" which causes California to fire at her
God. We recognize that the tragedy of the poem lies in
California's inescapable enmeshment in life and in her
humanity. California is simply a murderess, and the survivor is Christine (so-named with obvious significance), the
product of California's wild mysticism and Johnny's contemptible human nature. We may expect little from
Johnny's child, for she has "inherited . . . from his life a
wizened forehead."

In *Roan Stallion,* Jeffers gave convincing artistic shape
to the Revaluation of Values and the concept of the Over-

man. And once again the Nietzschean formulas proved unsatisfactory. Later Jeffers wrote *The Women at Point Sur,* as he said, "to show in action the danger of that 'Roan Stallion' idea of 'breaking out of humanity,' misinterpreted in the mind of a fool or a lunatic."[20] Such a statement clearly supports the argument that Jeffers is critical of what California attempts to do, and that these poems of the twenties are essentially examinations of philosophical positions, *Roan Stallion* being aesthetically one of the most successful.

The Tower Beyond Tragedy

What is power, how should it be used, and does it bring peace? These questions occupy Jeffers in his treatment of the story of the House of Atreus.

Clytemnestra, "craftier than queenly," knows that since she does not have the beauty of her sister Helen—"Troy's burning-flower from Sparta"—she must consciously exercise her wiles and use the strategems of power, if she is to exert any influence on events about her. In Agamemnon's absence, Clytemnestra has taken as lover the less warlike Aegisthus, and for understandable reasons she has repudiated her husband and the old belief in the gods, an alienation which was brought to a crisis by Agamemnon's sacrifice of their daughter Iphigenia. As the poem begins, we find Clytemnestra in command of Agamemnon's court, Aegisthus a subservient tool in the background, and Agamemnon returning to assassination at the hands of his wife.

Power and its use are strongly identified with Clytemnestra, who delights in her new role as absolute wielder of power over the court and her subjects. To Cassandra, whom Agamemnon has brought home as a prize of war, Clytemnestra brags about her power over the soldiers, "You know / I am holding lions with my two eyes" (p.

36).[21] When she says that, if necessary, she will kill her own children according to Cassandra's prophetic suggestion, the milder-mannered Aegisthus warns her of the dangers of her obsession with power:

> O strongest spirit in the world.
> We have dared enough, there is an end to it.
> We may pass nature a little, an arrow-flight,
> But two shots over the wall you come in a cloud upon the
>   feasting Gods, lightning and madness.
>
> (*RS, T,* p. 48)

After the king's murder, the dead Agamemnon returns to the scene by forcing his spirit into Cassandra's body and using it as a means of speaking from beyond death. For Cassandra, this is the ghostly climax of a series of invasions begun long ago by Ajax. Speaking through Cassandra, Agamemnon warns his people of the social danger of the queen's private wielding of power,

> I say if you let this woman live, this crime go
>   unpunished, what man among you
> Will be safe in his bed?
>
> .   .   .   .   .   .
>
> Law dies if the Queen die not.
>
> (*RS, T,* p. 41)

In addition, the captain of the troops warns the soldiers not to lose their bearings, "Companions: before God, hating the smell of crimes, crushes the city into gray ashes / We must make haste" (p. 43). Later Clytemnestra tells her subjects, "townsfolk: / You are not essential" (p. 49). One of the major themes in the first part of the poem is clearly that of individual license versus one's responsibility to society, upon which the resolution of the poem is based in part.

The first part of the poem has shown the turmoil of the

parents' generation—unfeeling sacrifice of one's child, infidelity in both parents, deceit, murder, and ruthless quest
for power. The second part, which tells of the children
Electra and Orestes and their revenge, is introduced by
Cassandra, who has seen much of the past and stands now
in the bloody present, looking into the future. What she
sees is not pleasant, for humanity is doomed to persist in its
ways:

> Where are prosperous people my enemies are, as you pass
>   them O my spirit
> Curse Athens for the joy and the marble, curse Corinth
> For the wine and the purple, and Syracuse
> For the gold and the ships; but Rome, Rome,
> With many destructions for the corn and the laws and the
>   javelins, the insolence, the threefold
> Abominable power.
>
> (*RS, T,* p. 55)

She goes on to curse Spain, France, and England; but

> there remains
> A mightier to be cursed and a higher for malediction
> When America has eaten Europe and takes tribute of Asia.
>
> (*RS, T,* p. 56)

Thus begins a vein of thought in Jeffers' poetry that culminates later in poems like *The Bowl of Blood* and *The
Double Axe*. Cassandra lays the blame at the feet of humanity and yearns for death to free her:

> but cut humanity
> Out of my being, that is the wound that festers in me,
> Not captivity, not my enemies.
>
> (*RS, T,* p. 57)

When Electra and Orestes return to Mycenae to avenge
their father's murder, they are grown up and are about to

begin the cycle anew. The second generation resembles the first, especially Electra, who perpetuates her mother's concern for power and her merciless maneuvering. Although both children are required to avenge the regicide, Electra practically wills the act through Orestes, who has some understandable reservations about killing his mother. It is Electra, not Orestes, who exploits the political advantage of their revenge, once it is accomplished; for Orestes believes it may be simply a private crime. She catches up Orestes' sword and cries, "Agamemnon failed here. Not in me. Hear, Mycenaeans" (p. 70). Orestes is momentarily deranged by his deed of revenge and wanders away from the court, leaving Electra to take charge. She says to the men, "Gather up the dead: I will go in; I have learned strength" (p. 72). Orestes returns later and says, "because I have conquered, the soft fiber's burnt out" (p. 74). Still hoping to educate her brother to play his new role as king, Electra tells him:

> O my brother
> You are Agamemnon: rule: take all you will: nothing is
>   denied you. The Gods have redressed evil
> And clamped the balance.
>
> (*RS, T*, p. 76)

Nevertheless, Orestes is disturbed by his dream in the forest. When he killed his mother, he insisted on using sexual imagery to draw a comparison between putting his mother to the sword and committing incest. Now he dreams that he has loved his sister. Electra accepts the implication of the dream, if it is a necessary condition to make a ruler out of Orestes, and she freely offers herself to her brother. "All that our Gods require," she explains, "is courage" (p. 78). Similarly, in the first part of the poem, Clytemnestra held her soldiers transfixed with a sort of

royal strip-tease while she justified the assassination of Agamemnon. Carpenter is quite correct when he observes that
she "conquers the wills of both her political subjects and
the men of Mycenae through the naked power of her
sex."[22] Like her mother, Electra offers her sex as a means to
power. If physical love is required to make Orestes king,
hers is his to enjoy. Like Clytemnestra's, Electra's sole interest in sex within the poem lies in its capacity to achieve
power—an example of Nietzschean sublimation recurring
in successive generations.

Electra desires to follow the course to power set by her
mother, and her characterization illustrates the possibility
of Eternal Recurrence, even though one of the objects of
the poem's action is to disrupt such patterning of events.
Whereas Nietzsche moved from the dualism of Dionysus
versus Apollo to the unified Will to Power, Jeffers, in order to make the point discussed below, has moved in this
poem from the Will to Power (i.e., Clytemnestra) to the
Dionysian (Electra) versus the Apollonian (Orestes). By
inverting Nietzsche's progression, Jeffers is able both to illustrate the hazards of the Will to Power recklessly exercised and to separate the impulse of greater value, Orestes,
from its involvement in the quest for power.

Orestes, after much self-examination, concludes that his
killing of Clytemnestra was not a crime. "Not the crime,
the wakening," he tells Electra (p. 80). "Yet we are divided," his sister declares, and Orestes replies, "Because I
have suddenly awakened, I will not waste inward / Upon
humanity, having found a fairer object" (p. 80). He returns to the subject of his dream, "the last labor / To
spend on humanity" (p. 80). The dream showed him that
people "all loved or fought inward . . . / Sought the eyes of
another that another should praise him; sought never his
own but another's" (p. 81). He concludes the speech:

It is all turned inward, all your desires incestuous, the
    woman the serpent, the man the rose-red cavern,
Both human, worship forever ...

                              (*RS, T,* p. 81)

and he breaks off. When Electra tries to dissuade him, Orestes says (not without some ambiguity in his use of the
term "humanity" in this context),

                   I remembered
The knife in the stalk of my humanity; I drew and it broke;
    I entered the life of the brown forest
And the great life of the ancient peaks, the patience of stone.
                             (*RS, T,* p. 81)

At this point Jeffers all but abandons Nietzscheanism in
favor of his own variety of materialism. Human nature is
contemptible for its petty preoccupations and fragility; so
Orestes, the Apollonian seeker of balance and shape in the
world, says, "I have fallen in love outward" (p. 82). Electra, who must continue to function in the world as she
found it, says these last words to Orestes, "Strength's good.
You are lost. I here remember the honor of the house, and
Agamemnon's" (p. 82). She stays and Orestes walks off "in
the clear dawn," and where or when he died "signified less
than nothing / To him who had climbed the tower beyond time, consciously, and cast humanity, entered the earlier fountain" (p. 82).

    Jeffers' own comment on the poem when he much later
dramatized it for production supports the present reading
of it. Orestes "escapes the curse," he wrote, of "the house
of Agamemnon ... a wicked house, corrupted by power,
heavy with ancestral crime and madness." He went on to
explain the hero of the poem.

Orestes, in the poem, identifies himself with the whole divine
nature of things; earth, man, and stars, the mountain forest

and the running streams; they are all one existence, one organism. He perceives this, and that himself is included in it, identical with it. This perception is his tower beyond the reach of tragedy; because, whatever may happen, the great organism will remain forever immortal and immortally beautiful. Orestes has "fallen in love outward" not with a human creature, nor a limited cause, but with the universal God. That is the meaning in my poem.[23]

Obviously, however, Orestes' decision to fall in love outward can satisfy no one but himself and perhaps the poet, for he has abdicated a position of responsibility to the Mycenaeans in favor of a very private quest. What is to become of such worthwhile citizens as Clytemnestra's captain, who seeks good answers in the face of adversity, when he finds that the old queen is replaced by Electra? Orestes' enlightenment is wasted when it is not applied to the lives of the Mycenaeans, for he also cuts the bonds of loyalty to his fellow man. His enlightenment, however, is not wasted for Jeffers, who has found in Orestes not only a possible solution to the Nietzschean formulas, but an inherent shortcoming as well.

The Women at Point Sur

An observation by H. L. Davis in his review of *The Women at Point Sur* focuses on the fundamental division in the poem's accomplishment and in its conception. "The most splendid poetry of my time," Davis announces. "Nothing written by this generation can begin to come up with it. . . . And yet—the poem itself is dead, as lifeless as a page of Euclid."[24] Davis' paradoxical evaluation of *The Women* reflects a fundamental conflict within the poem which one must face in reading it. There are strikingly moving passages in the poem, but they ornament an ideological structure rather than embody it.

In the Reverend Arthur Barclay, Jeffers has created his own Zarathustra, and this similarity between Barclay and Zarathustra may have been what prompted Cargill to label *The Women,* "an ill-digested reading of Nietzsche."[25] Gilbert, in his study of Jeffers, also recognized the presence of Nietzsche's influence in *The Women,* when he wrote, "Here the Nietzschean *'Will zur Macht'* becomes, through poetic vision, a prophesy."[26] These ideas, however, and Jeffers' treatment of them raised serious doubts in the minds of other readers whom Jeffers esteemed, and, in a letter to James Rorty, he agreed that there was "the need of an explanation." Jeffers had just read Mark Van Doren's review of *The Women,* and he wrote to Rorty that, if Van Doren, "a good friend" of his work, misunderstood the book, then the poem needed further explanation. " 'Tamar,' " he told Rorty, "seemed to my later thought to romanticize unmoral freedom [but]. . . . that way lies destruction of course, often for the individual but always for the social organism, and one of the later intentions of this 'Point Sur' was to indicate the destruction and strip everything but its natural ugliness from the unmorality." He went on to say that one of his primary intentions was to dramatize the *Roan Stallion* idea of "breaking out of humanity," if it were misinterpreted in the mind of a fool or lunatic. *The Women* is not "anti-social," he said, "because it has nothing to do with society." Like Ibsen's *Wild Duck,* which was meant to be a warning of his own ideas in the hands of a fool, Jeffers wrote, *The Women* "was meant to be a warning; but at the same time a reassertion." Jeffers listed six other "intentions" that he had in mind as he wrote the poem. It was (1) "an attempt to uncenter the human mind from itself," for there is no health for the individual or the society that is "introverted" upon itself, as our society "becomes more and more." The poet meant the poem to be a tragedy (2) "that is an exhibition of essential elements by the burning away through pain and ruin of inertia and the unessential." It was (3) "a valid study in psychology . . . sketching the growth of a whole system of emotional delusion from a 'private impurity' that was quite hidden from consciousness until insanity brought it to the surface." Therefore, Jeffers believed, the poem was (4) "a partial and fragmentary study of the origin of religions; which have been necessary to society in the past . . . yet they derive from a 'private impurity' of some kind in their originators." As a satire (5) "on human self-importance," the poem was related back to the first intention. Finally, the poem was (6) "a judgment of the tendencies of our civilization, which has very evidently turned the corner down hill." Jeffers concluded by admitting that these are "too many intentions," and that he should not expect the reader to "concentrate so long, nor so intently" on them.[27]

The ideological emphasis in *The Women at Point Sur* is further realized in the knowledge that at one time Jeffers considered the title *Metaphors Will Survive* from that phrase in the twenty-first line of the prelude. Later it was changed to *Storm as Galeotto,* referring to Canto 5 of the *Inferno.*[28] Either title would have stressed the abstract nature of the poem, which was already troublesome for some readers. The present title concentrates attention on the women themselves and on the misguided messiah, Barclay, who comes among them.

The prelude of the poem tells us that "Culture's outlived, art's root-cut, discovery's / The way to walk in" (p. 10). We are shown people involved in bestiality and sacrilege. (When, for example, Rod Stewart realizes that Myrtle Cartwright has decided to give herself to him, he "leads her into the barn." Their given names alone convey this

part of the poet's comment.) The brothers of Onorio Vasquez, the seer of visions, have shot a hawk and hung it on
the wall of a barn, and they taunt it, "Fly down, Jew-beak"
(p. 11). The prelude ends with Onorio's wish that he
could take the hawk's place, because "It is necessary for
someone to be fastened with nails" (p. 17). But, he concludes, "Jew-beak is dead" (p. 17). Thus is established the
rationale of the poem, which begins with a scene in which
Reverend Barclay descends from his pulpit and leaves his
congregation, having declared blasphemously, "Christianity is false."

Barclay withdraws to Point Sur, where he stays with the
Morheads and waits for his messianic talents to develop.
Having been told by a voice in the air that "God thinks
through action, how shall a man but through action?" (p.
24), Barclay regards all nature, "this show," as "God's
brain." He struggles with his metaphysical inquiry and the
notion that God thinks through action, concluding at last
that there are two alternatives for him:

> gather disciples
> To fling like bullets against God and discover him:
> Or else commit an act so monstrous, so irreparable
> It will stand like a mountain of rock, serve you for fulcrum
> To rest the lever.
>
> (*Women*, p. 33)

As he proceeds to gather disciples among the Indians
and to tell Natalia Morhead and Faith Heriot that, under
his new dispensation, their lesbianism is blameless, Barclay
reveals himself to be a crude parody of Nietzsche's Zarathustra. Intentionally, Jeffers changed the shrewd, severe,
and supremely ironical Zarathustra into an insane mimic
who is incapable of fulfilling the role to which he aspires.
Much of the violence and license, which at first seems gra-

tuitous, is meant to contribute to the portrayal of Barclay's irresolute and undisciplined mind. Hence a comparison of the two following episodes is relevant. Early in his break with convention, Barclay turns naturally to "freeing" the flesh and, finding that for eight dollars the Indian Maruca will accommodate his rebellion, he declares unblinkingly, "I have bought salvation" (p. 45). Having preached to his "multitude":

> I have come to establish you
> Over the last deception, to make men like God
> Beyond good and evil. There is no will but discovery.
> (*Women*, p. 64)

Barclay determines that the deed sufficiently monstrous to put himself "outside of good an evil" is to rape his twenty-year-old daughter, April. "God has come home to you," he proclaims from above her (p. 80). Whether or not these episodes are convincing, Jeffers tried to provide foreshadowing and a sense of development in Barclay's career.

Section 12 of the poem is an extraordinary apostrophe to the reader. Of the divine presence, the poet says:

> I made glass puppets to speak of him, they splintered in my
> hand and have cut me, they are heavy with my blood.
> .   .   .   .
> I
>   sometime
> Shall fashion images great enough to face him
> A moment and speak while they die.
> (*Women*, p. 73)

As the poem continues, the many sexual liaisons are revealed, April believes after her rape that she has become her brother Edward, and Barclay's messianic movement shows signs of deterioration. The poet returns in his own voice,

> I say that if the mind centers on
> humanity
> And is not dulled, but remains powerful enough to feel its
> own and the others, the mind will go mad.
> It is needful to remember the stone and the ocean.
>   (*Women,* pp. 97–98)

We recognize here Jeffers' intention "to uncenter the human mind from itself."

April, under the stress of her predicament, shoots herself —"turned the love inward"—and Barclay realizes that his disciples are falling away. He demonstrates his own durability by gathering "up in his hands a heap of red coals" from the oak fire. He says, "Heautontimoroumenos [literally "The Self-Tormentor"] repents," and heads north alone. Lying near death, three days later, at the mouth of a mine, Barclay concludes the poem, "I am inexhaustible." Behind him he left death, madness, sexual riot, and disillusionment—the fruits of his crusade against "false" Christianity—for he misunderstood the great responsibility of his first act of renunciation. Worse yet, as Jeffers emphasized, the Barclay type is inexhaustible, for religious zealots will continue to appear and to ignore the God manifest in nature.

Cawdor

Writing to his publisher, Horace Liveright Company, Jeffers tried to put *Cawdor* (1928) into perspective. "I think of *Cawdor* as making a third with *Tamar* and *The Women at Point Sur*," he wrote; "but as if in *Tamar* human affairs had been seen looking westward, against the ocean; in *Point Sur* looking upward, minimized to ridicule against the stars; in *Cawdor* looking eastward, against the earth, reclaiming a little dignity from that association."[29] After the irresponsible self-seeking of *Tamar* and the misguided saviorism of *The Women,* Jeffers turned to the role of the individual who must come to terms with life as it is on earth and thereby earn for himself dignity.

Cawdor is superior to *The Women* because its ideological premises are more clearly drawn and because the action of the poem rises directly from them. In *Cawdor,* young Fera Martial finds that the forces and events of her life have led her to loveless sex as a means of transcending her victimization by life. Severely taught by the example of her father's continual failure and disappointment, Fera is forced to use the only power she has in order to provide security for her aged father and herself.

Out of the smoke and ashes of a landscape recently charred by a forest fire, Fera leads her flame-blinded father, "a feeble old man / Marked for misfortune," into the farm-yard of Cawdor. Here in a steep canyon which opens to the sea is Cawdor's farm, the domain of an absolute ruler, an Old Testament patriarchal figure. Cawdor's sons, Hood and George, and his daughter Michal, children of a previous marriage, live in awesome respect for their father's tremendous physical strength and harsh discipline. Whereas Fera has always been the victim of life, Cawdor has been its master. He is the first of a series of Jeffers' enormously powerful men, who have little to say.

The proposal of marriage in the poem represents the intersection of two careers. For Fera, it is an opportunity to advance herself and secure her father's comfort; for Cawdor, it is the beginning of his decline because he stoops to pleasure. Fera accepts Cawdor's proposal, saying, "There is nothing under the sun worth loving but strength" (p. 15). The poet says of Cawdor's proposal that "The man who'd not be seduced" (p. 16) in his youth by passion or unreason "Now in his cooled and craglike years / Has humbled himself to beg pleasure: even power was better" (p. 16).

In the poem, sex is both a means to power, as in Nietzsche's principle of sublimation, and a contamination, and
these two attitudes bear directly upon the Hippolytus
theme represented in Hood, who as an avid hunter is in
communication with nature and who is unyielding before
Fera's sexual overtures.

Cawdor has more than the mere touch of "the windy
madness of Nietzsche" which Cargill attributes to it, as is
evident once Fera begins her overcoming by exercising the
Will to Power in all the ways available to her.[30] Safely married to Cawdor, a relationship which apparently holds no
conjugal satisfaction for her, Fera lusts after Hood, the
hunter. Hood is sexually attractive to Fera, and his submis-
sion would provide her with a foothold in her quest for
power within the Cawdor family. Hood, however, repeatedly rejects Fera's advances. It is after old Martial dies
slowly with the storm around him, a circumstance which
Fera feels reflects vaguely the old man's unappreciated
courage and nobility, that Fera goes directly to Hood, who
denies her. Hood has never slept with anyone, for "he love
the deer" (p. 40), the servant Concha Rosas tells Fera.

Fera Martial is filled now with her superiority, her craft-
iness, her own greater value, and also with the sense of the
greater value of her father, in spite of his repeated failure.
When she comes upon George and Hood, who have been
fighting but are now separated by their father, Fera announces somewhat ominously, "I'll have my will: quarrel
your hearts out," and to Michal she says, "I am better than
you all, that is my sorrow" (p. 57). At length Fera maneu-
vers Hood beneath the leafy branches of some laurels,
where she presses her seduction vigorously, but to no avail.
Just as Hood's capitulation before her passion seems inevitable, he stabs himself in the thigh and leaves "limping
from the Attis-gesture." Hood's resistance confounds Fera,

who asks him, "What do you love? What horror of emptiness / Is in you to make you love nothing?" (pp. 63–64). In terms of Jeffers' main thought, of course, Fera recognizes only a "horror of emptiness" in Hood. Hood, the chaste young man who moves with nature, has carefully, almost reverently, disengaged himself from old Cawdor's patriarchal grasp. He, too, is a rebel, but his rebellion is scarcely tumultuous; indeed, in the present context, one might characterize his rebellion as Apollonian, and Fera's as Dionysian. Furthermore, as the Apollonian, Hood is prepared to defend himself against the catapulting emotional impulses of his step-mother's carnality.

Hood gives a fresh, still-damp puma skin to Fera as a wedding gift, and she promptly dons it "like a garment," presumably indicating her new status among the Cawdors. Fera has already noted that the father and son have the eyes of predatory animals: "the same drooping eyes, like a big animal's / That never needs to look sideways" (p. 8). It is suggestive that both Hood and Cawdor are compared to predatory animals; they are the hunters not the hunted, and this trait in Hood may not be appreciated immediately in reading the poem. Whereas Cawdor's Old Testament patriarchalism, which has shown a weakening fissure of pleasure-seeking, is rigid, parochial, and moribund, his son Hood's character is freer and untroubled. It has been possible for him, like Jeffers' Orestes, to have "fallen in love outward."

After the scene in which Fera, wrapped in her lion skin, tricks Hood into firing at her, the action of the poem deteriorates. Recovering from her gunshot wound, Fera explains her behavior to Cawdor as being the result of her belief that she is no longer fit for him, since Hood, she says, has taken her by force beneath the laurels. Playing Theseus to his Phaedra, Cawdor hunts down Hood and attacks him even as the son protests, "I'm not hiding, I'll answer the law, not you" (p. 77).[31] Hood dies of the fall from the rock where his father struck him, and it is only later, although George and Michal had told him so, that Cawdor accepts the fact that Fera lied.

The theme of the law and self-judgment is continued in a scene in which Cawdor, his mind having rejected the fact of the murder, imagines that he is talking to Hood. The old man tells his son that he thought briefly of the sheriff:

> I know him.
> And a judge save me? I had to judge myself.
> Run to a judge was only running away
> From judgment; I thought I'd not do that; shame Michal
> And do no good.
>
> (*Cawdor,* p. 113)

Cawdor's line of thinking reappears in *Give Your Heart to the Hawks,* where it becomes a major theme. Like Oedipus he blinds himself; facing the mountains old Cawdor cuts out his eye balls with Indian flint blades, after sending a servant for the law. "These punishments," he says, "are a pitiful self-indulgence. / I'd not the strength to do nothing" (p. 125).

More clearly than in any other poem thus far discussed Jeffers enunciated in *Cawdor* the opposition of the old retributive, yet static, order represented by Cawdor, and the possibilities of Nietzsche's Overman concept represented (along with its failure) by Fera and of the Jeffersian hero represented by Hood. Both Cawdor and Fera sought to overcome themselves through different applications of the Will to Power. Unwittingly and through the weakness of his own pleasure-seeking, Cawdor admitted into his world a rival who dealt him corruption. In her recklessness, Fera failed simply because she exceeded herself instead of overcoming herself. Hood, who is caught between these two opponents, helped to define their positions, and yet himself represented still another line of action, which Jeffers favored.

The human action of the poem takes place before the brooding figure of Michal's eagle, which is wing-crippled and kept in a cage. Hood shot it down "the autumn / Before he went away," and now Michal must catch ground squirrels, which she brings to the fallen bird in its cage. Although she rejects the suggestion that the bird ought mercifully to be shot, Michal does admit that, "day after day," she has "to be cruel to bring him a little happiness" (p. 22). The eagle symbolizes the situations of both Hood and Fera. It is a lofty creature of nature brought low by human treachery to the miserable confinement of a cage. Like the eagle, Fera is crippled by a shot from Hood's rifle, and she finds herself similarly confined and tormented, although, she has asked for much of her own suffering. The eagle suffers his pain nobly; but Fera, who has been lectured by her father on the necessity of suffering and who herself lectures Michal, cannot in the end endure her allotment of pain. When Michal explains to her father why she finally had George shoot her pet ("It was unhappy, father"), Cawdor replies, "By God, if you go killing / Unhappiness who'll be left in the houses?" (pp. 121–22).

The passage of the poem which describes the eagle's death is one of the two that Jeffers included in the *Selected Poetry* to represent *Cawdor*. "The unsocial birds are a greater race," the poet says, and he goes on to describe the dying eagle's vision as its spirit flees this world (p. 114). As it mounts in spirals above Cawdor's farm, the eagle's spirit looks back at "the mountain-dividing / Canyon of its captivity (that was to Cawdor / Almost his world)" (p. 115) until it can see only

                                          A speck, an atomic
Center of power clouded in its own smoke
Ran and cried in the crack; it was Cawdor; the other
Points of humanity had neither weight nor shining
To prick the eyes of even an eagle's passion.
                                          (*Cawdor,* p. 115)

Of the members of his tragedy who survive, Jeffers' sympathies lie principally with Cawdor, who meets life with strength and who admits that life makes painful demands upon the individual. He understands what the poet meant in his apostrophe to the dead eagle:

Its prison and its wound were not its peculiar wretchedness,
All that lives was maimed and bleeding, caged or in
    blindness,
Lopped at the ends with death and conception.
                                          (*Cawdor,* p. 117)

Dear Judas

Jeffers' *Roan Stallion* and D. H. Lawrence's *St. Mawr,* which appeared at the same time, have similar themes. And Lawrence's *The Man Who Died,* a critical appraisal of Christianity, which he claims is deficient in humanity and to have been in continual decline since the death of the prophet, appeared the same year as Jeffers' long poem *Dear Judas. Dear Judas,* which together with *The Loving Shepherdess* serves as a transition from Jeffers' period of experimentation to the middle period of the thirties, is also a severe examination of the foundations of Christianity.

Lawrence's Christ returns laboriously from the dead (the difficulty he has in returning is symbolic of the problem of his reconciliation with man), and he is unpersuaded of the success of his mission on earth. In his teaching, he has ignored the fleshly side of man, he decides in retrospect, and now he discovers a nearly fatal disregard of his own carnality. Unless he takes into account his own flesh, he is incomplete, he discovers, just as in her way the sensualist Isis, whom he meets, is incomplete, but their subsequent union in a normal Lawrentian mode guarantees each of them balance, completeness, and duration.[32]

Jeffers' Jesus and Judas return two thousand years later to the events of the crucifixion, and Jesus is shown to be hungry for power over his followers, his personality having taken this bent because of gnawing misgivings about his legitimacy. In a crucial scene with Mary, Jesus repeats a question he has asked several times previously, "I am either a bastard or the son of God: who was my father?" (*Judas,* p. 30). Jesus' concern for his legitimacy and his quest for power in Jeffers' poem may have their origin in the satire on Christianity in Nietzsche's chapter "On Immaculate Perception," in *Thus Spoke Zarathustra,* where the people are criticized for hiding their carnality. "Behind a god's mask," charges Zarathustra, "you hide from yourselves, in your 'purity'; your revolting worm has crawled into a god's mask" (*PN,* p. 235). Earlier in the same chapter, Zarathustra announced, "Where is innocence? Where there is a will to procreate. And he who wants to create beyond himself has the purest will" (*PN,* p. 235). If we read *Dear Judas* with Nietzsche's ideas in mind, it is possible to see that Jeffers has carried the examination of Nietzscheanism, as it interested him in the twenties, back to the source of Christianity. The story of the career of Jeffers' Jesus is not a comforting one, for it reveals the Christian savior acting for selfish reasons out of a feeling of "private impurity" and taking advantage of the mass psychology of his followers (in spite of Judas' pleas to Jesus not to exploit them). These actions determine the character of the "Christianity" that both Nietzsche and Jeffers repudiated.[33]

The Judas of this poem is on the side of the people, and he hopes to prevent Jesus from misleading them. Judas loves Jesus for what he ought to be, but he recognizes the danger in Jesus' wavering and falling victim of his own psychology, i.e., the "private impurity" of his doubts of legitimacy. In return, Jesus castigates Judas for being "faint-hearted . . . brittle-hearted," and he expresses misgivings about hoping to build power on such a foundation as Judas. "All greatness is a wrestling with time," according to Jesus (p. 19), and, though he hopes to make "a power weaponed with love not violence" (p. 20), Judas sees him turning more and more to violence—culminating in the crucifixion, of course—"because they [the people] love destruction" (p. 23), which is "the dreadful key to their hearts" (p. 23). As Judas broods uneasily over the implications of Jesus' preaching, "my kingdom is not of this world. . . . This world is nothing" (p. 24), Jesus enters addressing a crowd:

> I bring not peace but a sword; the brother shall hate the brother and the child his father.
> The old walls must be pulled down before the founding of the new, the field must be broken before the spring sowing,
> The old wood must be cut before the young forest.
>
> (*Judas*, pp. 24–25)

It is then that Judas sees his "duty and destiny," and later Jesus admits that Judas' betrayal is necessary and will lead to awful consequences.

To his followers, Jesus declares that he prefers the Romans who "have courage and power and discipline" (p. 28), whereas the Jews have only "hatred and memories." But he adds, "how can I help but love you?" (p. 28). Throughout the poem, Mary has intimations of disaster, for, unlike Jesus and Judas, she has not "returned" in time to the historical events as they occurred, but is "living" them, as if for the first time. On another occasion when she avoids giving her son the facts of his paternity, she says,

> It is this ... it is this ... belief,
> Has lifted you up to over-dream nature, and scorn danger
>   and wisdom. Oh, it is secret. Be a prophet
> But not lay claim ... Be a king if you can, but not to go
>   mad.
>
> (Judas, p. 30)

The guilt of women who have children, especially sons, is a theme that appears in various guises throughout Jeffers' work. Mary, who is unable to account for her conception of Jesus, now regards it as sinful. Jesus chastizes her for her "weakness" of faith, and sends her away "Because faith is dead" (p. 31).

Hesitating before he undergoes the necessary violence of his crucifixion, Jesus muses over God, who is misunderstood "These years of the fall" (p. 32). "The mystery remains though," observes Jesus,

> He must have been lovely ... you daughters of Jerusalem
>   that you stir not up nor awaken my love ...
> He is lovelier than the desert dawns. Three ... four times
>   in my life I have been one with our Father,
> The night and the day, the dark seas and the little fountains,
>   the sown and the desert, the morning star
> And the mountains. . . .
>
> (Judas, p. 32)

The significance of *Dear Judas* as a poem marking the end of a phase in Jeffers' development is underlined here, for this passage is part of an overt examination of the origin of Christianity and of its power and weakness, the admixture of humanity and divinity. The rejection of Christianity for its weakness and deception in favor of Jeffers' materialism is apparent. In a parallel passage written almost twenty years later when he was settled in his beliefs, Jeffers has the old man in *The Double Axe* say to the universe,

> Dear love. You are so beautiful.
> Even this side the stars and below the moon. How can you
>   be ... all this ... and me also?
> Be human also? The yellow puma, the flighty mourning-
>   dove and flecked hawk, yes, and the rattlesnake
> Are in the nature of things; they are noble and beautiful
> As the rocks and the grass—not this grim ape,
> Although it loves you.—Yet two or three times in my life
>   my walls have fallen—beyond love—no room for love—
> I have been you.
>
> *(Double Axe, p.89)*

A comparison of the two essentially alike passages—the first ambivalent and questioning, the second resolved and secure; the first originating in orthodoxy and tradition, the second reflecting Jeffers' mature Inhumanism and preference for nature—illustrates the most significant development in Jeffers' thinking after he began his exploration of Nietzsche.

In *Dear Judas,* Jeffers portrays a Jesus who in a sense loses control of his mission. He comes to teach faith and love, but he is betrayed by the psychology of his adopted humanity, even before Judas gets his silver. The Christianity that Jesus has sown among men grows crooked; Jesus himself cannot help contributing to the problem. The sacrifice on the cross is wrong in the eyes of both Judas and Jesus, but it is necessary and irrevocable. Jesus tells us:

> and my poor Judas, who'll do his
>   office and break; and dreadful beyond these, un-
>   numbered
> Multitudes of souls from wombs unborn yet; the wasted
>   valor of ten thousand martyrs: Oh, my own people

Perhaps will stab each other in a sacred madness, disputing
    over some chance word that my mouth made
While the mind slept. And men will imagine hells and go
    mad with terror, for so I have feathered the arrows
Of persuasion with fire, and men will put out the eyes of
    their minds, lest faith
Become impossible being looked at, and their souls perish.
                                (*Judas,* p. 38)

The course of events is set, however, and will proceed in
spite of Judas, who reasons that "by doing the worst imag-
inable thing / I should be freed of tormenting pity" (p.
47). Lazarus tries to comfort Mary by saying, "Your son
has done what men are not able to do; / He has chosen and
made his own fate" (p. 48). To Judas, Lazarus gives assurance that his name will be forever coupled with that of Jesus: "you enter his kingdom with him, as the hawk's lice
with the hawk / Climb the blue towers of the sky under
the down of the feathers" (p. 48).

The Loving Shepherdess

As an ideological statement, *The Loving Shepherdess* is
important, but, in spite of the surprisingly large number
of its champions, it is difficult to defend the work as a convincing poem.[34] From the beginning the poem moves toward the allegorical mode, but it never satisfactorily estab-
lishes itself as more than fragmented allegory. The poem is
chiefly important because it obviously summarizes a period
of the poet's work. Clare Walker (a new character) and
Onorio Vasquez (a survivor from *The Women*) make a
stark pilgrimage through the Jeffers country of the twenties, and the poem mentions and comments on Arthur Barclay and his daughter April, Tamar's home site at Point
Lobos, and Cawdor's place with its new Japanese occu-
pants.

Early in the poem, we learn that Clare Walker (does the

name suggest "walking light"?) knows that whatever she
suffers now, as she leads her dwindling flock of sheep, it
will end in April. Thus the pastoral image moving toward
sacrifice at Easter is the first correspondence between the
story of Clare and that of Jesus in the preceding poem.
Later we learn that sometime in the past Clare gave herself
to her neighbor-lover, Charlie Maurice, who shot her father in an argument over the relationship between the
young people. Clare alibis for her lover and goes to trial,
but a bout of influenza saves her from the trial and causes
her to miscarry her recently conceived child. The attending physician warns her that a pelvic deformation would
have made full-term delivery impossible, and that a subsequent pregnancy will destroy her—"no life can pass there,"
he says (p. 94). For ill-disguised dramatic purposes, Jeffers,
the former medical student, fails to provide his doctor with
information about Caesarean delivery, and he underlines
this failure by permitting the Indian, Onorio, when he
hears Clare's story, to muse vaguely about an operation—
"it was called the Caesarean section" (p. 104).

After the trial, Clare lives quietly at home with her
sheep, until a shipwreck nearby brings survivors who dis-
possess her of her home and belongings, and she slips away
with the remaining sheep. A similar wreck occurs in *The
Double Axe,* and both appear to symbolize the shipwreck
of humanity and the subsequent exploitation of would-be
benefactors. In the case of the old man in *The Double
Axe,* the wreck serves to confirm his already critical estimate of the dubious state of humanity; but in the case of
Clare, who for many readers resembles a Christ-figure of
love and generosity, the wreck may symbolize the failure of
humanity to accept Christ. In other words, the people were
not following Christ's superior example, but were practic-
ing Christianity as described by Nietzsche and Jeffers.

Because her nomadic life with the sheep constantly exposes her to the weather, Clare falls ill, and an unnamed man takes her in and brings her back to health. Once she is restored, however, the man feels that he is entitled to the favors once enjoyed by Charlie Maurice, and Clare, in spite of her fears, yields again because she feels that her benefactor has a justifiable claim. This incident corresponds with the actions of Judas in the previous poem. Clare is betrayed in the act of love by a man who has "a frill of red hair / All around his face" (p. 99), a detail popularly attributed to the image of Judas.[35] As in *Dear Judas,* an act of love is both the acceptance of love and the acceptance of sacrifice. According to Jeffers, Clare, Judas, and Jesus embodied, respectively, three aspects of love, i.e., (1) "nearly pure, therefore undeluded, but quite inefficient," (2) "pitying," and (3) "possessive."[36] Subsequently, Louis Untermeyer agreed that "Clare's love is 'outward' and impersonal, Judas' is personal and pitying, and Jesus's is possessive and divided."[37]

Pregnant and doomed, Clare Walker eventually comes to the deserted house which was left eight years previously by Arthur Barclay, a preacher "claiming to be God" (p. 60). When she hears about it, Clare is appalled by the report of April's suicide. April must have been "crazy" to "spill / Her own one precious life," Clare says (p. 60). In Barclay's empty house, Clare gives herself freely to an inexperienced youth, Will Brighton (will brighten?), because, she says, "I want to leave glad memories" (p. 62). And when Onorio, the disillusioned visionary who meets Clare, asks what she is doing with her life, she replies, "I'm doing like most other people; take care of those that need me and go on till I die" (p. 66).

As they go along, Clare and Onorio are interrupted by the attacks of "A heavy dark hawk" upon a heron, which

Clare calls "the poor frightened fisherman." It is, of course, the symbolic hawk that Jeffers adopts in his poetry from now on (one remembers the wounded eagle in *Cawdor*) as the apotheosis of life and its intense desirability. Clare is horrified by the hawk, and she underlines the symbolism of the incident when she cries out, referring to the "frightened fisherman" heron, "Oh, what can save him, can save him?" (p. 68). The fisherman heron, the symbol of Christianity, is attacked by the fierce hawk, the symbol of new ideas about God and the world.

When Clare considers going back to Barclay's house for shelter, Onorio says, "Let no one go back there. . . . / God lived there once and tried to make peace with the people; no peace was made" (p. 70). Clare takes his advice and walks on to a farm where she offers herself to an old man who works there and who gives her the shelter that the farm-owner's sons have denied her. "I'd like to make you / Happier," she tells the old man (p. 77), but he declines in deference to the ailing owner who is dying in the farmhouse. Clare's flock continues to diminish, for she cannot provide adequate food or protection. But near Point Lobos, "Where Tamar Cauldwell used to lean from her white pony" (p. 113), Clare finds "much kindness," and she is nursed for many days and her sheep are cared for. By this time, she has left Onorio who, when he tries to follow her, meets a vision (presumably of Clare) that waves him back saying, "If I go up to Calvary ten million times: what is that to you?" (p. 112).

Before Clare and Onorio separated, he had suggested that she consider abortion, since otherwise she faces sure death. She rejects this idea as unthinkable because she relishes, in a way, the fact that now that she is in her "worst trouble" she also holds the child, "feeding on peace and happiness" (p. 102). She says, "I'd not steal one of its days to save my life" (p. 102), for part of her lesson (a theme that continues in Jeffers' subsequent work) is that intrauterine existence is the only peace and happiness that an individual may expect of life; yet Clare also tells Onorio that "all our pain comes from restraint of love" (p. 96). In the midst of her trials, she enjoys the realization that the child "is not mine, / But I am its world and the sky around it, its loving God" (p. 102). Clare's self-realization directs Onorio's next vision, but in the depths of his perception he can find only "his own eye / In the darkness of his own face" and he must admit to himself, "I can endure all things ... forever. I am he / Whom I have sought" (p. 106). Now he knows that "Clare loves all things / Because all things are herself" (p. 106). He regards Clare's pilgrimage as courageous and ennobling, but, he says to himself, "I remain from myself divided, gazing beyond the flaming walls, / Not fortunate enough, and too faint-hearted" (p. 107).

The poem ends quickly after Clare escapes from the well-intended detention and care of the family at Point Lobos, and far up the Carmel Valley, where the river becomes a brook, she watches "a salmon / Row its worn body up-stream over the stones" as it spends "all its dear flesh and all the power it has gathered ... To find the appointed high-place and perish" (p. 113). She recognizes, of course, in the salmon's fate "her own fate reflected," and when her labor begins along the San Joaquin riverbank, in "a thin April rain," she creeps down to the river and hides "her body / In a willow thicket" (p. 114). Like the Jesus of *Dear Judas,* she too has tried to overcome herself; but where Jesus is corrupted by power and destruction, "the dreadful key," as Judas calls it, in his overcoming, Clare performs many compassionate deeds of love while doomed by love and unable to care for her flock. Both individuals have risen to their appointed April high-places but by different routes. Jesus has been shown a savior troubled by his humanity and with his love corrupted; Clare is made absurd in spite of her essential nobility, for she suffers the additional hazards of allegorical abstraction.[38] Her poem ends,

> In the evening, between the rapid
> Summits of agony before exhaustion, she called
> The sheep about her and perceived that none came.
>   (*Judas*, p. 114)

In spite of her selfless devotion and care, as she lived out her dual pastoral role, she could not keep her flock. Clare's adventures are doubly important because they provide the poet with an opportunity to revisit the scenes of his earlier major narrative poems and to observe his characters from the changed perspective of time.

Shorter Poems

Apology for Bad Dreams first appeared in the May 1926 issue of *New Masses,* at a time when the *Tamar* and *Roan Stallion* volumes were already proven successes. In it, Jeffers reflected to some extent on his reasons for writing such books. He said that, because "This coast [was] crying out for tragedy like all beautiful places," he was moved to respond through his poems. He goes on:

> I said in my heart,
> "Better invent than suffer: imagine victims
> Lest your own flesh be chosen the agonist, or you
> Martyr some creature to the beauty of the place."
>   (*Selected Poetry*, p. 175)

As noted in the discussion of Jeffers' poetic theory, he preferred to create detached figures in his poems who, from the tensions of their opposed positions, presented his ideological statements. Consistent with both Jeffers' method of experimentation and my elucidation of that method, this poem records his intent to work out his quest, to analyze the usefulness of ideas, in imagined victims, lest his own "flesh be chosen the agonist." This intention is not exceptional among artists, but in the case of a poet who shows himself in his art to be more concerned with the experiment than with the artistic product such self-consciousness is noteworthy, especially in the light of his conclusion (in the same poem) that "remembered deaths be our redeemers; / Imagined victims our salvation."[39]

Another aspect of the role of imagined victims is revealed in *A Redeemer,* which appeared in the *Cawdor* volume. The narrator of the poem and his wife, who are traveling among the arid canyons inland from the fog-shrouded coast, stop at a farmhouse for water and meet there a man who has given himself the wounds of the "stigmata of crucifixion." He keeps the wounds open, since he believes "There never . . . was any people earned so much ruin," but, as he says, "I love them, I am trying to suffer for them." When asked if the stigmata are meant to signify the wounds of Jesus, the farmer replies contemptuously, "Religion is the people's opium. Your little Jew-God? / *My* pain . . . is voluntary." The farmer says that he lives "on the mountain making / Antitoxin for all the happy towns and farms, the lovely blameless children, the terrible / Arrogant cities." The narrator's wife asks the farmer's wife whether she is afraid:

> "Certainly not," she answered, "he
> is always gentle and loving. I have no complaint.
> Except his groans in the night keep me awake often. But
> when I think of other women's
> Troubles: my own daughter's: I'm older than my husband,
> I have been married before: deep is my peace."

The farmer in this poem may very well represent Jeffers, for the poet felt he was suffering for the people and making antitoxin, as it were, in his poems. Furthermore, the wife's description of the farmer fits Jeffers quite neatly, who was known among his associates for his gentle mildness which belied the violence of the poetry and whose wife, Una, was older than the poet and had been married before.[40]

Such poems as *Apology for Bad Dreams* and *A Redeemer* show how deeply committed to his ideas and poetry the poet was from the beginning of his production. Actually, no one can doubt Jeffers' sincerity; I am stressing his self-conscious commitment and the organically integrated search and experimentation of this period. The fact that the last poem of the volume preceding *Dear Judas*, i.e., *Cawdor*, is *Meditation on Saviors* again shows Jeffers' sense of continuity, for it serves as a prelude to the main topic of the poems *Dear Judas* and *The Loving Shepherdess*. Discussing the relationship of men and saviors, Jeffers wrote in *Meditation on Saviors:*

> The apes of Christ lift up their hands to praise love: but
> wisdom without love is the present savior,
> Power without hatred,
>
> .   .   .   .
>
> But while he lives let each man make his health in his mind,
> to love the coast opposite humanity
> And so be freed of love, laying it like bread on the waters;
> it is worst turned inward, it is best shot farthest.
> (*Cawdor,* pp. 156, 160)

Then Jeffers turned to the study of the savior in *Dear Judas* and *The Loving Shepherdess*.

The Humanist's Tragedy, which is included in the *Dear Judas* volume, shows Nietzschean influence. The poem follows very closely certain passages as well as the thought of Euripides' *Bacchae*. Pentheus, whose Apollonian attributes are strongly emphasized, falls victim to the followers of the Dionysian god at Cythaeron; among the followers is his mother, Agave, who leads the frenzied attack upon the intruder, whom she fails to recognize as her son. For Pentheus, the "end of being" is "To increase the power, collectedness and dignity of man." The Dionysian god, however, tells his women followers,

> But living if you will
> It is possible for you to break prison of yourselves and
>   enter the nature of things and use the beauty.
> Wine and lawlessness, art and music, love, self-torture,
>   religion
> Are means but are not needful, contemplation will do it.
>   Only to break human collectedness.

King Pentheus, as the absolute Apollonian, is no match in his rationalism for the Dionysian enthusiasts who slaughter him, and thus Jeffers reaffirmed his belief that either element alone is dangerous or inadequate. As the title and outcome of the poem's action suggest, however, he favored the group that can "break prison" of themselves and "enter the nature of things."

Determinism and Religion

From Tamar Cauldwell to Fera Martial and old Cawdor, individuals are seen to be seeking some power to overcome themselves as undistinguished parts of humanity. Tamar wants to break with "The withered house / Of an old man and a withered woman and an idiot woman." "What are we for?" she asks her brother (*RS, T,* p. 111). Peace O'Farrell, who is the embodiment of a grotesque biological determinism, leads a life that is chill and empty, and she longs to have it otherwise. To California, Christ has some-

thing to do with life; she is living, but what can Christ do
for her if Johnny is a part of the same humanity? So she
seeks identification with Him in the only way she knows
how—by a solemnly primitive parody of the descent of the
Holy Ghost to the Virgin Mary. Biological determinism directs in part the lives of Faith Heriot and Natalia Morhead
in *The Women at Point Sur*. Faith, who is shocked into a
hatred of men by an abortion paid for with money intended for her mother's cancer operation, finds her way to
Natalia's house. Natalia's husband, Randal, whose child
Faith has just lost, is now fighting in Europe, and the two
women become engaged in a robust homosexual relationship. In one of his more unfortunate lines, Jeffers observes
that Faith's "tropic nature / Knowing that no fence would
cage it found the other outlet"—lesbianism—"The love
without fear" (*Women*, p. 114). And Fera Martial, who
for too long knew failure before economic and psychological pressures, fails again in her final bid to master her situation at Cawdor's house.

The carefully drawn characters in Jeffers' poems dramatically illustrate the operation of the principles of late nineteenth-century materialism. They are frequently motivated by the forces of biological, psychological, and economic determinism, and either seek to escape these forces
or find themselves yielding to them. As commentators
like Waggoner have shown, Jeffers is a poet with an unusually broad acquaintance with contemporary scientific theories and terminology.[41] As a student of medicine, forestry,
and physics, Jeffers was aware of much of the scientific
thought of the day, and presumably his visits to his
brother, an astronomer at the Lick Observatory, kept him
at least casually informed about advancements in astronomy.[42]

Jeffers has confounded many of his critics, including

Waggoner, by employing the terminology of science in order to define, in a manner that sometimes verges on satire, his departure from or his opposition to a body of thinking —in this case the nineteenth-century materialism inherited by most of the poets of Jeffers' generation. *Such Counsels You Gave to Me,* which is the focal point of Waggoner's article, provides the best evidence of this artistic trait in Jeffers' work.

In his article, Waggoner quotes a letter he received from Jeffers which itself shows the confines of Waggoner's approach and the breadth of the poet's orientation. Jeffers writes:

> First, as to the importance of science for the artist and for the thinker. It seems to me that for the thinker (in the wider sense of the word) a scientific basis is an essential condition. We cannot take any philosophy seriously if it ignores or garbles the knowledge and view-points that determine the intellectual life of our time. (These data and view-points are not final, of course. A thinker might attack some of them successfully; but he must not be ignorant of them.)
>
> For the contemporary artist science is important but not at all essential. He might have no more modern science than Catullus yet be as great an artist. But his range and significance would be limited accordingly.[43]

The implications of Jeffers' statement are clear. Scientific thought is part of every thinking man's intellectual equipment; therefore, it must be part of any new philosophical inquiry which is serious and thoroughgoing. When Waggoner says that not enough emphasis has been given to the fact "that a particular set of scientific implications springing from nineteenth-century materialism has been the constant basis for Jeffers' thinking," I agree with him wholeheartedly; but he insists that the "constant basis" circumscribes Jeffers' thought, when actually it serves as a point of departure for new thinking.[44]

Science, therefore, must continue to appear in any poetry dealing with modern life, but, along with orthodox Christianity and other intellectual influences that tended to dehumanize man, science was often the object of Jeffers' "revaluation of values."[45] In his poetry, Jeffers sought to examine vigorously the escalating conflict between the opportunities for freedom of individual human choice and the deterministic theories and forces which affected this freedom. The burden of such poems as *Shine, Perishing Republic, A Redeemer, An Artist, Hurt Hawks,* and *Meditation on Saviors* is that Western civilization is moving toward decay, that Pauline Christianity aids and abets the process by fostering weakness in men, and that only superior men who have achieved self-mastery can hope to survive the collapse of society to build still another. The problem of what the proper mode of self-mastery was and what relationship the individual should have to the remainder of society remained. By applying the doctrines of Nietzsche, Jeffers was able to clear much ground, but ultimately the Nietzschean solutions were not satisfactory. As Nietzsche's Zarathustra implies in his sermons, the doctrine was more means than end.

In *The Women at Point Sur,* Jeffers wrote his *Zarathustra* and in *Dear Judas* his *Antichrist.* With *The Loving Shepherdess,* Jeffers began to turn toward considering, in the larger context of society, the examination which he began in the twenties with the individual. At this point, we should mention the sort of criticism of Jeffers which is exemplified by the comments of Sister M. J. Power in her chapter on Jeffers in *Poets at Prayer.*[46] She condemns Jeffers for trying to be both a pantheist and a deist, and for repeatedly taking God "to task," as she puts it. Her commentary is valuable, for it includes a letter (1 October 1934) which she received from Jeffers. Although he told her that he preferred to deal with such matters in verse instead of prose, Jeffers replied as follows to her inquiry about his "religious attitudes":

> I believe that the universe is one being, all its parts are different expressions of the same energy, and they are all in communication with each other, influencing each other, therefore parts of one organic whole. (This is physics, I believe, as well as religion.) The parts change and pass, or die, people and races and rocks and stars; none of them seems to me important in itself, but only the whole. This whole is in all its parts so beautiful, and is felt by me to be so intensely in earnest, that I am compelled to love it, and to think of it as divine. It seems to me that this whole alone is worthy of the deeper sort of love; and that there is peace, freedom, I might say a kind of salvation, in turning one's affections outward toward this one God, rather than inwards on one's self, or on humanity, or on human imaginations and abstractions—the world of spirits.
>
> I think that it is our privilege and felicity to love God for his beauty, without claiming or expecting love from him. We are not important to him, but he to us.
>
> I think that one may contribute (ever so slightly) to the beauty of things by making one's own life and environment beautiful, so far as one's power reaches.

Although this letter has been overlooked by other investigators subsequent to its publication in 1938, it is a clear statement of the position which I argue Jeffers' poetry describes after the period of trial and examination in the twenties.

4

jeffers and nietzsche,
the middle period

In Jeffers' first period of ideological development, his chief endeavor was to find a satisfactory approach to the problem of life as he saw it. The period ended with the volume *Dear Judas,* his revaluation (mainly under the influence of Nietzschean thought) of Christianity as a valid mode of human aspiration for the good. Beginning with *Thurso's Landing,* Jeffers focused on the problems raised in the poetry of the twenties and on the new theme of their impact in a broader social context. Between *Dear Judas* and *Thurso's Landing,* however, it is apparent that a profound change in attitude took place within Jeffers. As suggested above, the slim volume of short poems *Descent to the Dead* embodied this change. Whereas both the poems *Dear Judas* and *Thurso's Landing* belonged to the class of imagined victims which Jeffers mentioned in *Apology for Bad Dreams, Descent to the Dead* revealed that the poet had in fact permitted his "own flesh [to] be . . . the agonist." *Descent to the Dead* gives the reader a remarkable sense of the poet's unguarded self-disclosure.

Nietzsche's Influence in the Thirties

Descent to the Dead

For the reader who is searching for a continuity of Christian elements in Jeffers' development, nothing could be more apposite, after two major poems treating the theme of crucifixion, than the *Descent to the Dead* volume. Or Jeffers' poetic descent to the dead may be recognized as symbolically similar to Aeneas' descent to the underworld during which Virgil's hero learned about himself, his past, and his responsibilities in order to prepare himself for greater "public" adventures yet to come. The doctrines of Nietzsche do not necessarily constitute Jeffers' golden bough, but the metaphor may not be entirely inappropriate.

The poems were written in Ireland and Great Britain during a visit which Jeffers and Una made in 1929. Some years later, Jeffers was to remember that during the period in the British Isles he was "tired, and wanted to indulge . . . [himself] by playing dead for a few months." Because "the light and the life" in the islands seemed "to be keyed so much lower" than they were at his Pacific Coast home, the poet found it easy to imagine himself "a dead man in a country of the dead."[1] Indeed, as Jeffers wrote in *The Low Sky*, the clouds are often low in the British Isles and there appears to be little room for vulture or hawk flights—

> But one to whom mind and imagination
> Sometimes used to seem burdensome
> Is glad to lie down awhile in the tomb.

Most of the poems are occasioned by visits to ancient tombs and monuments of the heroic past; there Jeffers frequently chats in his poems with such figures as Ossian, the

king in the hill at New Grange, Shane O'Neill, Hugh Mc-
Quillan, and the dead at Iona and at East Lulworth. He
congratulates them on their deeds and envies their peaceful reconciliation with the earth. Jeffers regards the peace
of the tomb in a special way. Besides being a return to the
earth, entombment for him is also a return to the womb, to
one's origin. In *Ossian's Grave,* the poet wrote that he
found himself,

> In a uterine country, soft
> And wet and worn out, like an old womb
> That I have returned to, being dead.

Jeffers, who never disguised his high regard for things Irish
or Scottish, pictured himself as dead for the moment in
his ancestral land, where with the heroes of his own past he
sought counsel and identification. "We dead," he said, including himself among these heroes, "lived splendidly / In
the brief light of day." He added, "Enough has been felt,
enough done, Oh and surely / Enough of humanity has
been." The poet admired the heroic deeds of the past, and
deplored the weakness and fragility of "modern flesh."
Speaking as one who was dead, in *Antrim,* yet aware of the
brutal past of Ireland, "where men have so fiercely for ages
of time / Fought and survived and cancelled each other,"
the poet expressed his dread of returning to life and humanity: "I lie here and plot the agony of resurrection."

But in the next poem, *No Resurrection,* the voice of a
buried man announces that there is no point in returning
to the modern world where "friendship," "faithfulness,"
and "hatred" are no more than "metaphors." "Dead man,
be quiet," the poet advises, for he would be "A fool of a
merchant, who'd sell good earth / And grass again to make
modern flesh." The dead in *Ghosts in England* say, "Great
past and declining present are a pitiful burden / For liv-

ing men" and they feel "No pity for the great pillar of empire settling to a fall, the pride and the power slowly dissolving." By re-creating the past, Jeffers derived the authority he desired for his own "modern" outlook. Near Finvoy, County Antrim, Jeffers visited *The Broadstone,* which is "the availing hero's memorial, / And temple of his power." The poet indicated his great respect for the unknown hero by calling him "more than half God." Jeffers' attitude is not Carlyle's hero-worship, which Nietzsche emphatically abjured; it is the simple longing for a bygone day when men of heroic vision were also permitted heroic deeds. Is it not curious that a man with Jeffers' acquaintance with science should fail to acknowledge the obviously greater accomplishments of, say, Pasteur, Einstein, or Planck? Perhaps it is because the ancients more obviously overcame themselves, rose in their brief lives to eminence and power; before the "beauty of the world" reclaimed them in death, they were dynamic leaders of the affairs of men, and according to their abilities they hewed the future to suit themselves.

Jeffers used the ancient heroes as convenient metaphors, for they exemplified the message of *Inscription for a Gravestone.* "I am not dead," the inscription begins, "I have only become inhuman." The dead man beneath the gravestone is free of "laughable prides and infirmities. . . . [and] The delicate ravel of nerves that made . . . [him] a measurer / Of certain fictions / Called good and evil." He says, "I admired the beauty / While I was human, now I am part of the beauty."

In the poem *In the Hill at New Grange,* Jeffers talks to a dead king who tells the poet about the fierce love of Mary Byrne, who "used to be loving Jesus," but who preferred in the end the dead hero Shane O'Neill; about the burning of the Christian tower at Cloyne; and about the "rich merchant" who built his house on the mound of Bruce, the king buried above the legendary Cuchulain, both of whom look up with inexpressible ridicule at the "sweating merchant." The king cites incidents portraying the deadly conflict between the ancient culture and Christianity, between ancient bravery and modern irreverence and weakness. The poet then tells about Father O'Donnel, who races through his mass, hurriedly sends the people home, and "In the empty church . . . screams and spits on the Christ," striking the crucifix "Because the tortured torturer is too long dying; because the strain in the wounded minds of men / Leaves them no peace." The tormented priest craves to die, "To slip in the black bottomless lake and be still." It would also be best for modern man, the poet tells the old king, "For probably all the same things will be born and be beautiful again, but blessed is the night that has no glowworm."

The *Descent to the Dead* series reaffirmed the more significant of the Nietzschean ideas, which had begun to appear in Jeffers' work with *Tamar*. The Will to Power and Overcoming oneself are present in the tributes to the dead heroes, who are superior to the weak and ineffectual moderns with their reflections of a general cultural decline. Christianity, moreover, has lost its impetus in the minds of people like Mary Byrne, who reverts to the strength of ancient heroes; and, in the eyes of people like Father O'Donnel, it has failed in its promise to modern man. The tortured torturer is too long dying. Within two years, Jeffers was to publish his adaptation of the *Nibelungenlied,* a classic portrayal of the conflict of Germanic heroism and Roman Christianity, which is examined below.

Thurso's Landing

Thurso's Landing marks the beginning of Jeffers' second phase of development in which he tries to apply his theories to a broader segment of society. In various ways, critics have recognized a change in Jeffers' verse with the advent of this long narrative poem. Cargill regards the poem as one of Jeffers' masterpieces; he notes that, with the twenties behind him, "Jeffers, tasting the clean fresh air of better moral times, could write with more of human sympathy, like Sophocles, rather than madly and badly, like Nietzsche, or remotely and austerely, like Aeschylus."[2] I agree, of course, that Jeffers moved away from the remote and theoretical in Nietzsche and Aeschylus, but I should carry the poem's comparison in human sympathy forward to Euripides and his examinations of individual psychology and society. Granville Hicks concurs that *"Thurso's Landing* is perhaps the most human poem . . . [Jeffers] has written in the sense that its characters act from comprehensible motives."[3] Carpenter, who argues that the poet is at his best when he deals with myths of "archetypal appeal," as in the twenties, believes that the narrative poetry begins to slacken with *Thurso's Landing* because "after *Dear Judas* Jeffers wrote no more pure myths."[4]

Rorty was among those who gave the poem a socio-economic interpretation.[5] Reading the poem as an allegory of the thirties, he saw the great cable and iron skip stretched across the canyon as the symbol of "our stupid industrialism against which the suicide father shuts his eyes." The "hawklike mother" represents for Rorty "the harder force of pioneer America on the make, when it was still functioning and faith-whole." In Reave, "this force has become not strength but disease. He will not kill himself or permit himself to be eliminated—few capitalists die and none resigns." Furthermore, "Helen and Mark are like nothing so much as contemporary liberals." Rorty, who judges these characters to be "incredible" as human beings, is correct in seeing them as more the representatives of ideas.

In the following description of *Thurso's Landing,* Jeffers mentions the moral implications present in the poem:

> It is about as long as "Cawdor" and seems to me to be the
> best thing I have yet written. The scene is a canyon of the
> coast south of Monterey, widened by an episode into the
> Arizona desert. The time is perhaps more distinctly near
> the present than usual in my verses; the persons seem to me
> to be a little more conscious of the moral implications of
> what they do.[6]

In a subsequent letter from Jeffers to Alberts, much of the
thinking that characterizes *Descent to the Dead* and that
reemerges in *At the Birth of an Age* is implicit:

> It seems to me that the theme of the poem is courage, and
> its different colors or qualities, in Reave Thurso, in Helen,
> and in Reave's mother. This is not a Greek or Mediterranean
> theme but distinctly northern; perhaps for that reason the
> Viking name of the northernmost town in Scotland came to
> my mind as the family name of these people.[7]

In Chapter 2, *Thurso's Landing* was examined as a specific refutation of certain tenets of Schopenhauer's doctrines and as an endorsement or continuation of the Nietzschean line which has been followed through its development in Jeffers' work. Therefore, the discussion here is
briefer.

Helen Thurso, standing high on a ridge with Rick Armstrong, whom she is about to accept as her lover, looks into
the depths of the canyon where her husband, Reave, is, and
says, "Look down there: / What size Reave Thurso is
really" (p. 16). She goes on to explain, "What he's got's
nothing to him, / His game's the getting" (p. 19). As Rick
prepares to comfort her in a thicket, Helen complains that
she is "stuck in a rut: do I have to live there?" (p. 20).
Already there are overtones from *Tamar* and *Cawdor*, but
significant changes have been made. Reave (whose name

means "to carry off by violence") is a huge, enormously strong man, whose physical power Jeffers documents at every opportunity. As a personality, Reave is a curious amalgamation of the hypocritical David Cauldwell, the corrupted lip server of the Bible, yet without Cauldwell's self-defeating weakness, and of the stern, patriarchal Cawdor. Like Cawdor, Reave is the absolute ruler of his household, but, unlike him, Reave is unembarrassed by his fleshly appetites, for while Helen is away with Rick, the drab but serviceable Hester Clark takes her place. Reave's mother has "the alienation and tamelessness and sullied splendor / Of a crippled hawk in a cage" (p. 23), thus suggesting another antecedent in *Cawdor*. She obviously mistrusts Helen and suspects her adultery, and pointedly tells Reave that, strong as he is, "the mind inside [him] is a baby" (p. 25). From the beginning, Jeffers has cast serious doubt on the intellectual equipment that motivates the strong man, and the spokesman of this doubt is Jeffers' favorite hawk symbol.

Perhaps Jeffers is a little too obvious with his hawk and rock symbols, as when Helen adds to the description of Reave already given by his mother her remark to him that she despises the Landing, "Where nothing except poor Mark [Reave's crippled brother] is even half human, you like a stone, hard and joyless, dark inside" (p. 28). Helen also has antecedents in Jeffers' work, but, in the course of her irresponsible sexual rebellion, she is much less successful than Tamar and Fera Martial.

The earlier discussion of this poem noted that the generation of Reave, Helen, and Mark is trying to avoid the failure and surrender of their fathers. People should do something with their lives, they believe, not yield and give them up at the first disappointment. A large share of Reave's capacity for pain derives from his dread of failure. It is

Reave's extraordinarily severe attitude toward his father
that moves him to try to cut the cable and skip that still
spans the canyon as a constant reminder of his father. The
cable, Helen observes, has withstood earthquakes and fire,
but it will not hold against her husband: "That's the man
we're measured against" (p. 76).

Jeffers is still occupied with the Will to Power as it is
manifest in Overcoming oneself, but there are now important differences between the present representative of
Overcoming and his predecessors. Because the strength and
power are coupled with an infantile mind, there is a Nietzschean emphasis on the intellectual acceptance of the responsibilities accompanying the renunciation of old values. In the following speech to Mark, Helen indirectly
stresses the underlying Nietzscheanism of the poem, when
she compares the two brothers with the metaphor of her
love for them,

>   I am a
> Harlot of a rare nature. The flesh is only a symbol. Oh,
>   can't you see me
> Beaten back and forth between the two poles, between you
>   and Reave?
>
> .   .   .   .
>
> The one pole's power, that I tried to escape: that strong
>   man you know:
> And have been ... retrieved, and can't tell whether I hate
>   him
> Or what. The second, you can name better than I:
> The power behind the power, that *makes* what the other
>   can only
> Direct or destroy. See how wise I've grown.
>   (*Thurso*, pp. 54–55)

As an apparent Apollonian who is nevertheless incapable of controlling or influencing his Dionysian brother,

Mark is corrupted by an errant Dionysian impulse within himself when finally he lusts for his sister-in-law. And he hangs himself after heeding the Schopenhauerian whisperings of that "false prophet," the returned ghost of his suicide father.

In the scene where the cable is cut, Jeffers attests to his poetic skill in the effective presentation of his own ideas over the Nietzchean motif. The Thursoes assemble for the cable-cutting, including Reave's mother, who has already hinted to Reave that he can settle the adultery score with Helen by arranging to kill her with the falling cable. Reave refuses her prompting, but as he prepares to axe the cable "a small bright falcon" lands on it. (The association of the bird and the hawklike mother seems irrefutable.) Hoping to surprise the bird, Reave strikes the cable a blow, but only notches it, and the falcon is gone. Ironically, while Reave steps forward to make sure that Helen is in no danger, the wires part and strike him to the ground. When Helen gets to Reave she finds him "not dead but crawling . . . like the lizard in the desert" (p. 79). (The lizard, which Reave crushed in the desert, is a symbol of Rick's love affair with Helen.) Crushed and impotent after the accident, Reave is stripped of all defenses but his indomitable will; he is reduced to the status of victim before his mother, who does not interfere with his suffering because she feels it has value, and before his wife, who plots to shorten his pain by killing him. Jeffers addresses the reader in the midst of these thoughts about pain:

> No life
> Ought to be thought important in the weave of the world,
> whatever it may show of courage or endured pain;
> It owns no other manner of shining, in the broad gray eye
> of the ocean, at the foot of the beauty of the mountains

And skies, but to bear pain; for pleasure is too little, our
  inhuman God is too great.
                                                      (*Thurso*, p. 84)

Jeffers provides the lesson of California in *Roan Stallion*
brought up to date and made possible. If she could not actually put on "the shining and the power" of Christ, she
might have joined the people at Thurso's Landing and
shone like them in their pain. In Reave Thurso's death
scene, moreover, Helen strikes a note reminiscent of the
"heroism" in *Descent to the Dead;* she compares the death
of Reave with that of some king of Babylon:

                he was like a king in some ways, and
        if he had found any great thing to do
    He might have done greatly.
                                                      (*Thurso*, p. 121)

After Helen cuts Reave's throat in the act of kissing him
and after the hawk-mother watches Helen die of self-ad-
ministered poison, Jeffers concludes the poem by stressing
that such scenes

                      prove our nature
    More shining than that of the other animals. It is rather
        ignoble in its quiet times, mean in its pleasures,
    Slavish in the mass; but at stricken moments it can shine
        terribly against the dark magnificence of things.
                                                      (*Thurso*, p. 123)

Jeffers' Nietzscheanism has led him to a statement of his
own theory of the value of pain in human experience, and
this is one of his few poems in which the yearning for identification with a superior natural beauty is subordinated to
purely human concerns.

Give Your Heart to the Hawks

In his review of *Give Your Heart to the Hawks* (1933),
Morton D. Zabel criticized Jeffers for failing to come to

terms with human nature and for sending forth from his stone tower poems that reflected unpopular ivory towerism.[8] This is justifiable criticism, but it overlooks the work that leads up to *Give Your Heart to the Hawks* and necessarily ignores the line of development in these poems. The fact that Jeffers disregarded the Depression contributes indirectly, I suspect, to the tone of Zabel's criticism, but I believe that *Give Your Heart to the Hawks* is the best *poetry* of Jeffers' long poems.[9] Its opening situation is more complex than any of its predecessors, but its pace is easy and natural, unlike the terse, driving earlier narrative poems. From the beginning scene in the orchard with Fayne Fraser and her brother-in-law, Michael, to the murder of Michael at the beach party, Jeffers supplies realistic detail with confidence and skill. He uses distance with draftsmanlike care, and manipulates perspective to emphasize the dramatic action. The scope of the poem is wider than in earlier narratives; there are more characters (who are identifiable as distinct personalities), and they come from beyond the confines of one man's canyon. Michael, as a second son must often do, is about to go to the city; there are two waitresses "down from the city on their vacation" (one of whom, Sadie, has a three-masted ship tattooed on her stomach); and there is an assortment of neighbors. The main ideas of the poem turn out to be nearly the same as those in *Thurso's Landing*, but the stronger emphasis on society and its concern for the Frasers and that of the Frasers for society is intended by Jeffers to be a descent from the isolation of any stone or ivory tower.

"Give your heart to the hawks" (p. 30) is Fayne Fraser's advice to her husband, Lance, who has just killed his brother whom he found in dalliance with Fayne at the tail end of a drunken beach party. Her advice and her sudden transformation into a hard, quick-witted deceiver may be difficult for many readers to appreciate, for Fayne may eas-

ily give the first impression that she is an incredible and
deceitful bitch. Nevertheless, she is the heroine of Jeffers'
poem.

Old man Fraser is a thoroughgoing Calvinist for whom
the world has irrevocably fallen into sinful ways. At Michael's burial he prays:

> Oh Lord our God, when thy churches fell off from thee
> To go awhoring after organ music,
> Singing-women and lecturers,
>
> .   .   .   .
>
> I cried against them
>
> .   .   .   .   .   .
>
> I said, though all men forget thee thou hast a fort
> Here in these hills, one candle burning in the infidel world,
> And my house is thy people.
>
> (*Heart,* p. 36)

As the old Puritan continues, we begin to understand the
background against which the opening action of the poem
has taken place. The obvious allegorical significance of Michael's slipping a snake into the pant leg of Fayne's jeans
in the orchard and her throwing windfall apples at him in
retaliation goes beyond simple Freudianism. The fierce religious zeal of the old man has left its mark on the stolid,
grim Lance, who is bigger and stronger than either Cawdor or Reave Thurso. In spite of his father's blood-drawing
whippings at prayer time, however, Michael has retained a
healthy, light-hearted spirit. He is more or less engaged to
Mary Abbey, we find out after his murder; and it is reasonably clear that Lance, who has the taint of his father's en-
thusiasm, is responsible for driving an affectionate wife to
seek affection where it may be had—from Michael.

With ominous muscularity, Lance Fraser stalks through
the beach-party action. Although he drinks with his companions, his father's puritanism rankles in his mind. When

the men and women separate to swim nude, Michael joins the group; Lance cannot. When the curious group assembles to examine Sadie's frigate, Lance walks off in raging disgust—though he went to see for himself. And when Lance finds a man in his wife's arms, he caves in that man's head.

Fayne actually loves and respects her grave-minded husband, but it is not the love that flashes with warmth between two healthy young people in an orchard; it is a sense of serious responsibility, a sense of somber stewardship, as it were. In the impassioned instant of murder, Lance sheds the shell of his father's thinking, even as he forces that thinking to its severely logical conclusion; and Fayne immediately recognizes that her husband stands unprotected before society. What is good in him, his power and strength, she must preserve, as all the subsequent action of the poem indicates. Lance's violent act is a waste and a dissipation of his own value, and Fayne immediately supplies the alibi by which her husband's energy and potential may be saved and reshaped. Admittedly, at this point the characters become less believable, although Lance's mother and father continue as realizable human beings.

Michael's murder constitutes a renunciation of social justice, a point of no return, and to follow the alternative line of action, which Fayne chooses, it is necessary to play off the individual against society. What Lance has done he must bear himself, says Fayne.

> It's in ourselves and there's no escaping,
> The state of California can't help you bear it.
> That's only a herd of people, the state.
>
> (*Heart*, p. 29)

She persuades him not to go to Salinas to turn himself in, and then she commences his rehabilitation. When Mrs.

Fraser notices that Lance and Fayne no longer sleep together, she tells the daughter-in-law,

> He's just his father all over, crazy as hawks.
> They get to thinking Antichrist and the Jews and the wicked
>   Pope in Rome
> And scunner at every arrangement for human comfort.
>
> *(Heart,* p. 53)

If father and son are both hawks, the father is the hawk of
Calvin, but the son is the hawk of Jeffers with Nietzschean
flight feathers. Fayne is performing her Apollonian duty to
the Dionysian Lance. Fayne must rationalize the Revaluation of Values for Lance, or, weakened by the destructive
force of opposing tensions, he would surrender himself to
society according to old law.[10] The Calvinist principles of
accepting the responsibility for one's sins and of confessing
them publicly should apply in Lance's case, but such ideas
(excepting public confession) originate with Fayne, not
with old Fraser, the spokesman of orthodoxy. In a sense,
the balance of the poem is concerned with the education of
Lance, and the process is almost successful.

Fayne Fraser shows none of the personal irresponsibility
of Tamar, Fera Martial, or Helen Thurso. She is loyal to
Lance in their new relationship after the murder; she is
devoted to his ailing mother; and she tries, as well as she
can, to help Mary Abbey, who is drawn into the web of
Fraser affairs. As a matter of fact, Mary confesses that she
has always wanted to be like Lance and Fayne. For that
reason, the pattern of dissimilarities between the women is
significant. When the others drink at the party, Mary refuses; when Fayne recognizes the city girl's design on Michael, Mary denies it; Fayne swims farthest out, "Mary remained along shore" (p. 14); whereas Fayne prays for conception (after long denial from Lance), Mary seeks abor-

tion of Lance's child (an offshoot of his denial of Fayne);
Fayne leads Lance southward to a new life together, Mary
drowns herself in San Francisco Bay.

Fayne's role in the poem becomes clearer as she gives the
worried Mary much the same advice that she gave to
Lance:

> Do you think *you* with Lance
> Could strangle time? I am holding the made world by the
>   throat
> Until I can make it change, and open the knot that past
>   time tied. To undo past time, and mend
> The finished world: while you were busy teething your
>   young virginity. I have to control myself.
>
> (*Heart,* p. 61)

After a hawk (broken-winged) and cock fight—in which
Lance sees the hawk as himself—and the appearance of the
ubiquitous Onorio Vasquez, who tells Fayne of the Laurel
Spring that washes off blood of guilt, Fayne persuades
Lance to leave home for the southern Spring and to try to
begin life anew elsewhere. They do not leave before old
Fraser learns the truth about Michael's death, challenges
his "jealous" God, and appeals to Lance to give himself up.
Lance tells old Fraser he once wanted to surrender himself,
but now he prefers Fayne's advice to "give your heart to
the hawks." As Lance and Fayne travel, Lance becomes increasingly delirious from blood poisoning, which originated when he compulsively tore his hands on barbed wire
as he confessed the murder to his father. Trying to encour-
age her husband, Fayne says, "We have come out of the
world and are free, more hawk than human" (p. 100), and
near the end of the poem she summarizes their progress:

> Where you and I
> Have come to, is a dizzy and lonely place on a height; we
>   have to peel off

Some humanness here or it will be hard to live. If you could
    think that all human feelings, repentance
And blood-thirst too, are not very important in so vast a
    world;

.   .   .   .

                  We're going until the world changes,
    you and I like the young hawks
Going hunting; we'll take the world by the throat and make
    him give us
What we desire.

                                (*Heart,* p. 105)

Earlier in the poem, after Lance confesses to his father,
Fayne, now pregnant, makes two points as she tells him,
"Through *me* you go on, the other [i.e., Mary] threw you
away" (p. 91). After the infection-weakened and delirious
Lance throws himself to his death at the foot of a cliff,
Fayne concludes, "I could not keep you, but your child in
my body / Will change the world" (p. 107). There is a
suggestion of Eternal Recurrence in Fayne's statement, but
(though Nietzsche usually considered one or two generations an insufficient cycle) certain concessions may be necessary in reducing philosophical theory to poetry.

    When Jeffers does consider society and its relationship
to the sort of spirit which Fayne embodies, he produces
very much the same answers that he worked out in earlier
poems. He shows the ineffectiveness of monolithic religious orthodoxy, from which youth instinctively turns because it numbs and destroys vitality. In providing the obvious Garden of Eden overtones of the opening action (i.e.,
pastoral scene, the snake, the spoiled apples) and the name
of the brother, Michael, Jeffers may have had the twelfth
book of Milton's *Paradise Lost* in mind and meant to give
a perverse version of Milton's Michael. Lance and Fayne
have been led out of their static Eden by Michael's death;

leaving behind them the fiery sword of old Fraser's religion, they step into the world of trial and experience, in which Fayne is better equipped to guide her Lance. Jeffers' anticipation of the main action of the poem is skillfully handled. As the second section of the poem ends its relaxed narration of the swimming at the beach party, Fayne is drying herself by the fire and "watching with fascinated speculation of pain" the antennae of lobsters heating in a five-gallon tin as they "writhe at the sky, lives unable to scream" (p. 15). Jeffers prepares us for the many subsequent images of an entrapped life, and, by giving the lobster image to Fayne, he anticipates her reaction to the murder. The Dionysian character of the forces building up at the party is self-evident; it is an orgy that culminates in death, but Fayne is the one who imposes a kind of order on the chaos, quickly supplying whatever deception is needed to save the inherent value of her husband from unappreciative and shallow human social codes. The balance of the poem is the record of Fayne's (Apollonian) effort to salvage Lance's (Dionysian) power and to attain Overcoming for herself and her husband. Lance fails because he lacks heart, but Fayne is comforted by the thought that her unborn child (and therein a closer union of the characteristics of the parents) will change the world.

At the Birth of an Age

It is easy to see the significance of the title of Jeffers' next volume, *Solstice and Other Poems* (1935), but it is curious that he chose such an appropriate title at the time. The volume marks a solstice in Jeffers' poetry and in the thinking behind it. The sun of his interest in humanity, which had been moving upward in the three previous volumes, begins to sink back now toward the horizon. The subject of the book is the solstice of a civilization, as de-

picted in the title poem. *At the Birth of an Age,* which pre-
cedes *Solstice* in the volume, provides the background and
Jeffers' explanation of the phenomenon.

In the preface to the verse drama *At the Birth of an Age,*
Jeffers wrote that the story is derived "from the closing
chapters of the Niblung Saga." The theme of "self-contra-
diction and self-frustration" in Gudrun, he says, characterizes this culture-age, which has been "conditioned by
Christianity." When the poet singles out the "extremes of
hope and fear . . . [and] passion for discovery" of the age,
Jeffers reflects the observations of Nietzsche in his recon-
sideration of *The Birth of Tragedy;* but unlike Nietzsche,
who was dealing with ancient Greece, Jeffers sees the origin of these qualities of the age in "the tension between its
two poles, of Western blood and superimposed Oriental religion." He sees a shift in the polarity in modern times:
"the Christian faith is becoming extinct as an influence,
compensatorily the Christian ethic becomes more powerful
and conscious, manifesting itself as generalized philan-
thropy, liberalism, socialism, communism, and so forth."
Furthermore, he says, "the racial pole is weakened by the
physical and especially the spiritual hybridization that civilized life always brings with it." The poet also believes that
the perspective of his time is best for any explanation of
the phenomenon because "we live about the summit of the
wave of this age."

The point at which Jeffers takes up the action from the
Nibelungenlied forms part of a pattern. The first part of
Jeffers' poem, as he said, is an adaptation of the second half
of this Middle High German epic, in which Hagen leads
the Burgundians to meet Kriemhild, now the wife of Etzel
in Austria; there they will face her vengeance for Hagen's
murder of Siegfried, Kriemhild's first love. Jeffers fore-
shortened Hagen's life in order to use the dramatic con-

frontation between him and Kriemhild, but the full significance of Jeffers' Hagen is lost on readers unfamiliar with the earlier heroic figure's career. The hero Hagen in the *Nibelungenlied* represents the passing heroic standards that still survive in a world of dawning courtly traditions.[11] In both the *Nibelungenlied* and Jeffers' poem Hagen is an Overcomer, who by force and superior will power (beyond good and evil) guides Gunther and Siegfried in their affairs. His importance in the saga is symbolically emphasized when he must ferry the Burgundians across the Danube to a land which only he has previously visited. Hagen is often dark and troublesome, but even his murder of Siegfried can be seen as a necessary move of protection from the irresponsible and immature foibles of Siegfried and Gunther; to Gunther, however, Hagen is sworn in loyalty. Hagen's actions may be interpreted as genuine interest in the survival of the society as a whole. His sinking of the Nibelung treasure in the Rhine may be seen as putting beyond reach a great power (even the names of the successive possessors of the treasure were changed to Nibelung) which could easily fall into irresponsible hands—Kriemhild's in particular. Hagen's main task has been to weld together a dissolute and weak people, to make fighters out of them in order that they may best serve their rather dull-witted king, Gunther. At the point where Jeffers picks up the saga, Hagen is trying to guide the Burgundians through what he recognizes to be Kriemhild's trap to avenge her dead husband. They have come to Etzel's court where Kriemhild hopes to use her husband's Huns to achieve her revenge.

Between Jeffers' story and the *Nibelungenlied,* there are obvious differences and some which are more obscure. Jeffers uses the action and revenge motive of the German poem, but the names of the characters and some of the action prior to that in Jeffers' poem come from the *Volsunga Saga*, which is based on the Icelandic poem the *Poetic Edda*.[12] Hagen, Siegfried, Kriemhild, Gunther, and Etzel from the *Nibelungenlied* bear their respective *Volsunga Saga* names in Jeffers' poem—Hoegni, Sigurd, Gudrun, Gunnar, and Attila (Atli). Jeffers' Carling, the youngest brother, is not named in the *Volsunga Saga*, but he fits the description of Giselher, the youngest brother in the *Nibelungenlied*. Jeffers' notation that Brynhild enjoyed Sigurd "when he was a boy" (p. 39) comes only from the *Volsunga Saga*, as does the description of how the unpledged youth, Guttorm, ate "serpent" to acquire the courage to kill Sigurd. In the *Volsunga Saga*, Gudrun avenges her brothers and kills Atli, her husband; but in the *Nibelungenlied*, Kriemhild avenges her husband, Siegfried, and dies herself, with Hildebrand, Dietrich, and Etzel surviving in a world emotionally and socially altered by the conflicts of Hagen and Siefgried, of Hagen and Kriemhild, and of the Burgundians led by Hagen and Etzel's Roman-tempered people.

Jeffers' Gudrun dies as she does in the *Nibelungenlied*, and his Attila goes on to fight more battles and muse over the woman with the "harlot-gold hair" whom he once had. After this point, only halfway through the poem, Gudrun exists as "a thin, fractional, insubstantial" image, disengaged from her body, "neither seen by . . . [the living] nor seeing them" (p. 62). In time, Gudrun, who, as a living person, had begun to incline toward the example of her Christian slave Chrysothemis, finds herself on a peak with Christ, who is praying. She suspects that he may be the Roman God whom Chrysothemis has mentioned.

The first half of Jeffers' poem presents a rather telescoped version of Hagen, the heroic Overcomer who, after many a battle, has met his end at the hands of representatives of dawning Christian society. Like Thurso and Lance

Fraser, he has fought as hard as he could, but has won nothing durable or satisfying, except that he progresses toward whatever the end holds in store for him. Although Lance does not follow this pattern alone, I contend that Jeffers clearly shows the Apollonian Fayne leading the Dionysian Lance along this route. And whereas Thurso learns by himself and Lance learns within the admitted confines of social pressures, Hagen has shaped and led a fading, heroic society before the tide of Christianity swept northward from Rome. Furthermore, Jeffers has preserved in Gudrun the barbaric spirit of her age, somewhat mollified by the Christian example of Chrysothemis, who ignores Gudrun's suicide and prays:

> Dear Savior,
> care for her spirit.
> She was bewildered, and she was kind.
> She might have come to thee.
>
> (*Solstice*, p. 62)

Soon thereafter Gudrun's Shadow admits, " ... I think my deformity / Was only ambition: to fly at the highest" (p. 67). (Early in the poem Gudrun explained her marriage to Attila, "I have what I sought in marriage, that's power" [p. 23].) The second part of the poem is a colloquy of Gudrun's Shadow with the Young Man, whom she finds praying, and with the chorus of Singers.

The Young Man on the peak is related to Jeffers' Christ in *Dear Judas*. She asks him what he is praying for, and he replies, "I was deceived" (p. 70). He has failed his followers because he cannot "open the enchanted home" for them after their troubled lives of faithfulness: "I have stood here long / And seen my betrayed come to my feet, and bitterly seen the soul more mortal than flesh" (p. 72), and he concludes, "If Judas for a single betrayal hanged himself, / What for me, that betrayed the world?"

(p. 73). Then, as the clouds separate, a vast figure is revealed, bound and bleeding, which "resembles the Prometheus painted on the wall of the ruined house where Attila feasted," according to the stage directions of the verse drama (p. 76). The painting of Prometheus bound on Mount Elboros is the background before which Attila humbled the Bishop Lupus early in the poem. When Gudrun's Shadow sees the revealed Prometheus, she declares,

> Here is the dignity
> We adored in rocks and water,
>
> .   .   .   .
> Here is reality,
> All that any living eyes ever saw was phantom
> Shadows of this.
>
> *(Solstice,* p. 77)

The Singers say that Prometheus "is all that exists ... " and Gudrun's Shadow observes, "Hoegni had a glimmer of the beauty, he burned / A little pure, if pure killer" (p. 79).

The Hanged God, now identified as Prometheus, finally speaks to Gudrun's Shadow, the Voices, and the Young Man:

> Pain and their endless cries.
> How they cry to me: but they are I:
> let them ask themselves.
> I am they, and there is nothing beside.
>
> *(Solstice,* p. 88)

The Hanged God says that he could have had peace without pain, the perfect freedom, but "that's nothing"—

> I have chosen
> Being; therefore wounds, bonds, limits and pain;
> the crowded mind and the anguished nerves,
> experience and ecstasy.

> .   .   .   .
>   I torture myself
> To discover myself.
>
> *(Solstice,* p. 89)

The Hanged God explains that he has his peace, too:

>   it is in this mountain.
> I am this mountain that I am hanged on
> and I am the flesh
> That suffers on it.
>
> *(Solstice,* p. 91)

He ends his speech:

>   Without the pain,
>   no knowledge of peace, nothing.
>   Without the peace,
> No value in the pain. I have long strength.
>
> *(Solstice,* p. 92)

Both Gudrun's Shadow and the Singers accept The Hanged God's message, and she declares, "I will enter the cloud of stars, / I will eat the whole serpent again" (p. 92). The Singers agree with the decision of Gudrun's Shadow and say:

>   after I have rested as it were a moment
> Against the deep wells, and then
> I am willing to eat the whole serpent again ...
>
> *(Solstice,* p. 92)

Although other critics have recognized Jeffers' challenge to traditional Christianity, they have had difficulty in deciding how to interpret it. I must argue with Watts' reading of these last speeches, when he writes, "By sharing this repast [i.e., eating the serpent with The Hanged God], Gudrun attains to the same excruciating self-knowledge and to the same divine indifference to humanity."[13] Actually,

in the poem The Hanged God shares nothing with anyone
except the knowledge of his speech (quoted in part
above), which is a simple declaration of his discovery that
pain is necessary and that he is one with everything else—
he is the mountain he hangs from. His speech is singularly
free of proselytizing intent. The Young Man has confessed
himself a failure, a betrayer of his followers, and he sets
himself against the "merciless / God not my father" (p.
79) because, as he says,

> I see the ridiculous delusion
> that gave me power and the ways
> that led up to Golgotha,
> The delusion dies, the power survives it.
>
> *(Solstice,* p. 79)

He claims that the age is his because he bought it with
"the stubborn faith" of his people. He concludes,

> When men are happy
> Let them cut the crosses out of the churches,
> no man remember me.
>
> *(Solstice,* p. 80)

Gudrun says of him, "He is beautiful, this easterner, but
like a child / Desiring what men despise" (p. 80).

Gudrun and the Singers reject the Young Man for the
very reasons that he turns against himself. From a reading
of the closing speeches, there can be no doubt that The
Hanged God holds more meaning for them, but his way
demands strength and courage. To follow The Hanged
God, which is to reassert the values of Hoegni and his heroic world, Gudrun will eat the whole serpent again, and
the Singers say that they, too, are willing to do the same
thing. Gudrun and the Singers are ready to return to the
life that means violence, suffering, and heroic courage.

The salvation of Christian faith has been canceled by the Savior himself, but The Hanged God gives nothing except the knowledge of pain, which can only be met with extraordinary courage.

The dramatic structure of Jeffers' poem is broken at the point of Gudrun's death; the realism of the first part is replaced by the supernaturalism of the second. Only a poet more interested in ideas than in sound dramatic action could leave the vividly realized situation at Attila's court to ascend with disembodied Shelleyan voices to cloud-wrapped peaks to philosophize with a demoralized Christ and a Prometheus who is no longer interested in people. As long as Jeffers wrote realistically about his coastal neighbors, he had to leave them at death, but in this poem he pursues the dead Gudrun and supplies her with Jeffersian second thoughts about her career and that of Hoegni.

Solstice

The narrator of the poem begins his tale by pondering the "sombre magnificence of the coast [which] / Remembers virtues older than Christ." "Pride and ferocity," he says, "are virtues as well as love" (p. 94). They are a way of changing one's life in a world that has fattened into soft civilization, and the poet goes on to relate:

> I call to mind
> Against our meanness, the bitter crawling meanness
>   of human lives—not to damn all—Madrone
> Bothwell's white eyes and straight black hair;
>
> . . . .
>   She had power;
>   she was free and proud.
>
>   (*Solstice,* p. 94)

The poem, however, tells the "manner of her going away";

the giantess, Madrone, who is the fierce reflection of the
coastal grandeur about her, loses her intemperate struggle
with the agents of the society and civilization that she
scorns. In spite of a few striking descriptive passages and
some unusually stark action, Jeffers' adaptation of the story
of Medea to contemporary life remains gnarled and unin-
spired.[14] Madrone's identification with wild nature verges
on the psychotic, and the poet's description of the "dangers" of society is stereotyped and thinly drawn.

   The time of the poem is ten days before the New Year,
when Madrone learns that her husband has been awarded
the custody of her two children, Ronnie and Gloria, as the
result of divorce proceedings arising from her adultery.
Madrone despises her husband, who was "once no worse
than a drunken cowboy, a trick rider at dude-ranches" (p.
107), because he has proved to be weak-willed and a
drunkard ("I gave my virginity to a dog," she tells her
maid [p. 99]), and now they argue about who possesses the
power. Jeffers has endowed both characters with power—
Madrone's stems from her personality and her identification with nature; Bothwell's derives, not from within, but
from social institutions and conventions—from the courts
and public reaction to adultery. Madrone and her husband
were obviously mismatched, as the poet may be trying to
suggest in his description of Madrone's bath (after she has
abused her body among cactus and yucca spines to atone
for her "sins"):

                                        She washed her lacerated
        Body and all the heavy cordage of her nightfall hair,
            and stood up steaming in the cold twilight,
        Long-legged, deep-ribbed, great-shouldered,
            nothing soft, not even the dark-eyed breasts;
            but like a great engine

> Built for hard passions and violent labor,
>   and in the bone girdle of the hips
>   to breed warriors.
>
> *(Solstice,* p. 100)

In addition to his other shortcomings, Bothwell has proved inadequate before this imposing figure. Madrone turns to other men; among them, "she met and enjoyed that tall white Lance / Fraser in his youth" (p. 101). Madrone's adultery is motivated in part by her desire to embarrass her husband, but he merely hires a detective to record her assignations in order to take her to court.

When Bothwell arrives with his lawyer and detective at Madrone's home to take the children back with him, he explains without poetic inspiration,

> They'll have
> pleasures and advantages you cannot possibly:
>   radio, motion-pictures, books,
> The school, the church. And when they're
>   old enough to go up to college ...
>
> *(Solstice,* p. 106)

Madrone cannot see any value in such a life for the children; it means living in crowded cities where they will be deprived of their innate capacity to develop into strong individuals. "Better the babies died," she tells her husband, "than such lives for them" (p. 112). In addition to Bothwell's threat to "civilize" the children, Madrone learns that their home has been sold to a Mr. Black, who proposes "to develop the place as a resort." Madrone, however, envisions, "A stew-pot for nature- / Lovers and sick drunkards" (p. 105).

Madrone is stunned by these two blows, and her husband stresses the fact that now the power is his, implying

here as elsewhere that he has not always had it. Madrone
retorts,

> Your power? It is not your power but the world's.
>   I am quite alone, how can I fight
>   the law that you have
> Made for you . . . ?

(Solstice, p. 108)

"Do you think you can overcome me?" she challenges (p.
108), and in order to frustrate her husband's plans she
wrecks the engine of his automobile and throws away the
ignition key of her own car when he decides to appropriate
it. Ironically, the setting sun, shining through a rift in the
clouds, glints on the key, and the men find it. In this accident, Madrone sees divine intervention, and she says to
Bothwell, "He has given it to you" (p. 117). Henceforth,
she regards God as "my enemy."

Rather than surrender her children to society, Madrone
cuts their throats and escapes with their bodies into the
mountains. She buries them on a height from whence they
have a panorama of the scenic grandeur which they have
joined by virtue of their interment. Although her over-
turned car is found in a desert gully, Madrone is never seen
again, and the poet says,

> I think she had too much energy
>   to die. I think that a fierce unsubdued core
> Lives in the high rock in the heart of the continent,
>   affronting the bounties of civilization and Christ,
> Troublesome, contemptuous, archaic. . . .

(Solstice, p. 131)

The poet has assembled his usual themes and devices;
his intentions are clear, but his poem does not approach
success as a work of art. The ideas have thrust through the
fabric of the poem, but they lack the note of affirmation

that has been discernible up to this point. I think that Nietzschean attributes are evident in Madrone, but, as powerful as she may be, it is she who is overcome by the forces of society and by her unreasonable determination not to strike a compromise with them. Nobody wins anything in this struggle of forces. The children are dead as the result of a selfish sacrifice, which no burial at any scenic height can redeem. If the reader had any respect or sympathy for Jeffers' earlier strong characters who struggle to shape their own destinies, he would be quite likely repelled by Madrone, chilled by her obvious derangement.

In the two major poems of the *Solstice* volume, Jeffers reached a personal solstice as well, which marked the zenith of his affirmation of society and civilization. Jeffers had, in fact, come to a standstill. His Nietzschean characters are limited by their failure to be responsible to society, and in the balance of the volume's poems society itself remains decadent and contemptible.[15]

It is not surprising, then, to discover Jeffers' renewed emphasis on the "noble" world, as in *Life from the Lifeless,* in which he declares,

Spirits and illusions have died,
The naked mind lives
In the beauty of inanimate things.

But what about the cities, what will become of them? In *What Are Cities For?* Jeffers prophesizes that golden-rod will one day cover New York as "the earth has covered Sicilian Syracuse," and he interprets this observation for himself in the following manner:

You have seen through the trick to the beauty;
If we all saw through it, the trick would hardly entice us
    and the earth
Be the poorer by many beautiful agonies.

If there are times when Jeffers condemns modern civilization and incongruously even the Americans, who were
struggling out of the Depression, for their luxuries, he
holds "no bitterness," as he says in *Ave Caesar,* for "our
ancestors did it." Like the decadent Romans, Americans
"will learn to hope for a Caesar" to weld their weakened
nation together, a task which America's spineless indifference will facilitate, for "We are easy to manage, a gregari-
ous people, / Full of sentiment, clever at mechanics, and
we love our luxuries." Referring to this poem, Cargill
noted that some "reviewers guessed accurately enough his
potential, incipient Fascism."[16] And in the next poem,
Shine, Republic, Jeffers makes his position even clearer;
for, since "The love of freedom has been the quality of
Western man," he advises, "The states of the next age will
no doubt remember you, and edge their love of freedom
with contempt of luxury."

In *The Trap,* Jeffers says, "I am not well civilized, really
alien here," and attacks modern life:

I honestly believe . . .
Blind war, compared to this kind of life,
Has nobility, famine has dignity.

In the poet's judgment people as they are are not worth
keeping, and these sentiments are not endorsements of war
because war is good, but acknowledgments that, since the
world is arming itself, war seems a ready solution. Jeffers
makes this clear in the beginning of *Sign-Post:*

Civilized, crying how to be human again: this will tell you
how.
Turn outward, love things, not men, turn right away from
humanity,
Let that doll lie.

Orestes' discovery in *The Tower Beyond Tragedy* is reiterated here; it no longer exists only in the abstract, for it is given immediate application to everyday life. In the later poem, however, Jeffers preserves a semblance of Christianity:

Things are so beautiful, your love will follow your eyes;
Things are the God, you will love God, and not in vain,
For what we love, we grow to it, we share its nature.

In the *Solstice* volume the gospel of renunciation and endurance, of severity preferred to luxury, does not yet mark the end of a phase, but it is decidedly the turning point toward the bitterness and resignation that was soon to dominate the poet's work. Before Jeffers' second period came to a close, however, he was to present his *Selected Poetry* and *Such Counsels You Gave to Me*.

Such Counsels You Gave to Me

In *At the Birth of an Age* Jeffers was concerned with revising a Norse legend and projecting its implications into an abstract, supernatural debate, and in *Solstice* with an utterly macabre confrontation of society and a dubious champion of nature's splendors. In *Such Counsels* he returns to a realistic setting in which aberrant behavior is more readily understandable in terms of the facts and ideas in the poem. It is another examination of the Nietzschean Overman, his struggle and fall, but its most significant achievement is the hero's decision to assume the penalty which society will mete out for both his own and his mother's crimes.

Howard Howren, who is a medical student at Berkeley, returns to his father's farm to humble himself by begging for money to sustain him through his studies. Already physically exhausted and infected by tuberculosis, Howard has fought hard to earn his way and to stay at the top of his class, but he can no longer go on. As he arrives, he meets first his image (doppelgänger), then his mother, Barbara, who is much younger than her husband, and his sixteen-year-old sister, France. Howard argues that, given a fair chance, he can continue to show his superiority at school and to meet the other demands of intense student life. Throughout the poem there are notations of how he conquers the weakness of his body, but at one point, in a self-revealing dream, he sees himself as a dog to which he has nailed wings in the laboratory. The act of nailing on the wings is cruel, but how else, Howard wonders, can a dog be given flight? In the dream, the wings tear off and the dog falls "along the façade of a public building." Representing Howard's effort to overcome himself, the dream symbolically foreshadows the resolution of the poem—Howard's determination to surrender himself into the hands of social justice.

With labored reasoning unbecoming a brilliant medical student, Howard deduces, according to Mendel's laws of hereditary traits, that, because his sister's eyes are brown but the eyes of both parents blue, she is the result of his mother's adulterous union with a lover. This thought, interestingly enough, makes Howard's mother "more real and dear" for him "a living woman / With her own loves and lawlessness" (p. 21). If this information endears her more to him at the beginning of the poem, it is significant that her similar argument at the end ("Good and evil are too much mixed" [p. 68]) does not induce him to become her lover, as she desires.

Howard's father is simply not his son's kind of man. He is a rugged individual of unsophisticated ways and robust appetites. His son's dedication to science is beyond his comprehension, especially when the boy could come back to the farm and live a "good" life of outdoor work. Trying to provide a simple explanation, Howard tells his father,

> I want to know
> What life is; how it works. I want to discover new things
>   about it. I guess most of all I want to
> Succeed.
>
> (*Counsels,* p. 28)

About his research, Howard has some things to say that reflect some of Jeffers' own theories; Howard has

> opened a new chapter in bio-chemistry; the evolution of
> Pre-cellular life. That's my work: to begin a bridge
> Between broken-down rock and the virus of life.
>
> (*Counsels,* p. 31)

But these ideas are beyond his comprehension, and the father pleads "almost tenderly" for Howard to return to the natural beauty of his home.

Because old Howren, who is despised by his wife, refuses to provide his son with the money he needs, Howard is ripe for his mother's suggestion that he use the vial of potassium cyanide which he carries, should suicide be required, to give his father a "heart attack," since his death would release the property to his wife and son. In Howard's partial defense, Jeffers has Howard arrange a kind of cyanide roulette, but the father loses instead of the son.

Howard's mother, however, is not yet satisfied, for she takes up again her plan to have her son as her lover. Howard, who once told his father, "I don't want women, I hate their faces" (p. 31), is not interested in her offer, but, before he turns himself in to the authorities for the murder, he begs her to show him her "beautiful breasts. . . . And let me cool my face on the white snows. / My life will find its meaning" (p. 64). Howard's mother misunderstands his interest and renews her offer, from which he recoils, call-

ing her a whore and saying, "I know now, I've been your
creature all my life. The tortured ambition was yours, God
how you worked in me—" (p. 66). When he first came
home, Howard warned his mother to be careful, if she still
sleeps with her husband: "It would be cruel to breed another like me ... " (p. 16). Here is a tempered reflection of
Walter Margrave's indictment (in *Margrave*) of his father
for breeding him. Perhaps it is also significant that in a
brief subplot Howard's half-sister, France, invites her boy
friend, Ernie Crawford, to initiate her into the discovery
of physical love. France's objectives, obviously less preten-
tious than her brother's, may be purposefully drawn so as
to reflect adversely on her own adulterous origin.

Having resisted some of his mother's charms, Howard
begins to help her re-dress, and Barbara Howren begins to
scream—"while a cold inner eye . . . watched itself scream /
And watched the mirror of its mind split into fragments"
(p. 69). Her will, so long and so intently focused on its
objectives, simply shatters under the failure of this climac-
tic effort.

Running out of the house, Howard meets his doppelgänger again, which asks,

> Why did you not
> Complete your cycle? You returned to the breasts of infancy,
> Not to the womb of birth.
>
> (*Counsels*, p. 70)

Howard answers vaguely, "I loved her." The image has the
role of the Overman and the Will to Power in Howard,
and it takes him to task for denying his mother and want-
ing discovery:

> You are typical: your fever
> And your failure from the one fountain. You wanted
>   discovery

And then refused it, desired and yet not-desired, loved and
  yet hated.
The tension of the divided mind drove you on
And brought you down; that tension, the spurs and curb-bit
Of the present human world including its sciences.

(Counsels, p. 70)

The image criticizes Howard for losing control of the Will
to Power, i.e., the "tension of the divided mind," and it
accuses him twice of having "the split will." Howard's
doppelgänger represents another side of himself, and his
mother represents the opposite of himself. Howard has acknowledged that it was her ambition that inspired him to
succeed, but it is his own sense of propriety and justice
which bridles at her extreme means. In other words, she is
Dionysian and he is Apollonian, but he cannot control her
or join with her, which is the symbolic meaning of her incestuous offer. Howard's own awareness of the differences
between himself and his mother is represented by the self-
critical doppelgänger, which can judge and accuse but cannot act for itself.

This poetic device, which is used to illustrate the different aspects of the Nietzschean quest, is complicated, but
once explained in this manner, the final action of the poem
becomes plain. Thus, in the historical development of Jeffers' use of these Nietzschean ideas and their relationship
to general society, it is important to recognize the progress
marked by Howard's decision to defy his image and to
stand trial. "There are certain duties," he says to the image, "Even for ... modern man" (p. 72).

I feel that the poem is far from being the poor application of "only the rudiments of psychoanalytical thought,"
as Bernard DeVoto asserted, and regard it as a serious analysis and resolution of ideas that had occupied the greatest
part of the poet's work to date.[17] The poem coincides at

several points with Freud's Oedipus complex, but the controlling concern is the Nietzschean quest for Overcoming. A shrewd insight into the poet's design led Louise Bogan to comment that Howard is "unusual" because "he is moved . . . to a moral decision. . . . and chooses to expiate, not his own guilt, but his mother's."[18]

There are other poems in the *Such Counsels* volume, but they do not further develop the theme of the title poem. Instead, they prepare for the third period, which begins with the appearance of *Be Angry at the Sun* (1941). There will not be another Nietzschean Overman like Howard Howren; Bruce Ferguson in *Mara* and Hungerfield in the poem by that title are different breeds of men. The remaining poems—such as the artistically interesting *Steelhead, Wild Pig, the Fungus*—examine the motives of men like Hugh Flodden, who seems to have everything a man needs, or women like June Flodden and Florrie Crawford, who meet the perennial evil of the world with injured innocence and hateful retaliation, respectively. The pessimistic awareness that "surely one always knew that cultures decay" is carried in poems like *The Purse-Seine, The Great Sunset, Blind Horses;* and it is met by *The Answer—*

>   Integrity is wholeness,
>   the greatest beauty is
> Organic wholeness, the wholeness of life and things, the
>   divine beauty of the universe. Love that, not man
> Apart from that, or else you will share man's pitiful con-
>   fusions, or drown in despair when his days darken.

Among these poems is Jeffers' *Self-Criticism in February,* an honest appraisal of his work as well as a valuable guide to understanding it. In the poem, the poetic voice of the narrator converses with his public-conscious voice.

Against the charge that he has *"loved the beauty of storm disproportionately,"* the poet replies that the "present time is not pastoral, but founded / On violence, pointed for more massive violence." Why does he insist on poems

> *full of ghosts and*
> *demons,*
> *And people like phantoms ...*
> *And passion so strained that the clay mouths go praying*
> *for destruction* [?]

Because, the poet replies, that is the way life is. The worst fault charged, however, is that the poet has

> *never mistaken*
> *Demon nor passion nor idealism for the real God.*
>
> . . . .
> *If only ...* [he] *could sing*
> *That God is love, or perhaps that social*
> *Justice will soon prevail.*

Life is not that way, according to the poetry so far, and Jeffers repeats in this poem the principle that he derived from Nietzsche: "I can tell lies in prose." In addition to confirming my reading of the poems so far, Jeffers suggests, by the very act of self-examination, that as life gets grimmer for him so will the poetry for us. As he says in *Theory of Truth* (in *Selected Poetry*), "only tormented persons want truth." The fact that the world was preparing itself for World War II served only to confirm Jeffers' darkest prophecies and to intensify the torment.

jeffers and nietzsche, the final period

By the end of the second period of his development, Jeffers had demonstrated that the success of a Nietzschean Overman was short-lived and impractical because it failed to allow for the individual's responsibilities to society. The poet invariably found Nietzsche's doctrines opposed to social justice (which he also questioned more and more) and to the inevitable compromises of living in society. Yet certain lessons from these doctrines were still useful. As Nietzsche advised, the individual should continue to direct himself toward the Revaluation of Values, in order not to be deluded by forms and traditions. The doctrines of Antichrist were not only part of the Revaluation of Values, but they cleared Jeffers' way of moribund and stifling "Christianity," and sanctioned his own gospel of the beauty of things. The Will to Power was discarded as a principle no longer having practical application, but a moderated doctrine of the Overman still authorized firm independence and the intellectual fulfillment of the individual.

The drums of war had again begun their beat around

the world, their ominous roll coinciding with Jeffers' gradual self-realization of his ideas. This new awareness was apparent in a tendency of increasing momentum and justification to move away from society toward isolation and identification with a Nature that was unpolluted by the affairs of man. Current events provided daily proof of the poet's worst suspicions about the insistence of mankind on busying itself with aggrandizement, oppression, and meaningless luxury. The epic detachment characterizing many of the early long narratives gave way to personal emotional response that welled up almost uncontrollably in Jeffers. Generally, the poetry yet to be written was tinged with bitterness and contempt and with the meager consolation that humanity was on the verge of destroying itself, for the "culture-complex" (as Jeffers once referred to the age) was obviously running downhill.

Jeffers' reply to a questionnaire sent out by The League of American Writers indicated his mood at the end of his second period. In a letter dated 1 February 1938, the League sent the following questions to authors in an effort to put on record the sentiments of the writing community: Are you for, or are you against Franco and fascism? Are you for, or are you against, the legal government and the people of Republican Spain?[1] Jeffers' response was that, "As a neutral, I shall be in a minority of one, among the writers who choose to answer your questions. . . ." This remark reflects the temper of his poetry. As a matter of fact, however, Jeffers' reply appeared in the company of six other "neutrals": Eleanor Carroll Chilton, E. E. Cummings, Walter D. Edmonds, T. Swann Harding, Channing Pollock, and Stewart Edward White. The poet began characteristically, "I would give my right hand, of course, to prevent the agony; I would not give a flick of my little finger to help either side win." He went on to say that the

"legality of the government does not interest" him, for
"great changes were overdue in Spain." The "government's supporters are justified in fighting for them," but
Franco's people were also justified "in fighting for the
older Spain that they are more or less loyal to. . . ." Then,
as if in anticipation of the charge of fascism that some critics were soon to bring against him, Jeffers wrote: "As to
fascism: I would fight it in this country, but if the Italians
want it that is their affair. The same goes for Nazism. The
same for communism, from which the others learned their
methods."[2] As early as the spring of 1938, in a considered
statement on historical events, Jeffers thus clearly indicated
the direction his poetry was to take, as well as the basis for
his isolationism.

Later Nietzschean Influences
Mara

Between the first and last poems in *Be Angry at the Sun*
(1941), Jeffers demonstrates a significant change in attitude
toward the contemporary problem of the truth-seeking man.
The first poem, *Mara,* is about Bruce Ferguson, a "deceived
and jealous man / Who bawled for the truth, the truth,
and failed to endure / Its first least gleam." Actually, this
is an opinion of Ferguson which Jeffers included in *For
Una,* another poem in the book, where he added that Ferguson was in "some ways / My very self but mostly my an-
tipodes." The last poem is *Be Angry at the Sun,* which
declares that "public men publish falsehoods" and "America must accept . . . corruption and empire," and one might
as well "Be angry at the sun for setting / If these things
anger . . . [one]."

At the beginning of *Mara,* Bruce Ferguson is visited by
a phantom, the now-familiar doppelgänger. Ferguson, "all

wants fulfilled," is disturbed because "life in general looked dirty, senseless and destitute / In his dark times" (p. 4). The phantom looks exactly like Ferguson, and it asks him either "How long will you be satisfied?" or "How long / Will you endure it?" (p. 4)—the words are not clearly said. The rest of the poem is about Ferguson, who avoids truth even as he searches for it, until at last, hopelessly divided within himself, he takes his own life by hanging. An early episode in the poem reveals Ferguson's peculiar hypocrisy. As he is about to accept Mary Monahan's invitation to comfort her in her husband's absence, Ferguson tells her not to "call it love." He explains, "The girl I love is five miles from here" (p. 9), meaning his wife, Fawn. Mary, who is astonished, blurts, "Everyone knows she sleeps with your brother / When you're away" (p. 9).

It is true that Allen Ferguson and Bruce's wife are lovers, but, unlike earlier Jeffers' characters, they question themselves about their deceit and decide vaguely that their actions reflect the state of the world. Fawn even suggests to Allen that with time they can "make this clean" (p. 13). Ferguson, off in an upland pasture, is gnawed by suspicion, but he concludes his debate with himself:

> Either we are animals . . . clever in some ways,
> Degenerate in others, and follow instinct,
> Or else we are something else and ought to do otherwise.
>
> (*Angry*, p. 15)

Bruce's mother, who is taking care of ailing Andrew (her husband, who she believes suffers now for his past sins), also suspects Fawn of adultery. In Mrs. Ferguson's eyes, Fawn deceives Bruce just as Andrew deceived her; at one point she sees Fawn as Teresita Blaine, her husband's "other woman" of days gone by.

In an authorial intrusion, which recalls the apostrophe

in Section 12 of *The Women at Point Sur,* Jeffers asks the
Lord,

> out of these ordinary
> Elements of common life, these two or three persons
> Who not without cause question it,
> Can any discovery shine, or a hawk rise?
>
> (*Angry,* p. 26)

Bruce searches for discovery, but he fails to rise. He delivers a true Jeffersian sentiment as he punishes himself by
walking home from a dance, after sending Fawn and Allen
home in the car:

> You dark young mountains are going up in the world, we
>   the people going down. Why? Because
> Nobody knows the difference between right and wrong.
>
> (*Angry,* p. 41)

The phantom calling herself Mara joins Bruce and tells
him, "You used to want to know the truth about things.
. . . But now you are lost in passion" (p. 42). After Andrew's
death, Bruce moves into his father's room, abandoning
Fawn and devoting himself to study. He discovers Spengler's theory of the waves of civilization, and decides that
his own age is beyond the crest, headed down. Bruce has
studiously avoided checking on Fawn and Allen, often going out of his way to demonstrate his trust, as in walking
home from the dance; but, after drinking with whores in
Monterey, Bruce discovers more information which suggests his wife's infidelity. Going home, he breaks up before
the pressure of opposing images in his mind: "the one of
Fawn dead / With a sliced throat, the other of himself self-
hanged" (p. 64). He chooses the second option and hangs
himself in the barn; "He will no longer / Bawl for the
truth, the truth, though it were poisonous" (p. 64). The
poet observes that,

The cause is far beyond good and evil,

.   .   .   .

There are no angels and no devils,
Christ unopposed would corrupt all.

(Angry, pp. 65–66)

As Fawn says, however, Bruce's death "has given us freedom and happiness" (p. 66). When the self-questioning
idealist solves his frustration with suicide, the world of
Fawn, Allen, and presumably that of Mary Monahan feels
no loss, but rather a sense of liberation, freedom from conscience. Nevertheless, Jeffers ends the poem with a warning: "Look to it: prepare for the long winter: spring is far
off" (p. 67).

Except for the quest for truth, Bruce Ferguson is scarcely
recognizable as Nietzsche's Overman, for he is weakened
and unsure of himself in a troubled world; he is not its
master. In the poet's narrative, however, vestiges of Nietzscheanism appear as a critical frame of reference by which
Bruce and his world are judged. Bruce does not possess a
Will to Power sufficient to overcome his situation. Bruce's
world is the world as Nietzsche saw it; yet, having bawled
for the truth, Bruce could not bear it.

The Bowl of Blood

Jeffers takes up the theme of power again in the remarkable poem *The Bowl of Blood,* which is a daring application of his ideas to the forces and personalities of World
War II. This dramatic poem, which S. J. Kunitz said he
was "tempted to call . . . the greatest masque since *Comus,*"
takes place "northward of the Elbe, the Schleswig shore"
in a fisherman's cabin, where a woman conducts a seance
over a bowl of blood.[3] To her comes The Leader, quickly
identified as Hitler, who seeks advice about the future.
Three maskers represent the choric voice of the poet, and

one of them begins the poem by saying, "I do not know whether it is possible to present contemporary things in the shape of eternity" (p. 68). The reader is thus advised that Jeffers is following one of his basic literary principles, i.e., the duty of the poet to write for a future audience and to deal with eternal themes, if possible, in terms of everyday events.

Power, Jeffers says, "is a great hollow spirit / That needs a center" (p. 70). Introducing a change in the power theme, the poet decides that "the man does not have power / Power has the man" (p. 70). At this point, the skeptical Leader appears and muses over the extravagances in men and materials to which the necessity to win battles has driven him. He is staggered by these sacrifices, "And all the dawn-feeling dies" in him (p. 72), so now he looks for encouragement from the prophecies of the fishwife. The Leader objects to the ritual bowl of blood, but, as he is told by one of his aides, "No show without it" (p. 74). The parallel between The Leader's reaction to the required bowl of blood and his revulsion at the bloodshed necessary for the achievement of his political aims is self-evident. Hitler is thus sympathetically portrayed as the reluctant dictator, for "Power has the man" (p. 70).

The Leader summons the spirit of Frederick the Great to whom he identifies himself as "your own blood and successor." The spirit is unimpressed and wants to know where The Leader is leading the Germans. "From degradation and poverty to honor, wealth, power, / Vengeance and victory" (p. 76) is the reply. Napoleon is the next visitor, and The Leader severely criticizes him for engaging the Russians before settling with the English.

Here, Jeffers, who cannot resist the impulse to come front and center at least once in each poem, gives the Second Masker the following speech:

Before we proceed with the poem, I should like to point out to our friends here [the audience] that even Hitler, though all too mischievously occupied with human affairs, does have a sense of the other world, the inhuman one. This North Sea sunset that has just gone west; and the Berchtesgaden landscape, the nature-dreams of Wagner and so forth. It is romantic, therefore incompletely effective, but still it is one source of his power. If it were effective, it would lead to a crisp refusal of that kind of power, but of course it is merely romantic and makes him suffer. (*Angry*, p. 80)

From this speech, it is clear that Jeffers is not entirely absorbed in his own romantic delusions, as some of his critics have charged, for he insists upon the inferiority of the merely romantic outlook. The maskers discuss the "poetic" nature of Hitler, and they examine the terms "democracy" and "freedom," which they decide have only relative meaning. This discussion sets the scene for the entrance of Ernst Friedenau, a poet who was Hitler's youthful comrade. Friedenau had "prophesied / German re-birth" in former days and had otherwise "fed [Hitler's] flame" (p. 82). The maskers recognize as false Friedenau's advice to Hitler to "Wait for September" (p. 86) before advancing his campaign, but they remember that "God is less humane than Hitler, and has larger views. . . . God's spokesmen are often liars. God remains silent" (p. 86). Then what about civilization? A masker replies:

> Its ripening
> Is freedom's crisis. Men must keep in their minds
> The one way to be free: that's to be better armed
> And stronger than others, and not covet their goods,
> And stay frugally at home, death to invaders.
>
> (*Angry*, p. 87)

In this poem from the 1941 volume, strong independence and resolute isolation are Jeffers' recommendations

to a people anxious about their crumbling civilization. In
offering his peculiarly "cruel" kind of isolationism to a
nation on the verge of a world war, Jeffers invited censure
from many quarters (sympathy from others); but this judgment only settled him more resolutely in his own sense of
personal isolation from the world. Nevertheless, *The Bowl
of Blood* is not actually a radical departure from Jeffers'
chief ideas. Hitler, for example, says that he is innocent of
the war; he did not want it. He disavows all blame and
says the war was caused by

> Chamberlain the smiling moneyed man, Daladier
> The scared career-man, Churchill the bloody-minded
>   amateur,
> Roosevelt and his playboy envoys whispering them on.
>   (*Angry,* p. 90)

It is difficult, I suspect, for most of us to agree with Jeffers' assignment of the blame for the war; but if we can
see that in terms of his ideological system Germany represented new power and unity and the Allies represented
"over-ripe" civilization due for a purging by violence, we
shall have come a long way toward understanding the
poem as it was intended.

   Like so many of Jeffers' Overman types who reach the
point in their careers at which a reversal of some kind
seems imminent, the poet's Hitler curses "that night. . . .
the bed and the lust" (p. 92), when his mother conceived
him. This, too, belongs to a Jeffers pattern, which the psy-
choanalytically inclined critic may someday decipher.
From Friedenau, Hitler receives a final exhortation—"Hitler's name / Will take the sky of Caesar and Charlemagne"
(p. 93)—and The Leader leaves the seance firmly resolved
to fulfill his destiny. As discussed in Chapter 1, Jeffers believed that the poets also have their lies by which they sat-

isfy the exigencies of dealing with eternal themes. From the maskers, the reader knows that the poet Friedenau has given Hitler advice that will not only thwart the success of his campaign but will also guarantee far greater casualties. As Hitler leaves the cabin and the stage, the maskers ask the audience to "Watch this man, half conscious of the future, / Pass to his tragic destiny" (p. 93). They offer the consolation that "The storm that broke the old rotten tree / Was justified by a sprouting acorn" (p. 94), which is Jeffers' affirmation that the extermination of civilization by war will promote new, healthier growth. The maskers repeat this sentiment after they observe that "This man and the unconscious American / Are the two hands of the destroyer" (p. 94). The poet means that between Germany, which started the hostilities, and America, which must finish them, the required extermination will occur.

Just before he goes off stage, Hitler turns and cries, "Dogs! All that labor and faith / To die into mere bloody waste?" (p. 94), which suggests a dawning awareness of the implications of his actions. Referring to Hitler's outburst, a masker gives this advice, which concludes the poem: "We must not wake him. Sleepwalker, dream, / While the storm roars in the tree" (p. 94). The masker is clearly warning against an attempt to interfere with this "sleepwalker" whose delusion must be depended upon until the storm of war has run its course.

It becomes increasingly difficult to discern the Nietzschean influence in Jeffers' later work. With *The Bowl of Blood,* the theory that civilizations follow cycles, in which they ripen and go to seed, may be traced back to Nietzsche via Spengler. Jeffers' emphasis on Hitler's sense of another world, on the treacherous representatives of the Allies, and on the fault of the mothers who conceive such doomed Overmen, is peculiarly his own. Yet I suggest that

Jeffers could soberly work out and send forth such a poem because his own conception of the Revaluation of Values permitted him to think "beyond good and evil."

In *Come, Little Birds,* Jeffers makes it clear that he knows what he is doing and where he stands, for in a seance similar to that in *The Bowl of Blood* Jeffers meets his father to whom he says, "Forgive me. I dishonored and wasted all your hopes of me, one by one; yet I loved you well." It is difficult, he says in *I Shall Laugh Purely,* to "Keep a straight mind / In the evil time," but, as for the war, "all that pain was mainly a shift in power." It is not "the world's end, / But only the fall of a civilization." *Contemplation of the Sword* (i.e., God's fiery sword) reveals that the poet is anxious, in April 1938, about his two draft-age sons in the world of events leading up to World War II. To God, the poet admits, "now that this thing comes near us again I am finding it hard / To praise you with a whole heart."

"A great man must have a following," says Jeffers in his poem *Great Men,* whether that man be a Roosevelt or a Hitler. The poet continues:

No man standing alone has ever been great;
Except, most rarely, his will, passion or intellect
Have come to posthumous power, and the naked spirit
Picked up a crown.

He mentions Nietzsche and Jesus and wonders if they were honest while they were alive. He says to them:

You are not now.
You have found your following and it corrupts you; all greatness
Involves betrayal, of the people by a man
Or of a man by the people.

As early as *Dear Judas* Jeffers held this view of Jesus, but he is now considering Nietzsche in the same way. *Great Men* can reasonably be accepted as explicit acknowledgment of the diminishing Nietzschean influence that has been recognized in the poems of this period. The poet mentions that he prefers the alternative of joining a lonely quiescent Nature in order to be like "an old stone on the mountain, where no man comes / But only the wilderness-eyeing hawk. . . ." Apparently, Nietzsche's usefulness has all but come to an end.

Some of the opinion expressed in *The Bowl of Blood* is reiterated in the frequently anthologized *The Stars Go Over the Lonely Ocean,* in which the poet advises, "Keep clear of the dupes that talk democracy / And the dogs that talk revolution." He is resigned to uncorruptible isolation, and adds, "Long live freedom and damn the ideologies."

As Jeffers became increasingly disappointed with American foreign policy, he asked who was to blame for the state of affairs. No one, he says in *Shine, Empire,* for "Roosevelt's intentions were good, and Hitler is a patriot." The United States was thoroughly compromised and aimed at world rule, as Jeffers saw it; therefore, "Shine, empire."

The doctrine of the Revaluation of Values surfaces in *The Bloody Sire,* when the poet says, "Stark violence is still the sire of all the world's values. . . . Old violence is not too old to beget new values." From this point of view, the poet points out, there is little to grieve about when one considers the war. In the last poem of the volume, Jeffers explains that if someone is angered by political corruption and deceit, he may as well "be angry at the sun for setting."

The Double Axe

In 1948, Jeffers brought out *The Double Axe and Other Poems,* which revealed that the mood of *Be Angry at the*

Sun had emphatically intensified. Random House underlined the controversial nature of the work by including the
unusual Publishers' Note, which has already been quoted.
Jeffers believed that he spoke from a lonely eminence, and
his publishers assured him that this was so. The title poem
was curious, indeed, for, as nearly everyone agreed at the
time, it stressed ideas rather than poetry, and much of its
ideology was uncongenial.[4] Like *At the Birth of an Age,
The Double Axe* is divided into two distinct parts—sections entitled "The Love and the Hate" and "The Inhumanist." In the first part, Jeffers tells how Hoult Gore, a
soldier who was "killed on Meserole Island twenty days
ago" (p. 8), returns to his father's farm to denounce the
parent's American Legion engendered "insane talk / About
courage and honor" (p. 10). Not only does Hoult return to
discover that his mother, Reine, has a young lover, but to
find ironically that Bull Gore, his father, is at that very
moment attending an American Legion supper at Monterey. Hoult's bitterness about being tricked into an early
end by "the pimps of death" who led America into the
war knows no limit; and thus the scene is laid for erect-
ing a rather complex ideological structure, which, if it did
little for Jeffers' reputation as a poet, is interesting for
what it reveals about his thinking.

It is clear that Hoult regards himself as a sort of perverse
Christ arisen out of vengeance, not love, in order to settle a
personal score with society. When his mother doubts his
"resurrected" state, Hoult compares her with Thomas in
the Bible, and insists, by sheer force of will, that she put
her hand into his crushed side to see for herself. Later,
Hoult tells his father that they are not Christians, and the
son parodies John 11:25, saying, "I am the resurrection
and the *death*" (p. 28). It appears to be a fact that Hoult
is resurrected (the odor of his putrescent flesh lessens the

doubt), and he has brought death for his family. When Hoult comes down to dinner, he draws a picture of a rat-trap on a sea island, to which he adds the image of a man, drawn in red ink and catsup. Showing the picture to his parents, Hoult says,

> Take it in remembrance of me. This is
> my body
> That was broken for nothing. Drink it: this is my blood
> That was spilled for no need. Oh, yes: for victory:
> That rat-sucked hawk-egg.
> *(Double Axe,* p. 38)

During the deer hunt next day, Hoult shoots both his mother's lover and Bull Gore. Poachers nearby set fire to the underbrush with contraband tracer bullets, and Hoult, who feels himself burning with the last fever of his life, says to his mother, "I am burning up. Oh, oh, look down there! That's hell / And we are in it" (p. 49). Shortly thereafter soldiers from Fort Ord, who have come to fight the fire, find Reine holding her son's putrid corpse; she shoots herself with the rifle that killed the others.

Although at this point the poem seems to have reached a cul-de-sac, we soon realize that "The Love and the Hate" section has been a preparation for "The Inhumanist." In the second section we meet an old man, the Inhumanist, who is now caretaker of the property left by the Gores. Living alone, except for a double-bit axe with which he can converse and a mongrel bitch, Snapper, that adopts him, the old man attempts to live in peaceful isolation while he ponders the miserable quality of human life and studies the "transhuman" beauty of Nature and the universe, which he believes, "The human rare is bound to defile" (p. 57). The old man's solitude is not inviolable, however, for several people, usually associated with the flaws or cor-

ruptions of society, enter his world. As a result of these episodes, the Inhumanist's contempt of these unreconstructed
human beings is reinforced, yet he must retain control of
the double axe (possibly a symbol of the Revaluation of
Values) which, if it had its way, would kill all humans.
"Man is no measure of anything" (p. 61), he declares, and,
though he believes that God as seen through human institutions no longer merits reverence, he concludes that the
earth is God's prophet: "The beauty of things is the face of
God: worship it" (p. 105).

After these several encounters with uninvited visitors,
many of whom seek advice or sanctuary, the Inhumanist
delivers a kind of sermon which summarizes the conclusions he has reached and parallels the ideological growth
which I attribute to Jeffers:

> O future children:
> Cruelty is dirt and ignorance, a muddy peasant
> Beating his horse. Ambition and power-lust
> Are for adolescents and defective persons. Moderate kindness
> Is oil on a crying wheel: use it. Mutual help
> Is necessary: use it when it is necessary.
> And as to love: make love when need drives.
> And as to love: love God. He is rock, earth and water, and
>   the beasts and stars; and the night that contains them.
> And as to love: whoever loves or hates man is fooled in a
>   mirror.
>
> *(Double Axe,* p. 106)

Rejecting people who would be his disciples and charging his critics with failure to see reality, the old man has
learned that his isolation is good and that his custodian-
ship of the double axe is a serious responsibility. There are
only two remedies, he says at the end of the poem, for
"men's fouled lives"—surrender quickly to death (he dis-
approves of this) or adopt his Inhumanist position.

Returning to the poem to study its underlying ideological structure, we see that Hoult represents both a Christ image and, though more subtly, a Heraclitean figure. In this lone instance, Jeffers develops at length the ideas of Heraclitus—whom Lucretius refutes in Book 1 of *De Rerum Natura*—in order to establish his essentially Lucretian doctrine of Inhumanism. All but forgetting Nietzschean ideas in this poem, Jeffers follows the Inhumanist line of thought, which he announced in *Roan Stallion* and maintained during the second period of production as an attractive alternative to the Overman concept. The idea that "time is a ring" (p. 85) in the poem retains the notion of the cycle of events, but, unlike Nietzsche, the old man in the second section says that he has "heard some false reports / On the subject of God. He is not dead, and he is not a fable" (p. 93). The Heraclitean note is not unexpected; Jeffers mentions the pre-Socratic philosopher in other preceding poems, and there was to be a special acknowledgment to him at the beginning of the next volume, *Hungerfield and Other Poems*. In "The Inhumanist" section of *The Double Axe*, a visitor explains that he asks the old man for advice, "Because they say you have a harsh wisdom, unperfumed, untuned, untaught, / Like Heraclitus's Sibyl" (p. 70). The old man disavows knowledge of Heraclitus, but it is clear from the visitor's speech that Jeffers was familiar with Plutarch's comment on Heraclitus, as a comparison of the two passages reveals. Plutarch wrote, "The Sibyl with raving mouth, according to Heraclitus, uttering things mirthless, unadorned and unperfumed, reaches over a thousand years with her voice through the god."[5] The correspondence in language and ideas between these passages is striking. Other Heraclitean aspects of the poem are suggested by the lines containing the old man's celebration of the beauty of things, which he preferred to human beings. Heraclitus believed that men should try to comprehend the underlying coherence of things, which was expressed in the logos, the "unifying formula or proportionate method of arrangement of things."[6] This idea permits all things, which merely appear to be plural and totally discrete, to be united in a coherent complex of which men themselves are a part. In other words, the logos of Heraclitus appears to resemble Jeffers' doctrine of Inhumanism. But in spite of a discernible resemblance between Inhumanism and the ideas of Heraclitus, Lucretius is the ultimate source of Jeffers' Inhumanism (see Chapter 8). Upon further consideration of the poem, not only does "The Inhumanist" section begin to appear like the teaching of the Heraclitean logos, but Hoult Gore begins to appear like a Heraclitean warrior who has been killed in the heat of battle.

According to Heraclitus, fire is the chief constituent of the cosmos and the human soul itself is fiery, seeking to return at death to the ethereal fire, if it can. Some souls are less fiery than others, and this is explained as the result of "moistening"—that is, a soul that dies after an illness (which has moistened it and made it less fiery) simply dies, and that is the end of it. A warrior cut off quickly in the heat of battle does not suffer moistening, as it were, and he dies with the fieriest possible soul.[7] Heraclitus held, too, that such fiery souls may survive for a time after death as beneficent daimons before returning to the ethereal fire.

Hoult was killed quickly in battle on Meserole Island at a time, he tells us, when he yearned most for life. By sheer force of will he has risen from his grave and returned to rectify a fault in the world which he knew before his conscription. His actions in the poem may not at first be regarded as those of a beneficent daimon, but from his point of view his killing of Bull Gore, the representative of malignant patriotism that fosters unthinking human destruction, and young Dave Larson, who is the lover of Hoult's mother, are "good" acts in the sense that he has corrected an evil in society and thereby prepared for the coming of the Inhumanist. After Hoult has accomplished these acts of "correction," he feels himself slipping from life again. Appropriately, this feeling is manifest in the symptoms of high fever: his hand on Reine's wrist is "hot as fire," and he says, "I am burning up" (p. 49). Surrounded now by a brush fire that will soon consume all but the Gore house, Hoult excitedly tells his mother that they are in a fiery hell, the "boiler of life and death." As unrealistic as "The Love and the Hate" section is, it remains an interesting dramatization of the theories of Heraclitus, and its climax is a portrayal of the return of Hoult's fiery warrior soul to the ethereal fire that constitutes the cosmos for the Heraclitean.

How is Hoult's Heraclitean character related to the more explicitly stated Christ imagery? First, he represents Jeffers' most subtle rejection of the institution of Christianity. In his parody of Christ and the Last Supper, Hoult is not merely sacrilegious in bitterly attacking his religion in order to vent his emotions; instead, he is a "new" man who is disengaging himself forever from an exhausted tradition. Second, the overlay of Christianity which the underlying Heraclitean shrugs off in the course of the first section anticipates and reinforces the central image of the poem, the double axe. Early in "The Inhumanist" section, the old man explains the significance of the "double-bladed axe": "In Crete it was a god, and they named the labyrinth for it. . . . It was a symbol of generation: the two lobes and the stiff helve: so was the Cross before they christened it" (p. 54).

Jeffers is clearly continuing his attack on Christianity in this part of the poem, but the two respective sections represent a falling and rising of tradition. Christianity is brought low in Hoult's blasphemous parody, and the Heraclitean aspects implicit in Hoult's character rise to replace it, in the second section, with the Heraclitean logos. In the old man's explanation of the axe, this exchange of positions is confirmed: now he celebrates the logos and the ancient, generative symbol of the axe, and he notes that the cross had this function when it was adopted by Christianity. A significant episode late in the poem removes any doubt about Jeffers' portrayal of the casting off of Christianity. When three thieves come to steal the old man's gold, which actually exists only as a rumor, the double axe kills two of them. The third thief turns out to be the "man of terrors," who identifies himself to the old man, "I am your other self. The other half of yourself" (p. 101). The old man and the thief load the two dead men into a boat. As the man of terrors is about to shove it away from shore, the old man axes him so that he also falls dead into the funeral boat. The old man says,

> There . . . goes myself, my self-murdered half-
> self
> Between two thieves. It might be some tragic hero's death-
> voyage.
>
> (*Double Axe,* p. 103)

I suggest that in this episode we find the old man's symbolic counterpart of Hoult's parody of the Last Supper. The axing is an inversion of the events of the crucifixion, by which the Inhumanist symbolically murders his Christian self (who came to steal from him) and sends him paganwise in a funeral boat, lying like some tragic hero between two thieves, as Christ was crucified between two thieves.

The title of the first section of the poem, "The Love and the Hate," has troubled readers like Carpenter, who called it a misnomer.[8] Further consideration of the Heraclitean implications of the poem, however, may help to resolve such questions. In addition to the logos and the fiery composition of the cosmos, Heraclitus worked out an elaborate system of opposites in which each pair of opposites forms both a unity and a dualism. Seawater, for example, is good (for the fish which needs it to breathe) and bad (for the man dying of thirst).[9] In the light of Jeffers' theory that the poet's statement emerges from the tension of opposed ideas and/or structures, I believe that Jeffers meant "The Inhumanist" to grow out of the opposition of "The Love and the Hate," its unity and its duality.[10] The family situation described in the first section is rife with love and hate. Consider the love-hate ambivalence of Bull Gore's patriotic urging to go to war and his self-righteous indignation when he thinks that Hoult's corpse may be AWOL instead of just resurrected (indeed Hoult teases him into these emotional responses); consider Reine's pitiful adultery; and consider Hoult's own love of life which brings him back from the grave in order to vent his hatred and to improve the world by canceling out some of the "evil" he has known. "To god," Heraclitus believed, "all things are beautiful and good and just, but men have supposed some things to be unjust, others just."[11] The opposition of pairs present in "The Love and the Hate" is emphasized in the final detail of the old man's explanation of the double axe: "A blade for the flesh, a blade for the spirit: and truth from lies" (p. 54).

I have argued for the recognition of Heraclitus' influence in *The Double Axe* because, as the elements of Nietzsche's philosophy proved to be inadequate in some respects and often socially disruptive, Jeffers turned to an ideology that could still accommodate his Nietzsche-inspired view of men and outworn Christianity. Jeffers looked for a philosophy in which the self-sufficient individual could find comfort for himself as well as a high regard for the beauty of the world, without the manifest risk of extinction that plagued the Overman in Jeffers' other poems. Jeffers was still contemptuous of mankind for failing to fulfill itself, as Nietzsche had advocated, and he regarded war as one way of clearing away its decadence and heaped-up luxury. Even with war, however, the poet could find support in Heraclitus, who held, "It is necessary to know that war is common and right is strife and that all things happen by strife and necessity."[12] So at last Jeffers arrived at the alternative of "the beauty of things" which was present through much of the preceding poetry, but I must emphasize that the poet used only those ideas from Heraclitus which were compatible with the *De Rerum Natura* of Lucretius, whose influence on Jeffers was eventually greater than that of Heraclitus.

Recognizing the Heraclitean elements in this poem furthers an understanding of its main ideological structure, but it does not explain the relevance of some of the ancillary action of "The Inhumanist" section. As a measure of Jeffers' ideological development, some episodes, such as the old man's refusal to have disciples, should be compared with Barclay's Zarathustran concern with followers, but others can only be understood when seen as leading to or illustrating Inhumanism. Everything that I have said, however, about the Heraclitean origin of the ideas of the poem is supported by the poet's preface to the volume. The "burden" of the poem, he said, "is to present a certain philosophical attitude, which might be called Inhumanism." Inhumanism meant "a shifting of emphasis and significance from man to not-man," Jeffers continued; "the rejection of human solipsism and recognition of the trans-human magnificence." He explained further:

> This manner of thought and feeling is neither misanthropic nor pessimist. . . . It involves no falsehoods, and is a means of maintaining sanity in slippery times; it has objective truth and human value. It offers a reasonable detachment as rule of conduct, instead of love, hate and envy. It neutralizes fanaticism and wild hopes; but it provides magnificence for the religious instinct, and satisfies our need to admire greatness and rejoice in beauty.[13]

The shorter poems that constitute the remainder of *The Double Axe* volume are expressions, as Jeffers pointed out in the preface, "of the same attitude" described above. In *Cassandra*, Jeffers castigated the "religion-venders and political men" who pour new lies on the old, while he and Cassandra tried to remain "wise." *Pearl Harbor* criticizes America because, "The war that we have carefully for years provoked / Catches us unprepared, amazed and indignant," and the poem *Teheran* reveals little hope for the peace made there because Russia and America remain "two bulls in one pasture." Both *Pearl Harbor* and *Teheran* confirm the poet's diagnosis of a dying civilization which ignores the beauty of things as truly God's.

The titles alone of such poems as *Ink-Sack* (antipropaganda attack) and *Eagle Valor, Chicken Mind* communicate the level and intensity of Jeffers' topical poems. In *What of It?* Jeffers expressed unconcern for modern man and for such extravagances as the Bikini lagoon experiment, for man "has had too many doctors, leaders and saviors: let him alone. It may be that bitter nature will cure him." "The state is a blackmailer, / Honest or not," Jef-

fers declared in *New Year's Dawn, 1947,* his appraisal of the
state of affairs:

> There is no valid authority
> In church nor state, custom, scripture nor creed,
> But only in one's own conscience and the beauty of things.
> Doggedly I think again: One's conscience is a trick oracle,
> Worked by parents and nurse-maids, the pressure of the
>   people,
> And the delusions of dead prophets: trust it not.
> Wash it clean to receive the transhuman beauty: then trust
>   it.

And in *Original Sin,* he added, do "not fear death; it is the
only way to be cleansed."

The Double Axe is an important volume in Jeffers'
ideological development. As the minor poems in *The
Double Axe* and *Be Angry at the Sun* peevishly testify, the
crisis of war seems to have accelerated the shift in emphasis
(which was largely focused in the image of Bruce Ferguson's searching) from the earlier Nietzscheanism to the
subsequent dominance of Inhumanism. It is unfortunate
that much of the poetry of this period is superficial and
strident, for, arriving when it did, it found very few people
prepared to receive the work hospitably, and fewer still
who understood why it had taken the new direction.

Hungerfield

In 1950, Una Jeffers died. The poet's work, his letters,
and the reports of friends who knew the family all reflect
the great emptiness that Una's death brought to Jeffers'
life. She had served him as chauffeur and letter writer, as
well as affectionate wife, and she often put herself protec-
tively between the world and the poet in order to permit

him to use his time as he saw fit—to build the stone tower adjacent to their house, to care for the hundreds of trees which he planted on his property, or to write verses. Her intense appreciation of the world's natural beauty very possibly inspired the poetry Jeffers wrote and reinforced his regard for the beauty of things. Undoubtedly he would have recommended her courageously independent spirit as a guide for the redemption of diseased modern man.

In 1954, *Hungerfield and Other Poems* was published. The title poem, which had appeared two years before in *Poetry* magazine, is shorter than most of the narratives, and it is addressed (in an elegiac frame) to Una, whose death reminded the poet of Hungerfield, "the man at Horse Creek, / Who fought with Death" (p. 5). Hawl Hungerfield, who believes that he once won over Death in a hand-to-hand struggle in a French hospital during the war, sits by the deathbed of his mother, Alcmena, and waits to grapple with Death again and thereby save his mother's life. Hungerfield does win a second time, but he fails to understand that the old woman is prepared for and welcomes Death. She is angered by her son's disruption of the order of things, and repays him with lies and accusations that breed violence and more death in the family. Hungerfield's wife and son are drowned, and he kills his brother, Ross, for being negligent. Then Hungerfield, whom his mother has called a "worse monster" than Death, soaks the house with coal oil and sets fire to it and himself.

That death comes naturally when it should and that man is a fool to want it otherwise is the obvious lesson of *Hungerfield*. The poem, which is the product of Jeffers' reconciliation to his bereavement, ends by acknowledging that of Una "nothing human remains":

> You are earth
> and air; you are in the beauty of the ocean
> . . . you are alive
> and well in the tender young grass rejoicing
> When soft rain falls all night. . . .
>
> (*Hungerfield,* p. 23)

In addition to *Hungerfield* in this volume, there are *The Cretan Woman,* an adaptation of Euripides' *Hippolytus,* discussed in Chapter 7, and a handful of assorted poems. Together, the poems are a sobering indication that the poet is burnt out with nothing more to say, except to repeat his conviction that the beauty of things is preferable to man and his affairs. In *De Rerum Virtute,* Jeffers admits, "I believe that man too is beautiful, / But it is hard to see, and wrapped up in falsehoods." He says nothing more about the beauty of man, but I assume he means those rare instances, like the example of Reave Thurso, in which a man's suffering and pain make him shine briefly. Such men must be stripped, however, of their preconceptions about themselves, religion, science, and whatever else would keep them from realizing their greatest fulfillment. Nietzsche explained how this stripping away might be accomplished, but Nietzscheanism alone was not entirely satisfactory. Jeffers' doctrine of Inhumanism, as present in *The Double Axe,* I have traced in part to the Heraclitean logos or its more highly developed counterpart, the materialism of Lucretius. Nevertheless, having said that "man too is beautiful," Jeffers continued: "One light is left us: the beauty of things, not men; / The immense beauty of the world, not the human world." The beauty of things, according to Jeffers, "means virtue and value in them," but they are "in the beholder's eye." Beauty is "the human mind's translation of the transhuman / Intrinsic glory" of things. According to Jeffers' logic, the beauty of things is not accessible to everyone, unless the individual is willing to, and capable of, following the Nietzschean example of self-discipline and revaluation. By another route we have come again to the stalemate in Jeffers' ideological development which was implied in the fates that befell the heroes of his production's second period.

Other poems, such as *The Beauty of Things* and *The World's Wonders,* do little more than repeat the well-worn ideas set forth in *De Rerum Virtute.* In *Carmel Point,* Jeffers attacks suburbia, which swells outward like a tide from the cities, but, the poet assures us, "swells and in time will ebb, and all / Their works dissolve." Repeating a sentiment that he had expressed long ago to Rorty in a letter about *The Women at Point Sur,* Jeffers says,

>   —As for us:
> We must uncenter our minds from ourselves;
> We must unhumanize our views a little, and become
>   confident
> As the rock and ocean that we were made from.

Morro Bay, like several of the other poems, refers indirectly to Una's death and the changes that have taken place since then: for example, the change in the once beautiful bay which now "is brown-stagnant / With rotting weed" or the encroaching suburbs of *Carmel Point.* Part of this mood of resignation and impatient waiting is given interesting autobiographical documentation in *The Old Stonemason* and in *The Deer Lay Down Their Bones.* In each poem, Jeffers referred to the decision which he made thirty years earlier, or about 1920.[14] In *The Deer Lay Down Their Bones,* the poet accepted the hardships of old age and the emptiness of his life since Una's death, for even in these trials some value may be discovered. In the other poem, Jeffers pictured himself as the old stonemason, who had "much in common with these old rockheads" with which he built his house. He explained:

> I have shared in my time the human illusions, the muddy
>   foolishness
> And craving passions, but something thirty years ago pulled
>   me
> Out of the tide-wash; I must not even pretend
> To be one of the people.

Jeffers concluded that the granite stones will still be there tomorrow where they stand today, adding, in a note curiously reminiscent of the Reverend Arthur Barclay himself, "The old granite stones, those are my people."

The Beginning and the End and Other Poems

A year after Jeffers' death, Random House published *The Beginning and the End* (1963), a collection of forty-eight poems.[15] Most of the poems bring Jeffers' long-established opinions up to date by citing the cold war, the problem of the population explosion, the future of his granddaughter, Una, increased county taxes on his property, military activities at Fort Ord, and the wakening of Asia. He says in *To Kill in War Is Not Murder*, "As for me, I am growing old and have never / Been quite so vulgar."

The title poem of the book is a review of the Jeffersian history of the world. Life begins as a chemical reaction, the result of the union of the earth, "a female thing," and the "stallion" sun, from which amino acids and protein molecules grow to life and reproduce, "a virus / On the warm ocean." Such theorizing recalls the intended research of Howard Howren, in *Such Counsels You Gave to Me,* who also searched for the secret of life.

Man descended from the northern apes, not the southern ones, says Jeffers in *The Beginning and the End,* because violent changes in the northern environment induced similar violent changes in the nature of man, who "was made / By shock and agony" (p. 9). Jeffers warns us not to blame man because "a wound was made in the brain / When life became too hard, and has never healed" (p. 9). As a result of this psychic wound, man

> learned to butcher beasts and to
>   slaughter men,
> And hate the world: the great religions of love and kindness
> May conceal that, not change it.
>
> (Beginning, p. 9)

Father O'Donnel, in *In the Hill at New Grange (Descent to the Dead),* also mentioned that "the strain in the wounded minds of men / Leaves them no peace." Furthermore, *The Great Wound,* in the final volume, deals with the "mythology" of the scientists, with "The poet [who] also / Has his mythology," and with the myths on which stand church and state, thus completing the development of thought from the original trauma to the concealing mythology.

In *Ode to Hengist and Horsa,* Jeffers shows that he still believes in the cycles of civilization, when he says, "We have all history ahead of us." *Birth and Death* deals with the "population explosion," which "saps man's dignity," for men are "Breeding like rabbits" and "preparing for the great slaughter." The strident carping of some of these poems takes a different turn in *Let Them Alone,* which begins,

> If God has been good enough to give you a poet
> Then listen to him.
>   .   .   .   .   .
>   A poet is one who listens
> To nature and his own heart.

Obviously, Jeffers believes that the poet can help people become "one of God's sense-organs," as he says in *The Beginning and the End,* because

> This is man's mission:
> To find and feel; all animal experience
> Is a part of God's life.
>
> *(Beginning,* p. 10)

To the very end, Jeffers insisted on his peculiar reduction of humanity to a level that was usually below that of the beauty of things. After a revaluation of his received values, the poet asserted, man may hope to recognize the beauty which emanates from a God who is indifferent alike to this beauty and the plight of man. Jeffers was himself something of an Overman, who learned through the experiments of his poems, and redirected his own thoughts and those of his characters in the light of the results of these experiments. Having originally learned the merits of the Revaluation of Values, Jeffers explored Nietzscheanism, and, carrying the principle of Revaluation to its logical conclusion, he moved beyond most of Nietzsche's formal doctrine and aligned himself ultimately with Lucretian materialism.

6

the idea of culture ages

Parallel to the Nietzschean thought in Jeffers' poetry runs the poet's own doctrine of Inhumanism. As the Nietzschean ideas were tested and cast aside, their identity and influence waned, and the doctrine of Inhumanism grew to replace them, reaching full statement in "The Inhumanist" section of *The Double Axe* in 1948. Between these two controlling ideological positions were useful ideas and notions from other related systems of thought. Jeffers was especially attracted to those ideologies that contributed to and reinforced his theme of the "idea of culture-ages—culture-cycles—the patterned rise and decline of one civilization after another."[1] Since "Humanity is the start of the race . . . the mold to break away from," as Jeffers decided in *Roan Stallion* (pp. 19–20), it is understandable that he should look to those theories that suggest such possibilities. Although Nietzsche's doctrine of Eternal Recurrence, as Zarathustra described it, affirmed that human affairs follow cycles, there is little emphasis on a significant growth of the culture during each cycle, and the

Overman was conceived largely to transcend the ordinariness of man which these cycles seemed to guarantee. Strictly speaking, moreover, Nietzsche saw the period of each recurrence as a vast time span, possibly beyond historical record. The theory of Eternal Recurrence is not original with Nietzsche; other thinkers before him pondered over it. There is, however, a kind of genius in Nietzsche's presentation of a theory with so little practical substantiation. Like his Zarathustra, Nietzsche left to others the application of the theory. Nietzsche probably first got his idea from Heraclitus, as undoubtedly did Oswald Spengler, who in 1904 received his doctorate from the University of Halle for a dissertation on Heraclitus.[2] The ideas, however, of Vico's *The New Science* (1725), which describes the recurring phases of human development, had fairly well permeated those intellectual realms of Europe which were receptive to his "natural law of the gentes."[3] So it is not unexpected to find Jeffers' explanation of this interest in *Themes in My Poetry:*

> The idea of culture-ages—culture-cycles—the patterned rise and decline of one civilization after another—is a commonplace now, nearly as commonplace as death or war, but it held my thought and has been a frequent subject of my verse—"The Fall of an Age," "The Birth of an Age," and so forth. The idea was popularized by Oswald Spengler's book, "Decline of the West"; but it came to me much earlier, from my own thoughts, and then I found it formulated by the English Egyptologist, Flinders Petrie, in a little volume called "The Revolutions of Civilization," first published in 1911. Of course it was developed long before that, notably by Vico of Naples, Giovanni Battista Vico, who published his book in 1725. And there is a passage in Plutarch's "Life of Sulla," referring to the Etruscan acceptance of this idea,

which I versified in one of several pieces called "The Broken Balance."⁴

Jeffers then read the poem he had just mentioned, but let us consider now the contributions of Vico, Spengler, Petrie, and Ellis to Jeffers' ideology.

Giambattista Vico

The cyclical historians, who achieved preeminence in the liberal atmosphere of nineteenth-century romanticism as a reaction against the historical positivists, had as precursors men like the twelfth-century monk Joachim of Floris and Giambattista Vico, and in Spengler they reached their zenith of popular acceptance. Only very general statements can be made about Vico's influence on Jeffers, and the poet himself gives us little help in the manner of his reference to Vico, quoted above.

At the heart of Vico's teachings was the theory of *ricorsi,* or historical returns, which asserted that each period in the history of a nation resembled a similar period in the history of another nation, and that from such similarities it was possible to chart a typical course for the history of all peoples. The social evolution of peoples went through three stages, according to Vico: the age of the gods, the age of the heroes, and the age of man. In the age of the gods, man rose from bestiality and instituted the three prepolitical institutions of religion, marriage, and burial of the dead. A feudal aristocracy developed in the age of heroes that centered in "heroic states" in which weaker individuals gathered about the stronger, and a tension grew from the conflict between the plebeians, who wanted to change the state, and the patricians, who wanted to preserve it as it was. When the heroic states were transformed into democratic or "free popular republics," the age of man arrived, and the plebeians won rights to land tenure, legal marriage, legitimate children, citizenship, eligibility to office, and so on. Philosophy took the place of religion, and there ensued humanization and relaxing of established conventions and laws. Breakdown within or conquest from without brought on a reversion to barbarism, and a new cycle of three ages began.[5]

But the new cycle was not an exact repetition, for fresh cultural elements brought new intellectual and spiritual content to each *ricorso*. One of the negative aspects of the theory, however, was the idea that men who fell into bar barism from "rotting in this last civil illness" were turned into "beasts made more inhuman by the barbarism of reflection than the first men had been made by the barbarism of sense" (*New Science*, par. 1106). In general, however, each cyle showed improvement, so that Vico's *ricorsi* are better considered to be spiral than cyclical in character. Progressing according to the method of the geometrician, Vico sought and found in the new science "an ideal eternal history traversed in time by the history of every nation in its rise, development, maturity, decline and fall" (*New Science*, par. 349). Like Jeffers, Vico was drawn to Lucretius, especially to the fifth book of the Roman's Latin poem, for some of his ideas concerning the origin of social organization.[6]

The value to Jeffers of Vico's *New Science* probably cannot be usefully ascertained beyond the fact that it served as a model for a comparative study of cultures. For Jeffers, who believed he was living in the decline of a decadent civilization, there was confirmation in Vico's book of the symptoms of deterioration, but these theories were readily available from the works of such other scholars as Spengler. In Jeffers' poetry there are repeated references to the descent of man from apes, and such an idea could not have been derived from Vico's explanation of the origin of civilization, for he was not only Catholic but published the first edition of his *New Science* with a dedicatory epistle to Cardinal Lorenzo Corsini in Rome. The old man, for example, in Jeffers' *The Double Axe,* refers with contempt to man as "this walking farce, / This ape, this—denatured ape, this—citizen—" (p. 82). In *The Great Explosion,* Jeffers calls men "God's apes," and, in *The Beginning and the End,* he tells how man descended from northern "man-like apes," who suffered severe environmental changes; "the other anthropoid apes," Jeffers adds, "were safe / In the great southern rain-forest" (p. 9). Where Jeffers believed in complete cycles for all of Nature, preaching that human beings were an offensive evolution of Nature to which they would necessarily return as the result of their self-extermination, Vico could only go so far as to claim that the cycles of human history would repeat themselves.

Oswald Spengler

In *The Loyalties of Robinson Jeffers,* Squires begins a discussion of Spengler by stating that Spengler's influence, in part, "confirmed" in Jeffers "a set of dualisms intellectually related to that [the poet's] endemic fatalism: a dualism between Nature and history, a dualism between Nature and man, a dualism between culture and civilization" (p. 57). These particular claims about confirmed dualisms have the unfortunate effect of destroying the validity of Squires' other argument for the supremacy of Schopenhauer as an influence in Jeffers' ideology. As noted in Chapter 2, such dualisms contradict the basic premises of Schopenhauer's philosophy. The difference between man and Nature, which Squires emphasizes, is indeed a basic distinction in Spenglerian thought, but it is alien to Schopenhauer's view. As even the casual reader of Jeffers' po-

etry must notice, this duality between man and Nature is a
troublesome point for the poet, who ardently desires a
union with Nature and "the beauty of things." In *Meditation on Saviors,* Jeffers not only reveals his awareness of the
separation of man and Nature, but also asserts that man
should seek a union with Nature—it is better for man "to
love the coast opposite humanity."

Jeffers and Spengler had a number of thoughts in common on the subjects of Nietzsche and the organicistic view
of history, Caesarism and democracy, the future of the
twentieth century, and Nazi Germany and Hitler. In exercising a critical selectivity in his adoption of Nietzschean
ideas, Jeffers recognized some of their flaws and hazards,
and kept what he could use. Spengler also turned quite
naturally to Nietzsche, whose intellectual independence
and theories of cultures and civilizations he found congenial. One of the significant differences between the respective approaches of Spengler and Jeffers to Nietzsche is that
Jeffers took what he could from Nietzsche without at-
tempting to alter the system from which he borrowed.
Spengler, however, like many of the twentieth-century intellectuals who adopted Nietzsche, was often severely critical of the philosopher, and drew a picture of Nietzsche's
ideology that was considerably more rigid in outline than
Nietzsche ever meant his thinking to appear.[7]

During the 1920s, Spengler's *The Decline of the West*
was tremendously popular among readers with widely di-
versified interests. For a man of Jeffers' generally pessimistic outlook to respond to the book or its reception was to
be expected. To Jeffers, who saw himself living in a culture past its peak, Spengler's explanation of the cycles of
cultures was especially attractive. Spengler, whose aca-
demic background was in mathematics and the natural sciences, advanced a new, comparative method of historical

investigation; he proposed to reconstruct "long-vanished and unknown epochs, even whole Cultures of the past, by means of morphological connexions, in much the same way as modern palaeontology deduces far-reaching and trustworthy conclusions as to skeletal structure and species from a single unearthed skull-fragment."[8] By applying to history the biologist's concept of living forms, or the romantic's organicistic view of the world, he meant to enlist his "morphological" method. Each culture was thus considered to be an organism which passed through various stages from birth to maturity and decay. Spengler called his method "truly Goethian." Out of the morphological method evolved Spengler's central concept of history. H. Stuart Hughes writes in his book *Oswald Spengler:* "In defining history as '*a universal symbolism*,' Spengler proved that he understood the essence of Nietzsche's 'supra-historical' view—the establishment of certain supreme specimens of humanity as a historical ultimate, standing out above time and change" (p. 62). Spengler acknowledged his debt to Nietzsche in the preface to the revised edition of the *Decline*, in which he wrote, "I feel urged to name once more those to whom I owe practically everything: Goethe and Nietzsche. Goethe gave me method, Nietzsche the questioning faculty—and if I were asked to find a formula for my relation to the latter I should say that I had made of his 'outlook' (*Ausblick*) an 'overlook' (*Uberblick*)."[9] Having admitted Nietzsche's strong influence on him, Spengler went on to criticize his master. Spengler placed the state at the center of his historical scheme, whereas Nietzsche was hostile to the state; for Spengler the individual was subordinated to great historical movements, but for Nietzsche the individual represented the supreme moral value. Nietzsche was "the first to have an inkling," said Spengler, that each culture has its own moral system, but he failed to "place himself 'beyond good and evil' " (*Decline*, 1: 315, 346). Writing of his master, Spengler reveals both respect for and lively independence of his predecessor's philosophy:

> Consider the historical horizon of Nietzsche. His conceptions of decadence, militarism, the transvaluation of all values, the will to power, lie deep in the essence of Western civilization and are for the analysis of that civilization of decisive importance. But what, do we find, was the foundation on which he built up his creation? Romans and Greeks, Renaissance and European present, with a fleeting and uncomprehending side-glance at Indian philosophy—in short "ancient, medieval and modern" history. Strictly speaking, he never once moved outside the scheme, not [*sic*] did any other thinker of his time. (*Decline*, 1:24)

Spengler believed that "a strict morphology of all the morals is a task for the future," and that Nietzsche took "the first and essential step towards the new standpoint" (*Decline*, 1: 346). Apparently, Jeffers also concluded that there were severe limitations inherent in Nietzsche's philosophy, because nothing new actually emerged. Jeffers was certainly capable of making these judgments himself, but he could have found an outspoken ally in Spengler, who, still referring to the morphology of morals, wrote of Nietzsche:

> He tried to be at once sceptic *and* prophet, moral critic *and* moral gospeller. It cannot be done. One cannot be a first-class psychologist as long as one is still a Romantic. And so here, as in all his crucial penetrations, he got as far as the door—and stood outside it. And so far, no one has done any better. (*Decline*, 1:346)

From Nietzsche, Spengler took the concepts of "culture" and "civilization"—the former is a society's period of creative activity, the latter its period of theoretical elaboration and material comfort. The "style" of cultures, according to Spengler, was the "rhythm of the process of self-implementing," and that of civilizations the "expression of the state of completeness" (*Decline*, 2: 109). Egypt and China especially exemplify such completeness and have become "end-states," as Spengler called them. "They are land in petrified form," he continued, in a passage that might well have been the source of a similar opinion voiced by Jeffers' Phaedra in *The Cretan Woman* (*Hungerfield*, p. 50). In the same section of the *Decline*, Spengler makes some generalizations that could have influenced both *The Cretan Woman* and *At the Birth of an Age:*

> It is a mere incident that German peoples, under pressure from the Huns, take possession of the Roman landscape and so prevent the Classical from prolonging itself in a "Chinese" end-state. The movement of the "Sea-peoples" (similar to the Germanic, even down to the details) which set in against the Egyptian Civilization from 1400 B.C. succeeded only as regards the Cretan island-realm.... And thus the Classical is our one example of a Civilization broken off in a moment of full splendour. (*Decline*, 2:109)

There is no proof that Jeffers had this passage in mind as he wrote his two poems; but he was obviously familiar with the *Decline*, and, since these notions complement his own theories about "culture-complexes," the possibilities of direct influence are extremely attractive.

In Jeffers' *Mara*, neither the truth-seeking Bruce Ferguson nor his unfaithful wife, Fawn, can find meaning or moral certitude in their lives. Fawn senses that her moral decline is related to the times, and she blames her weakness on the state of the world. Bruce, however, withdraws to his deceased father's bedroom, where he restudies his old college books. In the solitude of the attic bedroom, Bruce Ferguson reads a passage from one of the books to his wife:

> A German professor
> Who thinks this bloody and tortured slave called history
> Has regular habits. Waves, you know, wave-lengths, separate
>   waves of civilization
> Up and down like the sea's; and the same sort of ... life,
>   arts, politics and so forth
> At the same level on each wave, you can predict 'em.
>   At present
> We're on the down-rip.
>
> (*Angry*, p. 52)

This explicit statement of indebtedness to Spengler amply
confirms *The Decline of the West* as a major source for Jeffers' ideas about culture-cycles and waves of civilization.
Although he did not stress the Nietzsche-Spengler distinction between culture and civilization, the theory of waves
is fundamental to the whole range of Jeffers' poetry.[10]

Spengler recognized in the course of historical cycles the
presence of what he called "Caesarism," and he believed
that democracy was a pious sham. By Caesarism, Spengler
meant "that kind of government which, irrespective of any
constitutional formulation that it may have, is in its inward self a return to thorough formlessness. . . . Real importance centred in the wholly personal power exercised
by the Caesar, or by anybody else capable of exercising it
in his place" (*Decline*, 2: 431). So it is not surprising to
find that Spengler also wrote that the notion of the Third
Estate was essentially a contradiction, defying positive definition, and having neither "customary-ethic" nor a symbolism of its own: "The Third Estate, without proper inward
unity, was the non-estate—the protest, in estate-form,
against the existence of estates; not against this or that estate, but against the symbolic view of life in general" (*Decline*, 2: 358).

Evidence of similar views held by Jeffers is not difficult to find. In *Meditation on Saviors,* he advises us to "Leave the joys of government to Caesar," but the world is "Bitterly afraid to be hurt . . . knowing it cannot draw the savior Caesar but out of the blood-bath." Jeffers, speaking of Americans in *Ave Caesar,* says, "they wanted freedom but wealth too. / Their children will learn to hope for a Caesar." Jeffers concludes this undisguised versification of Spenglerian ideas by saying,

> We are easy to manage, a gregarious people,
> Full of sentiment, clever at mechanics, and we love our
> luxuries.

An interesting variation on this theme occurs in *The Stars Go Over the Lonely Ocean,* in which Jeffers joins Spenglerian ideas to his own principle of isolated integrity:

> Keep clear of the dupes that talk democracy
> And the dogs that talk revolution,
> Drunk with talk, liars and believers.
> .   .   .   .
> Long live freedom and damn the ideologies.

If America needed Caesars to lead it out of its indolence, there was also the danger that it might fall victim to Caesars, and Jeffers, in *Shine, Republic,* warns us accordingly:

> Freedom is poor and laborious; that torch is not safe but
> hungry, and often requires blood for its fuel.
> You will tame it against it burn too clearly, you will hood it
> like a kept hawk, you will perch it on the wrist of
> Caesar.

By the time Spengler died in 1936, Jeffers could already hear the rumblings of the Nazi movement as it gathered its forces to launch the second of the wars of annihilation, which Spengler had predicted would occur as our "Faustian" culture went into more serious decline. At the risk of oversimplification, Spengler included charts and tables illustrating the comparative morphology of history which described the Western culture of the twentieth century as a period of "transition from constitutional to informal sway of individuals. Annihilation wars. Imperialism" (*Decline*, 1: Table 3, "Civilization"). According to Spengler, the twentieth century was to see great struggles between the "Caesars," while populations were eaten up in battles. It was clear to Jeffers, who lived through the World Wars I and II and died predicting a third, that Spengler's prophecies were coming true, but he regarded these catastrophes as desirable and beneficial purgings of decadent civilization.

Thus if one accepted the theory of cycles of history, one could also accept the Nazi movement in Germany as a part of the historical process, and since some agent in the world must serve as the instrument of historical process, Germany would serve as well as any other nation. Jeffers wrote in *Battle: (May 28, 1940)* that the conflict "is all in the whirling circles of time." It will make no difference, he said, "If England goes down and Germany up" because it is "all in the turning of time" and the "stronger dog will still be on top." Jeffers concluded his poem,

> If civilization goes down—that
> Would be an event to contemplate.
> It will not be in our time, alas, my dear,
> It will not be in our time.

The readers who declared that Jeffers was subversive, or worse, were undoubtedly unacquainted with his theories of the inevitable cycles of civilization, and they misunderstood his indifference to the identity of the victor. The poetry, moreover, has an air of familiarity—or recognition—

which reveals Jeffers' acceptance of contemporary events. In *The Soul's Desert: (August 30, 1939),* he warned, "They are warming up the old horrors," but implicitly acknowledged a variation of Eternal Recurrence. It is not "the world's end," he said in *I Shall Laugh Purely,* "But only the fall of a civilization."

Since past history revealed a cyclical character and since future history could be expected to follow a similar pattern, what matter the particular form? It could scarcely make a difference to a man like Jeffers, in the long view, which side won in a conflict, for a civilization in decline could only expect deterioration. Jeffers linked President Franklin Roosevelt and Hitler in a manner that appeared downright unpatriotic, but he apparently regarded them as representatives of Spengler's Caesarism, for either man, he said in *Great Men,*

> must have a following, whether he gain it
> Like Roosevelt by grandiose good intentions, cajolery
> And public funds, or like Hitler by fanatic
> Patriotism, frank lies, genius and terror.

In *Shine, Empire,* Jeffers tells America, "Hate no one. Roosevelt's intentions *were* good, and Hitler is a patriot. They have split the planet into two millstones / That will grind small and bloody."

Jeffers and Spengler obviously shared the opinion that America was being forced against its will into an imperial role, but on the question of Nazi Germany the two men took separate stands. It is not certain whether Jeffers read beyond the *Decline* in Spengler, but if he did he would have found Spengler to be a severe critic of the Nazi movement. In "Reconstruction of the German Reich" (1924), Spengler criticized the Nazis' racial theories because history had proved such ideas false. When he wrote the preface to *Politische Schriften* (1933), which included "Reconstruction," Spengler repeated *"with undiminished force"* his 1924 condemnation of Hitler. The leader of the national movement should be a "hero," he said, not a "heroic tenor." As a result of the coming into power of the Nazi party in 1933, Spengler cut short a criticism of the Nazis, which he was preparing, and published the fragment as the "first volume" of *Hour of Decision*. In it, Spengler said he could only view "with misgiving" the popular acceptance of Hitler's triumph, and his book was eventually regarded by the government as anti-Nazi.[11]

After writing *The Decline of the West*—even with the exaggerations and errors that scholars have found in it—Spengler was sure that he could accurately predict future history, and subsequently he could not resist the temptation to involve himself in political theory. Spengler's study of history taught him, for example, that a "Caesar" figure in Germany ought to help restore the nation to its rightful rank among other nations, but it also indicated that Hitler and the Nazi Party were taking a course already proved unsuccessful. Spengler's political writing criticized and sought to correct these errors. From his Inhumanist position, however, Jeffers took a still longer view of the events of modern history and apparently concluded that one form of disaster was as good as another, since civilization was intent upon its self-destruction.[12]

Whereas society could be tolerant of Robert Frost's opinion that to end the world either fire or ice would suffice, it was taken aback by such poems as Jeffers' *The Bowl of Blood* and *The Day Is a Poem,* which appeared in *Be Angry at the Sun*.[13] In *The Day Is a Poem,* Hitler is portrayed as a genius, but the basic consideration in Jeffers' masque *The Bowl of Blood* is the possibility, as he says, of the poet's presenting "contemporary things in the shape of eternity" (p. 68). Because, according to Jeffers,

> power is a great hollow spirit
> That needs a center.
> It chooses one man almost at random
> And clouds him and clots around him and it possesses him.
> *(Angry,* p. 70)

The subtle assimilation of several important ideas from various sources is apparent in *The Bowl of Blood.* Jeffers' own theory of poetry encouraged the attempt to see the shape of eternity in contemporary things. The various versions of the cyclical theory of history of Vico, Nietzsche, Spengler, and Petrie are blended to form what may conveniently be called the "Spenglerian" notion that the course of future historical development could be predicted on the basis of "morphological" correspondences between like civilizations. Furthermore, Spengler's historicism, which acknowledged the irresistible tides of the events of history as well as the occasional need for Caesars to lead the people in difficult eras, is joined to the vestigial concepts of Nietzsche's Overman (who overcame his limitations) and the Will to Power, which is related more to a specific individual (the Overman) than it is to impersonal historiography. Unlike Spengler, Jeffers reaffirms his Inhumanism when he says "that even Hitler, though all too mischievously occupied with human affairs, does have a sense of the other world, the inhuman one" (p. 80). And when Ernst Friedenau, who acts according to a paradoxical application of Jeffers' theory of the function of the poet, deceives his friend Hitler—the reluctant "Caesar," as Jeffers portrays him—he thereby assures greater world destruction and death; from a philosophical point of view, this extermination is ultimately to the advantage of the inhuman world, which Jeffers preferred.

Flinders Petrie

Sir William Matthew Flinders Petrie (1853–1942) wrote
The Revolutions of Civilization (1911) to which Jeffers
referred in *Themes in My Poems*. Flinders Petrie was an
English Egyptologist, who studied British remains at Stone-
henge and elsewhere from 1875 to 1880, was appointed
Edwards Professor of Egyptology at University College,
London in 1892, and founded the Egyptian Research Ac-
count, which in 1905 was reconstituted as the British
School of Archaeology in Egypt.[14] In 1923, Petrie was
knighted. Among his publications are *Religion and Conscience in Ancient Egypt* (1898), *Religion of Ancient
Egypt* (1906), *Egyptian Architecture* (1938), and *Egyptian
Science* (1939). A very capable and energetic individual,
Petrie revolutionized the techniques of excavation, and established a comparative method of evaluating small items
uncovered in diggings. Interesting in the context of this
study of Jeffers is Petrie's *The Pyramids and Temples of
Gizeh* (1883), the product of his findings at Gizeh, which
disproved once and for all the eschatological theories
which had prompted the expedition. Although outstand-
ing in his fieldwork and his technique of excavation, in his
scholarship Petrie was impatient of all authority and had
little interest or respect for the opinions of others. Thus, in
the face of all but overwhelming scholarly opinion against
him, Petrie held to his "long" Egyptian chronology, and it
is only in this respect that Spengler refers to him in a foot-
note.[15] There is, however, a striking similarity between the
theory of revolutions of society that Petrie worked out
from his discoveries in the field, and the morphological
method of Spengler, who ostensibly depended upon his
own reading in history.

In *The Revolutions of Civilization*, Petrie said that by

comparative study and the application of modern methods
man could read the past from artifacts. In looking at Wèst-
ern history, man had tended to see only the great age of
classical civilization—like a single enjoyed summer without
an ensuing winter; but, Petrie announced, history is a vast
series of winters and summers. Civilization is an intermit-
tently recurring phenomenon to be examined like any
other natural event. Selecting sculpture as his standard for
comparison, Petrie explained that in 7,000–10,000 years of
continuous Egyptian history, "we can discern eight successive periods of civilization, each separated by an age of barbarism before and after it."[16] Petrie's position between
Vico and Spengler becomes evident, both temporally and
ideologically. The series of charts and photographs which
Petrie included lie beyond the scope of the present discussion, but his conclusions are pertinent.

For Egypt, Europe, and England, Petrie worked out a
staggered series of periods of civilization; for example, the
fourth period of Egypt coincided with the first in Europe.
In spite of a wide variation in the particular stage of a civilization within the periods, they averaged 1,330 years. Because it was practically the same for different regions of the
world, Petrie felt that the length of the periods was due to
man's inherent constitution rather than to anything external. Studying his data, he saw the root of human progress
as "the widening of the outlook in the summer of each period, and the amelioration of the collapse in winter" (*Revolutions*, p. 106). In other words, Petrie regarded human
progress as a spiral rather than a circle. Furthermore, he
observed, his charts showed that the Eastern phase pre-
cedes the Mediterranean phase by about three and one-half
centuries, so that civilization gives the impression of always
coming from the East simply because the phase in the East
is a few centuries in advance of that in the West. Thus, ac-

cording to Petrie, on the upswing of a wave the East has reached a higher degree of civilization.

Petrie believed that only through the introduction of fresh blood could a fallen civilization rise from the trough between periods, and he cited the influence of various barbaric invasions to prove his point. Since, according to him, the foundation of every civilization is a mixture of races, Petrie urged the exploration of eugenic development to establish the distinctive types necessary to rejuvenate a civilization. "The future progress of man may depend as much on isolation to establish type, as on fusion of types when established," Petrie declared (*Revolutions*, p. 131). It is on this point of eugenics that Petrie, Nietzsche, Spengler, and the Nazi party went their separate ways.

In some of his other conclusions, Petrie reasoned that the world was becoming more civilized, in spite of the fact that successive intervals of barbarism produced no improvement in certain types of civilization. It was also apparent to him that another result of the widening of the phases to the present was the separation of the best periods from each form of culture. Consequently, as more recent phases space out farther, "the art is decadent before the mechanical ability is free, and before the wealth has grown"; hence, he continued, "the increasingly tasteless use of wealth by the late Mykenaean, the Roman, or the modern man" (*Revolutions*, p. 120). Moreover, when democracy has attained full power, Petrie reasoned in anticipation of Spengler, civilization begins a steady erosion during which the inferior peoples are gradually replaced by a fitter population, as was the case of the Roman Empire.

Although Jeffers could have obtained nearly the entire doctrine of Spengler from Petrie's book of 130-odd pages, the poet must also have looked into the two large volumes of *The Decline of the West*. Petrie, as well as Vico, believed in the spiraling progress of history, which Nietzsche and Spengler rejected. Nietzsche, as Spengler pointed out, recognized the cycles of Eternal Recurrence, but he did not produce such historicist theories about future civilizations as held by Spengler and Petrie. As a way of transcending the cycles of events, Nietzsche conceived the Overman, who detached himself from the civilization in which he originated; Spengler developed the concept of Caesarism, which was politically related to its social origin; and Petrie held not only that the period of a civilization was related to man's constitution rather than outside factors, but also that a general enrichment was evident in each successive cycle. Whereas the superior individual described by Nietzsche and Spengler was falsely appropriated by the Nazis as both authority and model for their doctrines of racial superiority, Petrie openly considered the possibilities of controlled eugenic improvement of races. Spengler, who criticized Nietzsche for slighting Asia in his philosophical considerations, was suspicious of the brown and yellow races, and advised against giving them technical knowledge lest it eventually be turned on the West. And Petrie, in his explanation of the three-and-one-half-century difference between the phases of Asia and the West, suggested why civilization appears to move from East to West.

Out of these closely interrelated ideas and attitudes, Jeffers formed many of his poems, and, since the influence of Nietzsche and Spengler has already been discussed, it may be sufficient to mention a few works that appear to reflect certain ideas in Petrie's *The Revolutions of Civilization*. Echoing the passage from Plutarch's *Sulla,* which Petrie also quoted (pp. 9–10), *The Broken Balance* describes a "Pealing of trumpets high up in the air" which sounds because "at the end of each period / A sign is declared in heaven / Indicating new times." The narrator of the poem reports, "I heard yesterday / So shrill and mournful a trumpet-blast," which he interprets as a like sign of impending change. He concludes the first section of the poem rather vaguely by saying that "When the republic grows too heavy to endure . . . When life grows hateful, there's power . . . ." In Jeffers' first period of ideological development, this is a typical expression of the concept of power, even though it still lacked useful definition. *The Torch-Bearers' Race* and *The Cycle* (both from the early period) present the idea that the torch of civilization is passed westward. And in *Hungerfield,* Jeffers observes, "Life is cheap, these days; / We have to compete with Asia, we are cheap as dust" (p. 4). The posthumously published *Prophets,* which declares "that as civilization / Advances, so wars increase," warns also of "huge Asia / Waking from sleep." Such poems as these reflect Petrie's theories about the cyclic trend of periods and about the movement of civilization from East to West.

The American tourists in *New Mexican Mountains* come "hungrily" to watch the Indian corn dances. They are "People from cities, anxious to be human again." Hoping for revitalization, the tourists find themselves almost instinctively held by the primitive rites. "Only the drum is confident," says the poet, for we must "remember that civilization is a transient sickness." Like Petrie, Jeffers expected new growth and death from the fusion of civilization and barbarism. In a later poem, *Teheran,* Jeffers expressed no hope for the peace made there; America and Russia remain "two bulls in one pasture," and—

> Observe also
> How rapidly civilization coarsens and decays; its better
>   qualities, foresight, humaneness, disinterested
> Respect for truth, die first; its worst will be last.

Havelock Ellis

Jeffers sent an inscribed copy of *Roan Stallion, Tamar and Other Poems* to Havelock Ellis, who had written a testimonial for the jacket of the book. Ellis mentioned this gift in a later letter acknowledging receipt of the "advance sheets" of the poem *An Artist* (1928).[17] Powell, Squires, and Carpenter merely noted this exchange between the authors, but we know that Jeffers "must have been familiar with most of Havelock Ellis's works," and, therefore, a brief discussion of them as possible influences may prove fruitful.[18]

Havelock Ellis is probably best known for his monumental *Studies in the Psychology of Sex* and least known for his editions of such authors as Marlowe, Chapman, and John Ford. Between these extremes fall several titles published or republished during the 1920s. *The New Spirit* (1921), *The Dance of Life* (1923), and *Fountain of Life* (1930) range from brief statements on to a sustained analysis of modern life. They do not form a philosophical system, but they do include numerous observations that were compatible with Jeffers' general outlook.

Ellis was an enthusiastic follower of Nietzsche. He wrote several articles on the German philosopher, and took the title and idea of *The Dance of Life* from Nietzsche.[19] From Nietzsche's idea that a man must make himself a work of art, as Ellis remembered it, grew the Englishman's conviction that morals and art are identical and both are life. Each individual must act like an artist, according to Ellis, letting the phenomena of his surroundings formulate his own truth. Any alien "emotional or practical considerations" must be checked or the individual will become "a bad artist and his work is wrought for destruction" (*Dance*, p. 232). In *Fountain of Life*, Ellis expands on the function of art; it alone can rise above the "categories of morality" to justify "the pains and griefs of Life by demonstrating their representative character and emphasizing their spectacular value," and thus redeem "the Pain of Life by Beauty."[20] One thinks immediately of *But I Am Growing Old and Indolent,* in which Jeffers refers to his decision three decades earlier to continue to examine life throughout his poetry and thus to be redeemed by fictitious victims.

Like the other "Spenglerians," Ellis, in *The New Spirit,* accepted the cyclical movement of history, and believed, with Spengler, that the "nineteenth century has seen the rise and fall of middle-class supremacy."[21] Referring to Nature's remarkable ability to economize, Ellis noted the constant renewal of old cycles, but clarified what he meant by cycle when he said, "Man has proceeded, not in a straight line, but in a spiral" (*Dance,* p. 196). In *Fountain of Life,* Ellis considered that it is the "feeble shrinking from Death and the flabby horror of Pain that mark the final stage of decay in any civilization" (pp. 158–59). Jeffers, as his readers know, reiterated this view throughout his career. In *Fountain of Life,* Ellis also describes the anxiety of the Cornish people of old who turned burial urns upside down because they feared that the departed dead would escape and return to earth. Although it could easily be coincidence, Jeffers, in *Ode to Hengist and Horsa,* mentions a similar practice to protect the living from the return of the dead. Both men agreed that superstitions like this had developed into a general fear of death in modern man.

Like Jeffers, Ellis grew up in an intense religious environment, and, like the poet, he soon turned from traditional religion to more liberal views.[22] He saw in scientific study the promise of a rejuvenated intellectual world, for, as he wrote, "We know that wherever science goes the purifying breath of spring has passed and all things are re-created" (*New Spirit,* p. 8). Under the influence of such works as James Hinton's *Life in Nature* (1862) and other later nineteenth-century examinations of religion and science, he began his rebellion which soon developed into a search for a truce between religion and science. In *The Dance of Life,* Ellis wrote that there should be no "opposition of hostility between mysticism and science," but, he added later on, "If at some period in the course of civilization we seriously find that our science and our religion are antagonistic, then there must be something wrong either with our science or with our religion" (pp. 191, 197). Although Jeffers' poetry often reflects his scientific training, it is frequently a matter of defining the modern world in terms of its prevailing scientific emphasis, and one gets the impression that the poet is convinced that whatever benevolent capacity science once had for man it is now perverted into new modes of destruction and debilitating mechanical conveniences.[23]

But, from another point of view, we may compare certain opinions which Ellis and Jeffers held about the truth of science versus the truth of art. For Ellis, just as for Shelley and Jeffers, imagination was a component part of all thinking, and, furthermore, scientific fictions were parallel with aesthetic fictions. "The poet," according to Ellis, "is the type of all thinkers: there is no sharp boundary between the region of poetry and the region of science." "Both alike," he added, "are not ends in themselves, but means to higher ends" (*Dance,* p. 102). Ellis wanted to show that Plotinus' dualism of spirit (good) and matter (evil) is being corrected by the scientific investigation of matter—including psychology. He also believed that Lucretius might be the first of moderns to identify mysticism

with science (*Dance*, p. 207). As noted earlier in the discussion of Jeffers' theory of poetry, Jeffers wrote, in *The
Great Wound*, that "The poet also / Has his mythology,"
his way of explaining things. Like the poet,

> The mathematicians and physics men
> Have their mythology; they work alongside the truth,
> Never touching it; their equations are false
> But the things *work*.

In *The Silent Shepherds*, Jeffers definitely favors the poet's
mythology, adding:

> Science and mathematics
> Run parallel to reality, they symbolize it, they squint at it
> They never touch it.

And he concludes the poem by considering what an event
it would be "If any mind should for a moment touch
truth." In *The Beginning and the End*, Jeffers compared
the poet and his poems to sense organs through which
people might receive impressions of the world around them,
and Jeffers clearly expected to find reality through poetry—
whereas Ellis sought it through scientific investigation.
Like Ellis, he believed in poetic and scientific fictions that
ran parallel to the truth, but poetry might yet run closer
to it.

The references which Ellis made to Plotinus and Lucretius tempt an examination of the similarity of the views Ellis and Jeffers held on Nature. Ellis was perhaps as enthusiastic as Jeffers about Nature; some of his prose passages on
the beauties of Nature rival passages in Jeffers. In his hope
that science could resolve Plotinus' dualism of spirit and
matter, Ellis anticipated Jeffers' Howard Howren, who
searched for the link between organic and inorganic matter,
but Ellis retained Plotinus' moralistic division of good and
evil into spirit and matter. Ellis thereby separated himself

from Jeffers, who held, in effect, that spirit was merely an extension of matter which was morally good. However, Ellis recognized in Lucretius possible reconciliations which also attracted Jeffers (see Chapter 8). In spite of their differences about dualism, however, Jeffers could have found among the aphorisms and observations in *Fountain of Life* statements in which Ellis revealed an attitude akin to Jeffers' toward Nature.

Nature created man as a creature to appreciate her magnificence, Ellis believed. "And she had to pay for it," he added, because "man proved a dangerous plaything. . . . Only one problem remains: How to dispose of him?" This is solid Jeffersian doctrine, and Ellis continued, referring to himself, "But once a creature stood here who saw and felt and knew that beauty. It will have been enough" (*Fountain*, pp. 344–45). In a late poem, *To Kill in War Is Not Murder,* Jeffers considers the future of his little grandchildren in the world he sees, and says of them, as he had been saying for years of his fellowmen,

> the enormous inhuman
> Beauty of things goes on, the beauty of God, the eternal
> beauty, and perhaps they'll see it.

Jeffers may also have read in Ellis' *Fountain of Life* the statement, "To see the World as Beauty is the whole End of Living" (p. 253).

"Behind the passing insanity of Man," wrote Ellis, sounding like a quote from any of several of Jeffers' poems, "the beauty of Nature seems to become more poignant and her serene orderliness more deeply peaceful" (*Fountain*, p. 216). And at the end of *Margrave,* Jeffers said of Nature, "It is very well ordered." He referred to the Nature he could see from his stone tower after describing the insane ambition and folly of Walter Margrave and the miserable

failings of Margrave's sister. In the midst of his afflictions
Walter Margrave's father had raged against the salmon
fishermen who wantonly destroyed the sea lions. For both
Ellis and Jeffers, insane mankind would go down before
the lasting grandeur of Nature. The restorative power of
Nature, to which all things transitory and human eventually return, is described by Jeffers in *November Surf*. Considering the respective dates of composition and the corre-
spondent attitudes toward Nature's regenerative capacity
to absorb humanity's decay and contamination, it is not
unreasonable to suggest that the poem owes a debt to the
following passage from Ellis' *Fountain of Life:*

> Alone but for a few meditative gulls, I sit among the rocks
> and dream of the miracle of this restless, antiseptic sea that
> for millions of years has been slowly and tirelessly absorbing
> all the rejected filth that the Earth and now Man can pour
> into it, and still to-day, as at the first, sends forth its fresh
> procession of waves in Purity and Joy, for the sacred lustra-
> tion of an Evil World. (p. 340)

From Ellis' various statements, then, Jeffers apparently
could have drawn considerable inspiration. Ellis had no
fully developed philosophical system of his own from
which Jeffers could borrow; but the men were emotionally
compatible in their regard for Nature, they shared theories
about the cycles of civilization, they recognized certain possibilities in Nietzsche's philosophy, they were equally concerned about the interrelationship of morality and art,
and, though they differed somewhat on the role of science,
their ideas of truth were all but identical.

the greek tragedians

Ever since *Tamar and Other Poems* first attracted the attention of established critics like Mark Van Doren, Jeffers' poetry has been compared, favorably or otherwise, with ancient Greek literature, especially with the Greek tragedians, Aeschylus, Sophocles, and Euripides.[1] In the course of his long poetic career, Jeffers amply substantiated his critics' recognition of classicial influences, for not only did he produce a version of the *Oresteia* by Aeschylus (*The Tower Beyond Tragedy*), two versions of Euripides' *Medea* (*Solstice* and the free adaptation titled *Medea*), and a version of Euripides' *Hippolytus* (*The Cretan Woman*), but he also adopted some of the chief ideas of Heraclitus, Lucretius, and Plato, and often referred to other classical authors.[2] Even though he once wrote that he wanted his lines "as formed as alcaics if that were possible," Jeffers was occasionally taken to task by his critics for not being a complete classicist or for not being a carbon copy of, say, Euripides or Aeschylus.[3] In fact, Jeffers was quite eclectic in choosing what he wanted from classical literature, taking only that which was useful and congenial to his own thought, or revamping a work to make it more nearly in accord with his own ideology.

This chapter is concerned with the major classical themes which appear in Jeffers' poetry and with their contribution to the central ideology that emerged during Jeffers' career. The role of Lucretius, who would ordinarily be discussed here, is examined in the final chapter. Jeffers, who apparently favored Aeschylean drama first, moved rapidly toward Euripidean models and what we may call the Euripidean view of the world and of the individual, after the style of Aristophanes' characterization (*The Frogs*) of Euripides, who Aristophanes claimed "taught all the town to talk with freedom. . . . To fall in love, think evil, question all things."[4] And after *At the Fall of an Age* (which is an enlargement of a note in Pausanias' *Description of Greece*), Jeffers dealt primarily with Euripidean materials, e.g., the Hippolytus theme and variations on the *Medea*.

On the eve of the opening of his *Medea* at the Geary Theater in San Francisco, Jeffers made some observations in the *San Francisco Chronicle* on the play and Greek drama. The dramas of Aeschylus and Sophocles, he noted, "began in a time of exultation when the great defensive war with Persia was triumphantly concluded." Jeffers shares the traditional scholarly view, which can be traced back to Thucydides, that a shift in the Athenian mood occurred, however, after the exhausting war with Sparta; and as Euripides in his tragedies foresaw during the age of Pericles, "the great dream was fading." Jeffers continued: "Aeschylus labored the theme of sublimity; the persons of his plays, and even the language, the great mouth-filling words, are larger than life. The work of Sophocles was valued for its nobility. . . . [but Euripides] presented real and understandable human beings, people you could identify with yourself, rather than ideal heroes, and demi-gods." In the period of disillusionment which followed the war with Sparta, the old "sublimity" of Aeschylus and the old "nobility" of Sophocles were replaced by the new "intensity and fury" of the plays of Euripides, Jeffers reminded his readers. His view, then, of these dramatists and their times is consistent with the conclusions of classical scholarship, but he also reveals a preference for Euripidean tragedy, founded, at least in part, in sympathy for the general sense of disillusionment which these plays convey. Jeffers observed, moreover, that part of Euripides' unpopularity in his own day may have been due to the fact that, unlike Aeschylus and Sophocles, who participated in both military and political campaigns, Euripides remained a "private man" and student "aloof from public life."[5] And to Euripides' actions Jeffers gave his approval.

Aeschylus

The Tower Beyond Tragedy

After the 1920s, Cargill said of Jeffers, the poet "could write with more human sympathy, like Sophocles, rather than madly and badly, like Nietzsche, or remotely and austerely, like Aeschylus."[6] If Cargill meant that in the thirties Jeffers focused more on the individual in a responsible relationship to his sociological environment, I agree with him completely. Jeffers abandoned Aeschylus, and I suspect he did so as a reaction against the traits which Cargill mentioned. As a matter of fact, the movement away from the Aeschylean view, as represented in the *Oresteia*, is evident within *The Tower Beyond Tragedy*, the only work by Jeffers that may truly be called Aeschylean.

Undoubtedly, the story of the House of Atreus portrayed in *The Tower Beyond Tragedy* first attracted Jeffers because it suited his theory that drama ought to evolve from conflicts within the family, and provided a ready-made power struggle with appropriate dramatic motivation. In most respects, Jeffers followed the *Agamemnon* as far as it goes, but since he wrote a verse drama not originally intended for theatrical production, there were significant changes. (Jeffers did later prepare an undated acting version which has been staged.) Instead of the long speech of the Watchman at the beginning of Aeschylus' version of the story, which creates a tense atmosphere of mixed joy and apprehension, and the dark suggestions of the Chorus that trouble is afoot in Argos, Jeffers swiftly introduces the dramatic situation, in the narrator's voice, and begins the action. The Aeschylean mood of awe for the gods, who move all things, has already dissipated, and Jeffers' opening lines concentrate on the individual psychology of Clytemnestra. Whereas Aeschylus' Cassandra and the Chorus exchange hints at length about the forthcoming murder and their fears about how these events will appear to the gods, Jeffers' Agamemnon is dead within two pages of the beginning of the poem. For Aeschylus, the murders of Agamemnon and Cassandra are the climax of the drama; for Jeffers, the king's death is simply a necessary condition for the following action. Furthermore, Jeffers' Cassandra, who does not die with Agamemnon, lives on to be invaded by the spirit of the dead king. In Aeschylus, the probable effect of the king's death on the gods is discussed before the murder; in Jeffers, the effect on the people of the shift of power is discussed after the murder. In other words, the people of Aeschylus' drama live in a world so constituted ethically that they may speculate with some confidence on the effects of a possible deed of violence; Jeffers' people find themselves without such "theological" guidelines, and forced to deal with a fait accompli. The difference in approach between Aeschylus and Euripides is that between speculation and necessity, and even in that part of his drama which is patently Aeschylean Jeffers is pressing his materials into a Euripidean mold.

After the murder of Agamemnon, Aeschylus' Clytemnestra attempts to convince the Chorus that the king's death is fair payment for his bold sacrifice of their daughter Iphigenia, and, of course, the *Choephoroe* and the *Eumenides* round out the trilogy and develop the conflicts created by the regicide. However, Jeffers' version, which all but starts with the murder, goes on to complete the cycle in one poem.

In the *Eumenides,* which describes the revenge of Orestes, Aeschylus causes Orestes to act according to the command of Apollo, so that Orestes, though he violates human law, may still claim divine sanction. Furthermore, as Philip W. Harsh has pointed out, Aeschylus appears to be interested not in finding a moral solution but in posing "a problem insoluble according to primitive law."⁷ Aeschylus' resolution of the murder may not have been completely satisfactory to his contemporaries, for both Sophocles and Euripides wrote their own versions of the revenge. In his *Electra,* Sophocles portrayed Orestes as an entirely admirable character; Aeschylus' version presents the deed as necessary but dreadful, and Euripides' account views the murder as an evil act which should not have been committed. Jeffers follows Euripides, for his Orestes is overwhelmed by the enormity of his act and wanders away in stunned distraction from the court of the Mycenaeans. Jeffers' Electra gives still more convincing proof of the Euripidean influence, for she bears a marked resemblance to other Euripidean female characters, who were often strong individuals. Being exceptional among Greek dramatists for his

nonstereotyped women, Euripides drew an Electra who
was a far stronger character than her brother. In Euripides'
drama, the sister actually guides Orestes' sword in the murder scene. Electra's extremely forceful personality supplies
the encouragement which Orestes requires, and her almost
psychotic behavior provides a precedent for the attributes
which Jeffers gives her.

Jeffers' Clytemnestra uses the sacrifice of Iphigenia as a
pretext for killing Agamemnon, but, although this motivation lingers in her speeches throughout the poem, she is
more genuinely absorbed in a quest for power which she
may wield and enjoy. By the time Agamemnon returns to
Mycenae, Clytemnestra is already well established in the
role she has cast for herself. Aegisthus, who is no Agamemnon, is a tractable partner; he fills out the royal household,
so to speak, but he may not be expected to challenge the
queen. Clytemnestra acts according to the Will to Power
and overcomes her enemies, all the while believing that
she is fulfilling herself, i.e., transcending the customary
limitations of feminine convention. Early in the poem she
compares her power with the prophetic power of Cassandra when she says to the prophetess, "I am holding lions
[i.e., the Mycenaeans] with my two eyes" (p. 36), and later
asks the Captain, "who was it that held / With her two
eyes the whole city from splitting wide asunder?" (p. 37).
Aegisthus himself calls Clytemnestra, "O strongest spirit in
the world" (p. 48). Before her people, the queen's Captain
also challenges the propriety of Clytemnestra's maneuvering.

In the earlier discussion of *The Tower Beyond Tragedy*
(Chapter 3), we saw that Jeffers reversed the procedure
that Nietzsche followed to arrive at the concept of the Will
to Power, which combined the earlier concepts of Dionysus
and Apollo. Jeffers began with the Will to Power embod-

ied in Clytemnestra and moved backwards in the Nietz-schean development to its constituents, the Dionysian and the Apollonian. Electra, who inherits her mother's craving for power and illustrates Eternal Recurrence, represents the reckless force of Dionysus, which lends its energy and impetus to the Apollonian element, i.e., to Orestes. Her Dionysian role is dramatically illustrated when she all but wills Orestes to murder his mother. A part of this overall design is the episode in which Clytemnestra, who knows her antagonists better than anyone, pleads for her life to Orestes, not Electra, and uses arguments intended to appeal to his Apollonian nature.

By the time Orestes returns, in the third part of the poem, he has learned something about himself during his self-imposed exile in the forest. First, he no longer regards the murder of his mother as a crime; it is an awakening, he says. Second, Orestes is finished with humanity: "I will not waste inward / Upon humanity, having found a fairer object" (p. 80). The fairer object is "the earlier fountain" or, as Orestes vaguely calls it elsewhere, "the life of the brown forest" (p. 81). Orestes' decision does not prevent Electra from offering him her incestuous love if it is required to make the youth a worthy successor to Agamemnon. Nor does Orestes' long defense of his decision change his sister's mind; her last words to him are, "Strength's good. You are lost. I here remember the honor of the house, and Agamemnon's" (p. 82).

Jeffers probably used the story of the House of Atreus because it provided the situation and motivation which he needed. The Atreidae lived under an ancient curse, and Jeffers' *The Tower Beyond Tragedy*, like Aeschylus' *Oresteia*, shows the climax of the family's cursed history and its resolution. For Jeffers' Orestes, who has "cast humanity, [and] entered the earlier fountain" (p. 82), the curse has been broken; but for his Electra, who still believes that strength is good, the curse is still in effect. Again, Jeffers approved of the decision which leads away from human frailty and excess (represented by Electra) toward peaceful identification with enduring and unblemished Nature (represented in Orestes' choice). It is significant, then, that Jeffers should impose on the legend a Nietzschean struggle of the Will to Power (illustrating the presence of Eternal Recurrence in the second generation of the quest as well as the presence of Dionysian and Apollonian forces). Furthermore, he demonstrated an early predilection for Euripidean thought when he incorporated into his own Electra much that originally belonged to Euripides' character.

Euripides

Cawdor

For obvious reasons, *Roan Stallion* may well reflect the tale of Pasiphae, the wife of Minos, or suggest the myth of Leda, but the poem is otherwise the original work of Jeffers. *Cawdor*, however, incorporates the Hippolytus theme from Euripides' tragedy. Fera Martial, like Euripides' Phaedra in *Hippolytus*, becomes the wife of an older man who has a family by a previous marriage. If there is a suggestion in old Cawdor of the earlier Theseus (Phaedra's husband), it is conveyed in his authoritarian bearing within the confines of his canyon-enclosed farm, which resembles Troezen, the setting of the Greek play, and in his casual philandering with Concha Rosas, the Indian servant, who may evoke the memory of Theseus' well-known amorous adventures.

Unlike Hippolytus, Hood Cawdor has not offended the goddess Aphrodite by refusing to honor her and by worshipping only Artemis, but before the action of Jeffers' poem begins, Hood has left his father's house to be a hunter. It is the occasion of his father's marriage to Fera that recalls him from his wilderness exile, and he comes home with a puma-skin wedding present for the bride. Later, when Hood is accused of violating his father's bed, he cannot plead for the intercession of benign gods, but he responds with a modern equivalent by protesting his father's attack, "I'm not hiding, I'll answer the law, not you" (p. 77). As the result of Cawdor's violence, Hood dies, like Hippolytus, his body mangled among the rocks; Cawdor, like Theseus, has been misled by a deceitful wife.

At this point, the two works begin to diverge to their own ends, but the validity of the parallels, which have just been cited, is not diminished. Fera Martial, who has suffered much with her father at the mercy of forces beyond her control, decides that to join Cawdor will guarantee security and some measure of power over the problems which have beset her heretofore. She errs, as we have seen, by overemphasizing the value of power, as she reveals when she says that strength is the only thing under the sun worth loving. Phaedra is the unwitting victim of Aphrodite's plan to chastize the unbelieving Hippolytus, and in that sense she is not responsible for her love of her stepson; besides, she has in her some of the troubled blood of Pasiphae. But Fera is conscious of her victimization by external forces, and she is guilty of seeking more from life than sufficiency, i.e., having found security and peace, she demands still more. It is in this way that Jeffers dramatizes the error of Fera's Nietzschean Will to Power.

Breaking loyalty to her husband's bed, Fera calculatingly pursues Hood with the hope of establishing a liaison with the younger man. In Hood's bedroom, where Fera

(Latin for "wild animal") has tracked the hunter, the youth rejects his stepmother's advances again, and she observes in passing,

> Your breast's more smooth
> Than rubbed marble, no hair like other men in the groove
> between the muscles, it is like a girl's
> Except the hardness and the flat strength.
>
> (*Cawdor*, p. 43)

Earlier, Concha Rosas tried to explain to Fera that Hood sleeps with no one, "He love the deer / He's only a boy and he go hunting" (p. 40). This explanation accords very closely with Euripides' characterization, which Harsh has emphasized in his study of the Greek play. Hippolytus is a youthful hater of women, for "there is no hint of sexual perversion anywhere in the play or the legend . . . many passages prohibit such an interpretation."[8] Jeffers preserves the same character traits in his poem, in spite of the doubts which Fera expresses. Beneath the shadowy laurels, Fera makes her strongest bid for Hood's cooperation, but she loses again and asks, "Is it men you love? / You are girl-hearted, that makes you ice to me?" (p. 63). She is wrong, as Jeffers carefully demonstrates, for, as she becomes more insistent, Hood stabs his knife into the muscle of his thigh to break the power of Fera's seduction. When he leaves the laurels, Hood is "limping from the Attis-gesture." According to Catullus (poem 63), Attis, a Phrygian deity, was the son of Nana, daughter of the river-god Sangarius. When Attis wished to marry, Agdistis, who loved him and was jealous, drove him mad, so that he castrated himself and died.[9] Symbolically, Hood has castrated himself to neutralize Fera's appeal, and he will soon die as a result of it.

Phaedra hangs herself in Euripides' play when she discovers the Nurse's duplicity, for she is ashamed of her Cretan heritage, which she blames in part for her trouble, and wishes to be an honorable woman. Guilty of no overt sin, she is still compelled to commit suicide, for, as she says early in the play, "My hand is clean: but is my heart, O God?" Thus Phaedra anticipates Hippolytus' famous line, " 'Twas but my tongue, 'twas not my soul that swore."[10] Fera Martial also tries to hang herself, but her attempt is apparently motivated by despair, for Hood is dead by then from his father's violence. When Fera, who has been revived from attempted suicide, visits Hood's grave, she says, "It was I that killed you. The old man / Who lives in hell for it was only my hands" (p. 103). Can this be Jeffers' conscious echo of the Euripidean line?

In the discussion of *Cawdor* in Chapter 3, I argued that of the three ideological positions—represented by Fera, Hood, and old Cawdor—Jeffers favored that of Hood, in spite of the fact that he at first seems to be a failure by dint of his early death. Nevertheless, in view of the poetry to follow in the thirties, Hood, always pure and honorable, independent and closely allied with a beneficent Nature, should be acknowledged as the hero of this poem, just as Hippolytus is the hero of Euripides'. That Hood is able to resist the malicious design of the Nietzschean Will to Power in Fera and at the same time seek independence from the patriarchalism of his father is, as already noted, a part of Jeffers' examination of Nietzscheanism. While Hood remains pure and honorable, Fera demonstrates the flaw of Nietzsche's principle of sublimation, and she wins nothing, thereby discrediting those aspects of Nietzscheanism which she embodied. But both she and Hood have carried out their respective Revaluations of Values, so that only selected aspects of Nietzsche's thought have been rejected.

Old Cawdor, like Theseus, realizes too late what he has

done, but, unlike Theseus, he takes justice into his own hands when he blinds himself for his crime, saying, "These punishments are a pitiful self-indulgence. / I'd not the strength to do nothing" (p. 125). In the earlier discussion of the "death flight" of the dead eagle's spirit (a dual symbol related to both Fera and Hood), there was the poet's further comment on men like Cawdor, who are diminished until they disappear amid the grandeur of Nature. In Jeffers' poem, both Fera and Hood rebel against their worlds and seek their own solutions. Fera is ruthless and destructive, and achieves nothing of value for herself. Hood also appears to achieve nothing; but he has remained chaste, he has identified with Nature, which is superior to his father's values, and in his associations with Fera and his father he has shown the duplicity and irresponsibility of both the other rebellion and the conventions from which he and Fera took their respective departures. In Hood, Jeffers adapted Euripides' Hippolytus and portrayed a possible solution to the human dilemma, as well as the possible hazards.

The Humanist's Tragedy

The Humanist's Tragedy, a poem included in *Dear Judas,* is an adaptation of Euripides' *Bacchae.* Jeffers took a long and problematical play, telescoped its action, and simplified its argument. Euripides' Pentheus, King of Thebes, seeks to suppress the worship of Dionysus because he believes the worship involves sexual improprieties. His opposition to the new cult of Dionysus gains impetus when a messenger reports that the king's mother, Agave, is among the god's worshippers at Cythaeron. In the Greek play, Pentheus is represented as a mortal who interferes with the worship of a god (somewhat like Hippolytus versus Aphrodite), but, in the course of the action, Dionysus intoxicates

Pentheus, who then reveals his own prurient interest in the Dionysian rites. Euripides' exposure of the psychology of Pentheus is lengthy, subtle, and actually still open to interpretation, but it is apparent that Pentheus is the victim of his own unhealthy interest in the exotic rites of the new religion. There is pitiful irony in the emphasis Cadmus gives to the admirable qualities of Pentheus, but this occurs after the worshippers, led in their madness by Agave, mistake Pentheus for a lion and decapitate him. In a sense, Pentheus, like Theseus, is guilty of hubris.

Jeffers' Pentheus is much more simply drawn, but he is also a victim of his inflexible outlook and the maddened rage of his mother and her fellow worshippers. The poet's repeated emphasis is on a rational and self-composed Pentheus—

> Not like a beast borne on the flood of passion, boat without
>   oars, but mindful of all his dignity
> As human being, a king and a Greek.
>
> > *(Judas, p. 122)*

Pentheus satisfies himself with the thought that, "The generations . . . aspire. They better; they climb; as I / Am better than this weak suggestible woman my mother." The end of being, the king affirms, is "A more collected and dignified / Creature." Dionysus, however, urges his adherents to break from the prisons of themselves and to enter the nature of things—"to break human collectedness." Pentheus loses his life as he challenges the authority of the new religion, for his inflexible posturing proves no match for the enthusiasts. The "tragedy" of Jeffers' poem is double-edged (as it is to some extent in Euripides), for Pentheus, the humanist, with all his admirable qualities, is sacrificed to his rigid views. At the same time the cult of Dionysus, which expounds aims that reflect to some degree those of

Jeffers himself, is guilty of a crime of excess. As noted in the previous discussion of the poem in Chapter 3, Jeffers illustrated the necessity of fruitful cooperation between the Dionysian and the Apollonian (i.e., Pentheus).

Give Your Heart to the Hawks and *Solstice*

In Jeffers' characterization of Lance Fraser, the hero of *Give Your Heart to the Hawks,* it is possible to recognize a touch of Euripides' Pentheus, for Lance, who resembles Pentheus in demeanor, shows a similar prurience under the influence of liquor.[11] I have described Lance as Puritanical like his father at first, and, with drink, he becomes agitated by breaches of propriety. He goes to look at Sadie's tattoo, but hurries away self-righteously. He suspects his wife and brother, and apparently finds confirmation of his suspicions. In this case, however, Lance does cooperate with his wife and permits her to attempt to save him from himself.

In his *Mythology and the Romantic Tradition in English Poetry* Professor Douglas Bush, who is a severe critic of the quality of American literature, writes that in Jeffers "we have . . . the most striking of the many proofs we have had that Latin and Greek cannot make a classical artist out of a romantic, in this case a decadent romantic."[12] Unfortunately for Jeffers, Bush goes on to attack the extremely vulnerable *Solstice,* which shows "that characters who exist and act in a moral vacuum have no trace of significance" (p. 524). "When we think of Medea and then of Mrs. Bothwell," Bush writes, "we may be glad that the ancients had got beyond behaviorism" (p. 524). It is useless, I think, to try to defend the poem's artistic merits; but it does show Jeffers' developing social awareness—his willingness to introduce the concerns and values of society into his verse. In *Solstice,* Jeffers meant to oppose the decadence of metropolitan life with pride and ferocity, "virtues older than Christ" (p. 94). We can recognize what Jeffers tried to do with the Medea theme, but his personal message at the end remains unbelievably dramatized and incredibly motivated.

Medea

In 1944, Judith Anderson asked Jeffers to write an adaptation for her of Euripides' *Medea*.[13] The poet must have warmed quickly to the idea, for the verse drama was published in 1946; but a failure to reach an acceptable financial agreement with the New York producers prevented the play's production until 1948. With Miss Anderson and John Gielgud as its stars, the play was a popular success both in New York and on nationwide tour. For Jeffers, the legend of Medea proved especially attractive because in some respects it illustrated ideas which he held, and it gave him a chance to write a play for a strong actress who could give the lines of his tragedy the force and "poetic" quality which he claimed in "Poetry, Gongorism, and a Thousand Years" to be most desirable. In the *San Francisco Chronicle* article, Jeffers claimed that, as a rule, he did not like to hear his verses read, but, having heard Miss Anderson's Medea, he was pleased with the result.[14]

In his version, Jeffers broke up most of the long speeches by Medea, Jason, and the Messengers, and substituted shorter exchanges of information between characters, but without resorting to the common dramatic device of stichomythia. He deliberately gave the speeches a realistic quality, since he realized that the rhetoric of the Greek play's psychology was too formal for the taste of modern audiences. He also provided speaking parts for the two sons of Medea, and the success of this technique is evident in a scene with Jason which quickly develops the father's love for the boys and strengthens the argument which he had given Medea for his marrying Creüsa. In a clever bit of stage sense, Jeffers made another change in the original. Medea's dragon-drawn chariot had for centuries invited the attacks of Euripides' critics, and Jeffers knew that his audience would never accept this device literally on the stage. Instead, he gave Medea, who is portrayed as an Asiatic versed in witchcraft, two lamps—"two fire-snakes"— which effectively keep Jason at a distance in the closing action and prevent his following Medea.

As Jeffers' play opens, the Nurse and the Chorus of women are pitying Medea, whom Jason has abandoned for Creon's daughter, for now she faces exile along with her sons. Medea scorns their pity because "Pity and contempt are sister and brother," and she "will not die tamely," since, as she tells them, "I am not a Greek woman" (p. 11). The distinction made here between Medea's "barbaric" Colchan origin and Greek civilization anticipates the defenses of both Euripides' and Jeffers' Jasons, but in the later play this distinction receives quick emphasis and reflects Jeffersian attitudes toward comparative civilizations. When, for example, Jeffers' Medea discovers that she has been overheard by the Nurse and the Chorus, she says,

> I understand
>   well enough
> That nothing is ever private in a Greek city; whoever
>   withholds anything
> Is thought sullen or proud ... [*with irony*] undemocratic
> I think you call it.
>   (*Medea,* pp. 13–14)

Anticipating Jason's speech, Medea adds that "justice, at least on earth, / Is a name, not a fact" (p. 14). Since Jeffers himself was under fire at the time for his attacks on civilization and democratic society, there is double irony

in Medea's remarks and in Jason's recital of the advantages
he has given Medea in exchange for her well-known feats
in the search for the Golden Fleece. To Medea, Jason
says:

> I carried
> you
> Out of the dirt and superstition of Asiatic Colchis into the
> rational
> Sunlight of Greece, and the marble music of the Greek
> temples: is that no benefit? And I have brought you
> To meet the first minds of our time, and to speak as an equal
> with the great heroes and the rulers of cities.
>
> (*Medea,* p. 38)

Euripides' Jason, in a corresponding speech, mentions that
he has given Medea the advantage of living in Hellas according to law and justice instead of by will of force in
Colchis. In either play, these speeches are insulting enough
to Medea, but I want to point out the subtle change which
Jeffers has made. First, he has Medea anticipate the
speech in her thoughts about justice, and, second, Jason
emphasizes rationality, balance, and intellectual superiority, i.e., the qualities of mind from which the institutions
of justice and law may be expected to arise. But, from her
point of view as an abused foreigner, Medea sees only the
institutions, the facades of the minds which Jason describes
and the realities with which she must deal, and they lack the
nobility that Jason attributes to them. There is also a suggestion here of the Nietzschean contempt for institutions
that merely protect weakness and obscure pettiness.

Jeffers is careful to remain within the Euripidean framework of the play, but there are other Jeffersian alterations.
Where one would expect Jeffers to minimize such arguments as Jason's to the effect that what Medea has done for
him she has done simply as an instrument of Venus, these

arguments are not only retained but to some extent reinforced by additions. For example, when a woman of the
Chorus tries to prevent Medea's slaying of her sons, she
calls (without authority) that a god is outside, as if that
information would stop her. When she sends the boys to
Creüsa with deadly gifts, Medea says that the gods are smil-
ing to see such "open undisguised traps . . . take the proud
race of man" (p. 77) and to the Chorus she explains, "God
and my vengeful goddess are doing these things" (p. 79).
Clearly, Jeffers is trying to distinguish between the contrasting modes of respect accorded divinity. Medea's deity
closely resembles that of Jeffers—severe, aloof, powerful,
and indifferent. But the deity of the civilized Greeks—Jason and the Chorus—is a god of convenience whom they
seek to manipulate to serve their own ends. To the Chorus,
which tries to dissuade her, Medea answers, "I do according to nature what I have to do" (p. 80), adding the Nietzschean thought that, "Only a coward or a madman gives
good for evil" (p. 81). Hence Medea intends to express
great contempt for Jason when she says, after his speech in
which he attributes all of Medea's sacrifices for him to the
undeniable will of the goddess Venus,

> Here it is: the lowest.
> The obscene dregs; the slime and the loathing; the muddy
>   bottom of a mouthed cup: when a scoundrel begins
> To invoke the gods.
>
> (Medea, p. 39)

In Medea's eyes, Jason has just exposed the baseness of his
"civilized" theocracy, the same grounds upon which Nietzsche and Jeffers attacked Christianity.

At the end of the poem, when the Nurse says of Medea's
crime, "It was destined when she was born" (p. 98), there
is a hint that she and the Chorus have learned nothing after all. In their platitudes and attempts to smooth things

over, they appear unchanged. Jeffers' Medea, however, who said earlier, "I am alone against all" (p. 31), leaves the abject Jason in Corinth, saying, "Now I go forth / Under the cold eyes of the weakness-despising stars:—not me they scorn" (p. 107).

With nearly surprising adroitness, Jeffers took the already congenial tragedy of Medea and gave it his distinguishing impress with both skill and restraint. Before leaving Jeffers' *Medea*, we should note at least one instance of an interpolation from the poetry of Sappho. In Medea's last speech before she goes into the house with her children, having decided that they must die, she says,

> Evening brings all things home. It brings the
> bird to the bough and the lamb to the fold—
> And the child to the mother.
>
> (*Medea*, p. 96)

Medea's speech indicates the actual coming of evening—the stage darkens throughout the action of the murders and Jason's discovery scene before the mysterious lamps—and Jeffers has her recite an often-anthologized poem by Sappho variously titled *Evening* or *Invocation of Hesperus:*

> All that the glittering morn hath driven afar
> Thou callest home, O evening star!
> Thou callest sheep, thou callest kid to rest,
> And children to their mother's breast.[15]

The Cretan Woman

The Cretan Woman is based on the *Hippolytus* of Euripides, but there are important changes. Jeffers probably had Agnes Moorehead in mind for the part and was simply trying to produce another exciting play with a strong female leading role, because his Phaedra, unlike Euripides', lives longer than Hippolytus, almost to the end of the poem.[16] Euripides is concerned with Hippolytus, with

honor, and with inequality between men and gods. Euripides' Phaedra and Hippolytus, who are beset with the
mischievous design of Aphrodite, struggle to be honorable
and decent, but they perish in their effort, and Theseus is
brought low by his inability to understand what is happen-
ing, although his actions appear to be justified.

In his version, Jeffers preserved the controlling motivation of Aphrodite's revenge and also attempted an unexpected bit of social criticism. Euripides is noted for his social commentary, as in the discussion of the role of women
in Medea's speech or in Alcestis' examination of human
fidelity, but Jeffers created a Chorus of filthy and impover-
ished wives, who have drinking husbands and little food at
home. (One of the women observes late in the play that
rich men ought to be able to buy security.) Indeed, the
Chorus is present at Phaedra's gate simply because they are
awaiting a royal dole, which gives them an interesting perspective from which to observe the troubles of their superi-
ors.

In his attempt to write a strong play that would sustain
his Phaedra to the end and give her ample room in which
to move, Jeffers has sacrificed some of the moral tone of the
original. Besides prolonging the debate between Phaedra
and her stepson, Jeffers has given a clear picture of Hippolytus' homosexual nature.[17] By investing his Hippolytus
with this attribute, Jeffers introduced what Phaedra herself calls an "impediment of nature"; it precluded the ultimate necessity for Hippolytus to make moral choices, and
thereby weakened his role, something Euripides carefully
avoided. Jeffers departed from his model in two other significant ways. Unlike the Phaedra of Euripides, Jeffers'
Phaedra quickly and clearly confesses to Hippolytus her
passion for him. The love of Euripides' Phaedra might
have gone unidentified had it not been for the interven-

tion of her less idealistic Nurse. And whereas Euripides' Phaedra and Theseus do not meet on stage, Jeffers' husband and wife do meet, quarrel, make up, and quarrel again. As a result of these structural changes, Jeffers may have enhanced the psychology of his characters, and perhaps he made them more "realistic" for modern audiences, but he has lost, it seems to me, the intense intellectual air of the original play at the human level.[18] What could Jeffers have gained by these changes? The answer is obvious: Jeffers seized upon Euripides' play as the opportunity to reiterate his own message.

The Phaedra of Euripides is the victim of Aphrodite's revenge on the unfaithful Hippolytus (and so is Jeffers'), but she is also the unlucky inheritress of the legendary Pasiphaean predisposition to violent passion. Thus the psychology of Euripides' Phaedra is partly explained by inherited traits, but Jeffers' Phaedra makes no such claims upon legend. Instead, she is clearly portrayed as the representative of a different civilization from that of Hippolytus and Theseus. Early in the play, Jeffers' Phaedra is described by Selene, her waiting-woman, as "royal-born, / Of the most highly cultured family in Europe!" (*Hungerfield*, p. 31) and shrieking at the "mere smell" of raw meat. In her attempt to persuade Hippolytus to accept her love, Phaedra, in a speech that softly echoes a Nietzschean argument, says to the youth:

         —Listen to me: I am a civilized person,
  Hippolytus, in exile here
Among savages: the fierce little cutthroat tribes of Greece,
    feudists and killers. Lovers of tragedy! —We Cretans
Love light and laughter. We like things refined and brilliant;
    bright games, gay music, brave colors.
     · · · · · · · · · ·
—I tell you, Hippolytus, there are two heads of civilization
  on earth: Egypt and Crete: but holy Egypt

Is so old, so old, stone-stiff and pious
In the petrified desert: we Cretans
Can be passionate still. We have hot blood, we love beauty,
    we hate bigotry,
We know that good and evil and virtue and sin—are words,
    tired words: but *love* is more beautiful than sunrise....
                                    (*Hungerfield*, pp. 49–50)

Phaedra not only considers herself more civilized than the
Greeks, who have an obvious moral advantage over her in
the play, but she also insists that she is representative of
the civilization which she describes, not an exception to it.
Furthermore, three civilizations are contrasted at different
stages of maturity: old Egypt, "stone-stiff and pious";
Crete, "passionate still"; and Greece, "Lovers of tragedy."
According to Jeffers' theories of cycles or waves of civilization, Egypt is in a trough, Crete is passing a crest, and
Greece is ascending. Unlike Medea, who came "Out of the
dirt and superstition of Asiatic Colchis into the rational /
Sunlight of Greece" (*Medea*, p. 38), Phaedra comes to
Greece from civilized Crete, where good, evil, virtue, and
sin are tired words. Jeffers, then, gives Phaedra the attributes of decaying civilization as well as the space in which
to display them dramatically.

In his *Medea*, Jeffers explored some of the relationships
between men and gods, and in *The Cretan Woman*, with
its underlying theme of divine revenge, it was natural that
he should continue his examination of the subject. Before
Phaedra uses the argument of superior civilization quoted
above, she tells Hippolytus that people must accept what
the gods send—

                        They send sickness or health, evil or
    good, passionate longing
Or the power to resist it. We have to do
What the gods choose.
                                    (*Hungerfield*, p. 47)

Hippolytus replies, "Not entirely," for he denies her "civilized" sophism, saying, "We have to *suffer* what they choose: but we control our own wills and acts / For good and evil" (*Hungerfield*, p. 47). Phaedra appears later to have learned this lesson from Hippolytus, for, after he is dead and Theseus explains the murder with the remark that "Some god came into me" (*Hungerfield*, p. 83), Phaedra replies to her husband: "How cowardly it is in men, to say / That a god did it! *You* did it. [*a pause*] And *I* ... deluded you" (*Hungerfield*, p. 84). Another lesson which Phaedra may have learned from the Greeks is shown in a later speech. Watching the lamentation of Theseus, who has killed his blameless son, Phaedra says, referring to her husband:

> ... I have almost come to the
> Greek opinion: that there is nothing
> Nobler than a great man in his mortal grief. Or ... [*she begins to weep*] a loved beautiful youth ...
> Suddenly slain.
>
> (*Hungerfield*, p. 85)

In her speech, Phaedra reiterates what Jeffers had said about Cawdor and Thurso and their successors, who suffered greatly and well. And in Phaedra's afterthought about the slain Hippolytus, can there be another trace of the Heraclitean doctrine regarding people who are quickly killed as it appeared in the first part of *The Double Axe?*

In his study of Jeffers, Gilbert wrote over three decades ago: "Jeffers, as does Euripides, reflects the feelings of a changeful epoch in an outgrown culture that is gradually disappearing. He himself is a genuine offspring of our age of transition."[19] With Gilbert's judgment no one would wish to quarrel, and this chapter has shown that Jeffers continued in his predilection for Euripidean themes and that he reshaped the originals to convey his own message and theories. His rendering of the *Oresteia* of Aeschylus was cast in a Euripidean mold to incorporate the Nietzscheanism which Jeffers explored during the twenties. Euripides, who is remembered as much for his examination of society and individual psychology as for his questioning of irresponsible gods, also attracted Jeffers as strongly in the last period of his work as in the twenties and thirties. Euripides, whose themes occasionally converged with those of Nietzsche, presented Jeffers with useful models for the development of his own ideology.

8

the order of nature

So far in this study of Jeffers' use of ideas, I have emphasized the philosophy of Nietzsche and the related ideologies of the "Spenglerians" because together these ideas constitute a key to Jeffers' own doctrinal position. By tracing what I have referred to collectively as "Nietzscheanism" in the poet's major work and by studying his disposition of the various principles associated with this body of thought, I have attempted to show how the poet's own doctrine evolved through successive periods of trial and was influenced by coinciding historical developments. As the original force of Nietzsche's ideas in the poems of the twenties waned in the subsequent volumes, another ideology, which the poet called Inhumanism, developed to all but replace the Nietzscheanism. In *The Double Axe,* the various lines of thought contributing to Jeffers' Inhumanism come together for the fullest expression of the validity of its tenets.[1] In the preface to this volume, Jeffers described Inhumanism:

[The poem's] burden, as of some previous work of mine, is to present a certain philosophical attitude, which might be called Inhumanism, a shifting of emphasis and significance from man to not-man; the rejection of human solipsism and recognition of the transhuman magnificence.... This manner of thought and feeling is neither misanthropic nor pessimist, though two or three people have said so and may again. It involves no falsehoods, and is a means of maintaining sanity in slippery times; it has objective truth and human value. It offers a reasonable detachment as rule of conduct, instead of love, hate and envy. It neutralizes fanaticism and wild hopes; but it provides magnificence for the religious instinct, and satisfies our need to admire greatness and rejoice in beauty.

Nietzschean thought was never discarded altogether, for elements of it can be traced down to, and including, the posthumous volume of poems. The poet's "thirty-year-old" decision, which I have mentioned on several occasions, meant adopting Nietzsche's philosophy and using it as the beginning of the search for "new discovery." New discovery occasionally involved the testing and discarding of those Nietzschean ideas—for example, the original conception of the Overman—which proved to be more of a liability than an asset to the evolution of the poet's ideology.

Lucretius

Inhumanism depended on Nietzscheanism to clear away certain preconceptions, but it drew inspiration from Lucretius' great poem *De Rerum Natura*.[2] As an identifiable intellectual position, Inhumanism first appeared in *Roan Stallion*, when Jeffers announced that the crust or mold of humanity must be ruptured to free the inner man. In this poem, Jeffers demonstrated that it is precisely her human qualities that inhibit California's complete liberation from socialized behavior, in spite of the fact that briefly she had access to suprahuman experience and a consequent identification with the divinity in nature. Reverend Barclay, in *The Women at Point Sur,* is intended to show the irresponsible misinterpretation of the " 'Roan Stallion' idea." As we shall see, however, the language of Barclay's incitement to his people ("be your desires . . . flame . . . enter freedom") is pertinent to the argument being developed here.[3] In *The Tower Beyond Tragedy,* the problem of transcending human nature is more explicitly stated in Aegisthus' warning to Clytemnestra to beware of passing altogether beyond nature, and his metaphor is that of an arrow-flight going too far beyond the wall of humanity. Elements of these images are also present in the poet's advice, in *Meditation on Saviors,* that the human mind that loves the coast opposite humanity is healthiest—"it is worst turned inward, it is best shot farthest" (*Cawdor,* p. 160). Through his association with Clare Walker, in *The Loving Shepherdess,* Onorio Vasquez becomes aware that there is no annihilation in store for him, only the possibility of change. He compares himself with Clare, who loves all things because she can identify with them, and in the light of his shortcomings in this respect he concludes, "But I remain from myself divided, gazing beyond the flaming walls, / Not fortunate enough, and too faint-hearted" (*Judas,* p. 107).

What is the relevance of these passages to the discussion of Lucretius, since they come from poems written by Jeffers during the twenties, when Nietzsche's influence is most obvious? All these images occur in important ideological cruxes, and for the most part they have in common the notion of passing beyond a formal limit in the sense of transcending a barrier or enclosure—but not in the sense of Nietzschean transcendence, which always remains intellec-

tual and abstract. These images remain insistently concrete
—perhaps farfetched—and imply a change in state. In addition to the wall element—"the four walls of humanity" referred to explicitly in *The Torch-Bearers' Race*—there is a
second element of "flame" in most of the quotations.
The "flaming wall" image comes from the beginning of
Book 1 of Lucretius' *De Rerum Natura*. In Jeffers' poems,
the image usually occurs at that point where the Nietzschean exploration of the human situation falters and
where the Inhumanist position is presented, tentatively or
conclusively, as a desirable alternative. It is curious that
the "flaming wall" image occurs in Lucretius when he
sounds most like Nietzsche or Jeffers. Praising the service
to mankind of his master Epicurus, Lucretius recounts
how Epicurus, "extra / processit longe flammantia moenia
mundi."[4] "When the life of man lay foul to see and gro-
velling upon the earth, crushed by the weight of religion,"
Lucretius tells us, Epicurus dared to confront superstition
and religious conservatism and with "the eager daring of
his mind to yearn to be the first to break through the close-
set bolts upon the doors of nature" (p. 179). Continuing
his praise of Epicurus, Lucretius tells us that Epicurus
"passed on far beyond the fiery walls of the world, and in
mind and spirit traversed the boundless whole; whence in
victory he brings us tidings what can come to be and what
cannot. . . . And so religion in revenge is cast beneath
men's feet and trampled, and victory raises us to heaven"
(pp. 179–80). Lucretius immediately proceeds to discuss
the impiety of religion, citing, in a striking passage, the
sacrifice of Iphigenia as one of the most flagrant abuses of
religion so far recorded. And in Jeffers' work, we recall,
the earliest appearance of the wall image is in Aegisthus'
speech to Clytemnestra in *The Tower Beyond Tragedy*. It
is apparent that Lucretius commends Epicurus for what,

from a Nietzschean point of view, might be called Epicurus' Revaluation of Values and his Antichrist position. The similarity between Lucretius and Nietzsche, however, in no way diminishes the validity of the earlier discussion of the influence of Nietzsche on Jeffers, because, of course, Lucretius does not postulate the Overman or sublimation or the Will to Power or Eternal Recurrence. Lucretius does, however, endorse Epicurus' rebellion from traditional views and confining religious orthodoxy. In effect, Epicurus cleared the way for the new, and apparently sometimes unpopular, views of Lucretius, just as Nietzsche showed Jeffers some of the preparatory steps in developing his own doctrine of Inhumanism.

Let us consider further the "flaming wall" image in Jeffers' work. Several references have already been made to the passage in "The Inhumanist" section of *The Double Axe,* in which the old man, sickened by humanity and its spiritual impoverishment, addresses himself prayerfully to the beauty of Nature. The puma, the hawk, the dove, and even the rattlesnake are noble and beautiful because they "are in the nature of things," but the old man feels he is unable to participate completely in the many-splendored beauty of Nature. He is not entirely disappointed, however, for he says, "two or three times in my life my walls have fallen—beyond love—no room for love— / I have been you" (p. 89). The old man has on rare occasions broken away, like California, from the mold of humanity and passed, unlike Onorio Vasquez, beyond the four walls of his humanity. Instead of gazing, he has gone beyond the flaming walls. Following the poet's advice in *Meditation on Saviors,* the old man has loved the coast opposite humanity. The salvation of man's spirit depends upon his ability to discard his illusions about himself and the rest of humanity and upon his capacity to concentrate on honest and appreciative identification with the superior value of Nature.

When Jeffers, in his final volume of verses, explained the nature of things in *The Beginning and the End,* he described how the "virus" of life grew from protein molecules which gathered and multiplied in "the ammoniac atmosphere" until they formed cellular structures, thus isolating the life within from the outside world. Jeffers then proceeded to relate the origin of life to Lucretius' image:

> But why would life maintain itself,
> Being nothing but a dirty scum on the sea
> Dropped from foul air? Could it perhaps perceive
> Glories to come? Could it foresee that cellular life
> Would make the mountain forest and the eagle dawning,
> Monstrously beautiful, wings, eyes and claws, dawning
> Over the rock-ridge? And the passionate human intelligence
> Straining its limits, striving to understand itself and the
>   universe to the last galaxy—
> *Flammantia moenia mundi,* Lucretius wrote,
> Alliterating like a Saxon—all those Ms mean majesty—
> The flaming world-walls, far-flung fortifications of being
> Against not-being.
>
> (Beginning, p. 6)

The source of the metaphor which I have been tracing and the significance which I have attributed to it are unquestionably confirmed in this late poem.

Earlier in this study I referred to Jeffers' materialism, as Santayana used the term in his essay on Lucretius. Materialism, like any system of natural philosophy, according to Santayana, "merely describes the world, including the aspirations and consciences of mortals, and refers all to a material ground." Santayana observed that Epicurus, whose philosophy Lucretius adopted and modified, was remarkable for his mercy and mildness, and his horror of war and suffering; for ordinarily the naturalist "will believe in a certain hardness, as Nietzsche did; he will incline to a certain scorn, as the laughter of Democritus was scornful."[5] Lucretius restored a certain hardness to Epicurus' materialism, and Jeffers made it harder still. *De Rerum Natura* shows how Jeffers adapted it to suit his doctrine of Inhumanism.

On the topics of religion, of the creation of the universe, of the world as organism, and of the nature of being, Jeffers and Lucretius may be usefully compared. A fine distinction must be made between Lucretius and Jeffers on the subject of religion. Lucretius saw religion as a superstitious impediment to man's understanding the world because he believed that, although they existed somewhere in space, the gods had nothing to do with the creation of the universe. The world and its life came into being by the accidental collision of atoms, as Democritus described it. But if the gods had made the universe for man and given him the "glorious nature" of the world, Lucretius says to Memmius, his patron, it would be foolish to imagine that they did so to merit the gratitude of mankind, because the thanks of man could not possibly benefit them (p. 441). Furthermore, the obvious imperfections of the world refute the notion that it is divinely made (p. 443). Schopenhauer must have known that these arguments came from Lucretius' *De Rerum Natura*, especially Book 5, for he rejected pantheism on precisely the same grounds.[6] Jeffers, who wrote in *To His Father*, "Christ was your lord and captain all your life, / He fails the world but you he did not fail," could not, however, accept all of Lucretius at this point. Jeffers could condemn institutionalized Christianity, but he could not give up God the creator.[7] By striking a compromise with Lucretian philosophy, Jeffers retained for himself the idea of a divinely created universe, and added the idea that God feels no obligation toward man and remains indifferent to man's situation. On the notion of pantheism, Jeffers had to make a corresponding adjustment. Lucretius said that the world was made up of atoms of matter and space in combinations of varying density, and no god could be held responsible for them. Jeffers believed that God is manifest in all created things, and that to recognize the beauty of Nature is to reverence the God in Nature. Such poems as *Sign-Post, Air-Raid Rehearsals,* and *The Double Axe* reveal Jeffers' attitude toward the divinity of things, and, in *Look, How Beautiful,* the poet says that the beauty of Nature is God's signature. Jeffers' logic is simple enough: he accepted the atomic theory of Lucretius, but if God created the atoms which are present in all things, then by the act of creation all things are by extension divine.

Finally, Lucretius believed that the world was newly made and, because of his limited conception of organicism, that the continuing growth and improvement of certain arts proved his argument. Unlike Jeffers, Lucretius had none of the doctrine of nineteenth-century Darwinism available to him; consistent with his atomic theory, Lucretius denied the possibility of what we would call evolution of species, but he did recognize in Nature a simple adaptation in the life processes of growth and decline. In *The Beginning and the End,* as well as in other poems, Jeffers studiously sought evolutionary links to demonstrate that life originated from an accidental combination of elements—an assumption Lucretius would have favored—and then went through changes of species (e.g., ape to man); Lucretius, however, could not accept this latter theory because he classified atoms into finite species.

Lucretius had an interesting explanation of the renewal of things. If Nature had not set some limit to decay and disintegration, he argues, all things would eventually be destroyed beyond recognition. Nature has apparently set limits to the breaking up which it will allow, "and at the same time fixed seasons ordained for all things after their kind, in the which they may be able to reach the flower of their life" (p. 45). When Jeffers wrote, in *The Answer,* that the "greatest beauty is organic wholeness," he probably did not draw his organic ideas from Lucretius, since such theories were available, more fully developed, from the historicists with whom he was acquainted. He might have been impressed, however, by the effort Lucretius made to account for and to defend the concept of organicism.

An examination of Lucretius' ideas about the nature of being discloses that Jeffers' search for the "virus" of life may not be as alien to Lucretian thought as at first it may appear. The earth is and always has been insentient (p. 271), says Lucretius, and it is apparent that, since the earth is the mother of many beginnings, whatever is sentient is nonetheless composed of atoms that are insentient (p. 281). Anticipating by centuries the second law of thermodynamics, Lucretius resolutely holds that there is no annihilation of matter; thus death must mean nothing more than the redistribution of a being's atoms in new combinations and in other forms. "What once sprung from earth," Lucretius writes, "sinks back into the earth, and what was sent down from the coasts of the sky, returns again, and the regions of heaven receive it" (p. 289).

Jeffers' scientific training taught him the principle of the conservation of matter, and over and over again his poems affirm that there is no annihilation. Plainly, the secret, then, of escaping from the mold of humanity in order to mingle one's atoms with the greater splendor and divinity of Nature is death. Death is the event that leads to the rearrangement and distribution of a being's atoms among those from which they originally sprang. Death is nothing

to be feared, both Lucretius and Jeffers agreed, because
there is no afterlife of punishment. For an individual with
Jeffers' temperament and regard for humanity as a transient sickness, death is the ultimate stage of Inhumanism;
it is the way for Onorio to unite with himself beyond the
flaming walls, and death, after all, is the passport to the
coast opposite humanity. In life, an individual may press
against a rock—as in *Sign-Post*—and hope, with Wordsworth, to feel the divinity in it. But where Wordsworth's
pantheism was simply the assurance of God's benign presence in the world of Nature, Jeffers' pantheism offered the
undeniable opportunity to join the divinity of Nature.
Thus the dead man lying beneath Jeffers' *Inscription for a
Gravestone* exults, "now I am part of the beauty." In *Ani-
mula*, the poet says,

> The immortality of the soul—
> God save us from it! To live for seventy years is a burden—
> To live eternally, poor little soul—
> Not the chief devil could inflict nor endure it.

Using the analogy of death and *The Shears* with which his
"flower-greedy daughter-in-law" has snipped off a rose, and
taken it indoors to join the life that the flower watched
through a window, Jeffers draws the lesson:

> —So we: death comes and plucks us: we become part of the
>   living earth
> And wind and water whom we so loved. We are they.

In *Hungerfield,* a poem about a man who tried to interfere with the process and promise of death, the poet's apostrophe to his dead wife appears less bizarre, certainly more
reasonable, in the light of his adaptation of Lucretian philosophy. To Una, who he knew had an unmatched admiration for Nature, Jeffers says:

> You are earth
> and air; you are in the beauty of the ocean
> And the great streaming triumphs of sundown; you are alive
> and well in the tender young grass rejoicing
> When soft rain falls all night, and little rosy-fleeced clouds
> float on the dawn. —I shall be with you presently.
>
> (*Hungerfield*, p. 23)

In Lucretius, Jeffers discovered escape from the carapace
of humanity, the consolation of union with divine Nature,
and, apparently, a satisfactory reunion with those loved
ones already dead. Hence his longing for death cannot be
regarded as morbid despair but, rather, as the anticipation
of promised fulfillment. Obviously, both Schopenhauer
and Jeffers read Lucretius attentively and then went their
separate ways. To confuse them on these issues is foolhardy
and wrong-headed.

As a final comparison of Jeffers' work with *De Rerum
Natura,* there is the passage in "The Inhumanist" section
of *The Double Axe* in which the old man ponders the
form in which God exists. Of course, God does exist, the
old man declares, adding,

> there is not an atom in all the universes
> But feels every other atom; gravitation, electromagnetism,
> light, heat, and the other
> Flamings, the nerves in the night's black flesh, flow them to-
> gether; the stars, the winds and the people: one energy,
> One existence, one music, one organism, one life, one God:
> star-fire and rock-strength, the sea's cold flow
> And man's dark soul.

> Not a tribal nor an anthropoid God.
> Not a ridiculous projection of human fears, needs, dreams,
> justice and love-lust.
>
> (*Double Axe*, p. 53)

In this passage, Jeffers' Inhumanist acknowledges the essential unity of one existence and one God, and disavows all religion and ritual, either institutionalized or private. Lucretius has a comparable but not exactly parallel passage, in which he takes men to task for the false religion and superstitious beliefs that lead them to blame gods for their mortal condition:

> Ah! unhappy race of men, when it has assigned such acts to the gods and joined therewith bitter anger! what groaning did they then beget for themselves, what sores for us, what tears for our children to come! Nor is it piety at all to be seen often with veiled head turning towards a stone, and to draw near to every altar, no, nor to lie prostrate on the ground with outstretched palms before the shrines of the gods, nor to sprinkle the altars with the streaming blood of beasts, nor to link vow to vow, but rather to be able to contemplate all things with a mind at rest. For indeed when we look up at the heavenly quarters of the great world, and the ether set with twinkling stars, and it comes to our mind to think of the journeyings of sun and moon, then into our hearts weighed down with other ills, this misgiving too begins to raise up its wakened head, that there may be perchance some immeasurable power of the gods over us, which whirls on the bright stars in their diverse motions. (p. 495)

Although there are other inviting correspondences between the ideologies of Jeffers and Lucretius on the questions of atomic theory, the nature of the soul, the psychology of sensation, the use of sex, and the beginnings of civilization, they are less impressive because of the more likely influences of Spengler, Petrie, and Ellis. Furthermore, these similarities are sometimes obscured by the theories and discoveries of modern science. For Jeffers, it was enough that *De Rerum Natura* nourished his own Inhumanism.

Spinoza

Having attempted to analyze the Nietzsche-Lucretius axis at the center of Jeffers' Inhumanism, I should like to consider briefly the possible philosophical influence of some of Spinoza's carefully reasoned metaphysics of naturalism. In the poet's work, there is no explicit internal evidence to support the supposition that Spinoza's might have been an affective voice. But from the repetition of certain themes in the poetry and from one explicit external statement we may infer that the similarities in themes and in questions raised suggest at least the implicit influence of Spinoza. Perhaps Spinoza's influence is less obvious because his writing, unlike that of Nietzsche and Lucretius, is predominantly abstract, lacking the powerful images and lively language of Nietzsche and Lucretius, and therefore left Jeffers with less concrete data (i.e., images, language, and striking conceptualizations) that he could assimilate into his own work.

In his *Ethics* (pt. 1, props. 4 and 5), Spinoza repudiated the common Jewish and Christian idea of a creation which necessarily implies a dualism, i.e., Creator and creation, for he held that a monistic conception of creation must follow the acceptance of his theory of the unique, infinite, and all-inclusive substance which he referred to as *Deus sive Natura* (God or Nature).[8] For his contemporaries Spinoza's *Deus sive Natura* implied horrifying pantheism. But this concept, as Spinoza intended it, never was meant to validate any associations with mystical intuitions or with a poetic and romantic feeling of the splendor and unity of Nature, for he dissociated the word "God" from all traditional figurative epithets that insisted on anthropomorphic and personal images. Instead Spinoza moved coolly and logically to the reasoned position that God and Nature cannot be distinguished, and that man is a part of Nature. Summarizing Spinoza's views about the relationship of man to Nature, Stuart Hampshire wrote: "To Spinoza it seemed that men can attain happiness and dignity only by identifying themselves, through their knowledge and understanding, with the whole order of nature, and by submerging their individual interests in this understanding."⁹ With remarkable insight, which he cautiously calls "no more than speculative," Hampshire pondered whether this aspect of Spinoza's naturalism could not be "the surviving spirit of Lucretius against a greater background of knowledge."

It is precisely this "spirit of Lucretius" in Spinoza which might have drawn Jeffers to him. To consider what these different inquiries have in common, the reader has only to recall the insistence of Jeffers' characters or narrators to declare, in *Intellectuals,* for example, that God includes everything in existence, or in *Sign-Post* that "Things are the God, you will love God," or in "The Inhumanist" section of *The Double Axe* the old man's belief in the oneness of all things, or in *Fog* the worshippers' faith in the oneness of God and things. Orestes, in *The Tower Beyond Tragedy,* has always troubled readers and thereby troubled Jeffers as well, who believed that he had made Orestes a sufficiently clear character. When Powell was preparing his study of Jeffers in 1931, he asked if Orestes was akin to that part of Buddhistic thought which holds that man's knowledge of himself is limited "whilst [he] remain[s] immersed in this all-undermining dream of Selfhood?" Jeffers wrote back:¹⁰

> I feel for much in Oriental thought, though I don't enjoy reading any Oriental book except the bible. But the Indian feeling that the world is illusory and the soul—the *I*—makes it, is very foreign to me. The world seems to me immeasur-

ably more real. Am I wrong in thinking that the Oriental mystic identifies the world with himself, and my "Orestes" identified himself with the world? The former imposes a human mind on an imaginary world—attributes to it his own "love," for instance, or desire of love; the latter let in the inhuman mind of the world (Deus sive natura—Spinoza's phrase) to obliterate his human one.[11]

Asked to explain a problematical point in his poem, Jeffers goes directly to Spinoza and the concept which Orestes illustrates.

Although Jeffers readily acknowledged what Spinoza denominated *Deus sive Natura*, he lamented the historical and cultural basis of man's jejune existence which divorced him from a real union with divine Nature. Georg Christoph Lichtenberg, the eighteenth-century German physicist and satirist, once described Spinoza's philosophy as the religion of the future, and one may say that Jeffers is Spinoza's twentieth-century evangelist. For Jeffers, modern man exists in a fallen state which is irreligious in mode. In Jeffers' view, modern man has, in effect, driven himself out of the garden of Nature, not because of pride or the sin of intellect, but simply because he lacks feeling, an appreciation of the splendor of Nature, a true evaluation of the superficiality of his decadent culture, i.e., failure of plain moral fiber, and finally because he lacks a kind of heroism.

Like Spinoza, Jeffers also tried to repudiate the anthropocentric interpretation of the universe.[12] In *See the Human Figure,* Jeffers warned: "to see the human figure in all things is man's disease," and we recall the poet's statements in a letter to James Rorty and in *Carmel Point* which urged that man must uncenter his mind from himself.[13] Quite plainly Jeffers believed that modern man's chances of redeeming himself are gravely limited by his insistent and ultimately self-alienating anthropocentric view of the

universe. Although Jeffers felt that the source of modern
man's malaise was his (often unconscious) alienation from
Nature, he was apparently convinced that certain rare individuals might succeed in getting beyond the mold of humanity, in breaking the boundaries of humanity, in loving
the "coast opposite humanity" by following the spirited example of his many hawk symbols and by recognizing the
everlasting permanence of Nature represented in his rock
symbols.

It appears, then, that Jeffers and Spinoza present striking similarities in their beliefs that the beauty, strength,
serenity, and values of God are identical with Nature because there can be no distinction between the Creator and
the creation. Spinoza developed a philosophy to show
man's position in the scheme of things. Jeffers, however,
was trying, less systematically to be sure, to demonstrate
how modern man had fallen out of his position in the
scheme of things and how he might effect his reinstate-
ment. Spinoza was religious in his outlook; Jeffers, perhaps
because of the temper of his time, was irreligious. I think
that it is a revealing symptom of the age in which the poet
lived that, though he could have shared some or all of the
ideas produced by a kindred spirit like Spinoza in an earlier period, he felt compelled to conduct his own quest and
to propose the dramatically individualistic solutions presented in his poems. For example, Jeffers would have dis-
agreed with Spinoza's belief that man was meant to live,
not as an isolated individual, but in a society where he
could strengthen his love of God by sharing it with others.[14]
It was the disease and empty religions of society which
prompted Jeffers' rebellion and search for new discovery.
Insofar as he endorsed the Nietzschean concept of the
Overman as a method by which the individual could overcome cultural and social stagnation and lifelessness of the

spirit, Jeffers differed with Spinoza again, for Spinoza argued that to think of a person fulfilling or failing to fulfill a purpose or design was to imply the existence of a Creator distinct from his creation. Furthermore, Spinoza claimed that, as man's knowledge and understanding of Nature and of his human nature as part of Nature increased, man would necessarily abandon the notion of free will. On this point, Jeffers also differed with Spinoza, for Jeffers tested and adapted the Nietzschean principles of Will to Power and Revaluation of Values, tempering them with Lucretian materialism.

Even though there was apparently no explicit Spinozan influence upon the ideology of Jeffers' poems, I believe, nevertheless, that the above comparisons tend to illuminate further the ideological tensions and the prevailing themes of alienation and loss not only in the work of Jeffers but in a large part of the literature of the first half of the twentieth century as well. Granted the similarities in temperament and philosophical goals of these two men, I interpret what they had in common and the manner in which they diverge ideologically as a manifestation of the more severe sense of spiritual deracination in the modern world—deracinated to the point that Inhumanism appeared practicable.

Robinson Jeffers used the various concepts of Nietzsche's philosophy to clear away outworn intellectual traditions and religious preconceptions in order to develop his own doctrine of Inhumanism. That Nietzscheanism was a useful—though sometimes limited—tool for Jeffers is now obvious. That his Lucretian-derived Inhumanism and its insistence upon transhuman magnificence flourished from inception is equally clear. Hence readers acquainted with both Nietzsche and Lucretius may achieve a more sensitive appreciation of the tumultuous grandeur and severe individualism of Jeffers' poetry. Readers who perceive Jeffers' unswerving faith in the order of Nature are better prepared to give a late poem like *Vulture* a fair reading. In this poem, Jeffers tells of resting on a hillside and of attracting the investigation of a soaring vulture. The man, though old, is not yet ready for death, but he considers the possibilities of the incident—and muses:

>   To be eaten
>   by that beak and become part of him, to share those
>   wings and those eyes—
> What a sublime end of one's body, what an enskyment; what
>   a life after death.

The proper study for the reading of Jeffers, then, is *Thus Spoke Zarathustra* and *De Rerum Natura*.

reference matter

notes

Chapter 1

1 Niven Busch, "Duel on a Headland," *Saturday Review of Literature* 11 (9 Mar. 1935): 533. Jeffers discusses Inhumanism in the preface to *The Double Axe and Other Poems* (New York, 1948), pp. vii–viii.

2 *Tamar and Other Poems* (New York: P. G. Boyle, 1924). With the addition of the poem *Roan Stallion*, this volume was published the following year as *Roan Stallion, Tamar and Other Poems* (New York: Boni & Liveright, 1925).

3 Radcliffe Squires, *The Loyalties of Robinson Jeffers* (Ann Arbor, 1956). Certain revisions of the 1956 edition and a new preface in the second edition, an Ann Arbor Paperback in 1963, mention the last volume of verse.

4 Squires, *Loyalties,* p. viii.

5 Squires, *Loyalties,* p. ix.

6 Cf. Frederic I. Carpenter, "The Values of Robinson Jeffers," *American Literature* 11 (Jan. 1940): 353–66; and "Death Comes for Robinson Jeffers," *University Review* 7 (Dec. 1940): 97–104, reprinted in Carpenter's *American Litera-*

ture and the Dream (New York: Philosophical Library, 1955), pp. 144–54.

7 George Sterling, *Robinson Jeffers: The Man and the Artist* (New York, 1926), pp. 2, 8.

8 "Harrowed Marrow," *Time* 19, no. 14 (4 Apr. 1932): 63–64.

9 Benjamin De Casseres, "Robinson Jeffers: Tragic Terror," *Bookman* 66 (Nov. 1927): 262–66.

10 Melba Berry Bennett, *The Stone Mason of Tor House: The Life and Work of Robinson Jeffers* (Los Angeles, 1966).

11 Robinson Jeffers, "A Few Memories," *Overland Monthly* 85 (Nov. 1927): 329, 351.

12 Robinson Jeffers, *The Selected Letters of Robinson Jeffers*, ed. Ann N. Ridgeway (Baltimore, 1968), no. 122 (5 Aug. 1927), p. 115.

13 Jeffers, *Themes in My Poems* (San Francisco, 1956), p. 7.

14 L. C. Powell has stressed this facet of the poet's life in "The Double Marriage of Robinson Jeffers," *Southwest Review* 41 (Summer, 1956): 278–82, and in his *Books in My Baggage* (Cleveland, 1960), pp. 139–47: identical articles based on an address delivered at Occidental College in 1955.

15 In the last years, Jeffers' work was severely limited by failing eyesight, and the task of selecting the poems for the volume fell largely to Mrs. Melba Berry Bennett, his friend and biographer. Cf. *The Stone Mason of Tor House*, pp. 236–38.

16 Jeffers, *The Double Axe*, p. vii.

17 The article was printed later by the Ward Ritchie Press, Los Angeles, 1949.

18 P. B. Shelley, *A Defence of Poetry*. In August 1966, Donnan Jeffers, the poet's son, granted me access to the remains of his father's library, but he had warned me previously that it was his mother's custom periodically to destroy or to give away to friends or libraries those books which, for one reason or another, had outlived their usefulness (Donnan Jeffers' letter to me, 24 Mar. 1965). From an inspection of the books, it became apparent that many of them belonged

to Una Jeffers, who had gathered both the works of and works on Shelley and Byron. For more on Una Jeffers' interest in Shelley, see Mrs. Bennett's *The Stone Mason of Tor House,* p. 163.

In spite of the inviting similarities between Jeffers' views on the roles of the poet and of poetry and the views of Whitman in the 1855 preface to *Leaves of Grass,* I concur with other commentators on Jeffers, who, following both internal and external evidence, see Milton, Shelley, and Yeats as the chief formative influences.

19 Robinson Jeffers, *The Selected Poetry of Robinson Jeffers* (New York, 1938), p. xiv.
20 Robinson Jeffers, foreword to D. H. Lawrence, *Fire and Other Poems* (San Francisco, 1940), p. viii.
21 Jeffers, *Selected Poetry,* p. xiv. Originally written for another purpose in 1922, these remarks first appeared in print in S. S. Alberts, *A Bibliography of the Works of Robinson Jeffers* (New York, 1933), pp. 109–14. See also L. C. Powell, *Robinson Jeffers: The Man and His Work* (Pasadena, 1940), p. 52.
22 Letter to Graham Bickley, University of California, Berkeley, in 1932, in Bennett, *Stone Mason,* pp. 151–52.
23 Jeffers, *Selected Poetry,* p. xiv.
24 Ibid., p. xv.
25 Ibid., p. xvi.
26 Cf. the early *To the Stone-Cutters* and the later reference to "flower-soft verse" in *Harder than Granite.*
27 Jeffers to H. H. Waggoner, 21 Nov. 1937, quoted by H. H. Waggoner in "Science and the Poetry of Robinson Jeffers," *American Literature* 10 (Nov. 1938): 287.
28 As Squires suggests in *Loyalties,* pp. 23–28, Jeffers felt certain psychological compulsions which might be traced to his youth, to the pattern of his life between college days and his marriage to Una, or to his parents. There seems to be no simple answer to explain the defensive tone which Jeffers' isolationist views occasionally assume.

29 Jeffers, *Selected Poetry*, p. xv.
30 "Poetry, Gongorism, and a Thousand Years."
31 Bennett, *Stone Mason*, p. 151.
32 Ibid.
33 Ibid., p. 153.
34 Robinson Jeffers, foreword to Powell's *Robinson Jeffers*, p. xvi. See also next note.
35 Bennett, *Stone Mason*, p. 152. In his tractate *Of Education*, Milton described poetry as "simple, sensuous, and passionate."
36 Powell, *Robinson Jeffers*, facing p. 55.
37 Jeffers, "A Few Memories," pp. 329, 351.
38 Powell, *Robinson Jeffers*, p. 118. See also Alberts, *Bibliography*, p. 150.
39 Herbert Klein, "The Prosody of Robinson Jeffers," M.A. thesis, Occidental College, 1930; this is still the most comprehensive study on the subject. See also C. C. Cunningham, "The Rhythm of Robinson Jeffers' Poetry as Revealed by Oral Reading," *Quarterly Journal of Speech* 32 (Oct. 1946): 351–57.
40 See Alberts, *Bibliography*, p. 147, and Powell, *Robinson Jeffers*, p. 106.
41 Cf. Jeffers' claim to F. I. Carpenter, "I think it is the business of a writer of poetry, not to express his own gospel, but to present images, emotions, ideas, and let the reader find his good in them if he can." Carpenter, "The Values of Robinson Jeffers," p. 356.
42 Benjamin Miller, "Toward a Religious Philosophy of the Theatre," *Personalist* 20 (Oct. 1939): 371.
43 Jeffers, *Selected Letters*, ed. Ridgeway, no. 272 (Feb. 1938), p. 262.
44 Cf. Jeffers, *The Double Axe*, p. vii, where the poet stresses his concern with presenting "a certain philosophical attitude."
45 Friedrich Nietzsche, *Beyond Good and Evil*, in *Basic Writings of Nietzsche*, trans. and ed. Walter Kaufmann (New York, 1968), p. 326.

Chapter 2

1 R. W. Short, "The Tower Beyond Tragedy," *Southern Review* 7 (Summer, 1941): 144, "cannot see any sense in" referring to Jeffers' work as Nietzschean. Oscar Cargill, *Intellectual America: Ideas on the March* (New York, 1941), p. 752, in a chapter entitled "The Freudians," refers to *The Women at Point Sur* as "ill-digested reading of Nietzsche." Charles Cestre, "Robinson Jeffers," *Revue Anglo-Américaine* 4 (Aug. 1927): 493, regards the poet as "un disciple émancipé d'Emerson, qui s'est mis à l'école de Nietzsche."

Benjamin De Casseres, "Robinson Jeffers," pp. 262–66, calls Rev. Barclay, in *The Women at Point Sur,* "Zarathustra-Satan, an illuminated incarnation of the New Evil," and *Roan Stallion* "the mystical dream of Nietzsche." James G. Fletcher, "The Dilemma of Robinson Jeffers," *Poetry* 43 (Mar. 1934): 339, says that Jeffers' "anti-human God... probably derived from Nietzsche." Rudolph Gilbert, *Shine, Perishing Republic: Robinson Jeffers and the Tragic Sense in Modern Poetry* (Boston, 1936), cites Nietzsche on pp. 80, 92, 96 (tragedy), 185 (dream and tragedy).

Horace Gregory, "Suicide in the Jungle," *New Masses* 10 (13 Feb. 1934): 18–19, says, "What he has written since 1925 seems to show that... he turned to Nietzsche and Greek drama for relief." Horace Gregory and M. A. Zaturenska, *History of American Poetry, 1900–1940* (New York, 1946), in the chapter "Robinson Jeffers and the Birth of Tragedy," pp. 400–403, 407, minimize Schopenhauer in favor of Nietzsche, refer to Nietzsche's *The Birth of Tragedy* as providing the basis for Jeffers' conception of reality, as well as supplying the Midas story from which sprang *The Tower Beyond Tragedy,* and conclude: "The great poet in [Jeffers] cannot get clear of Nietzsche's philosophy." Horace Gregory, "Poet Without Critics: A Note on Robinson Jeffers," in his *The Dying Gladiators and Other Essays* (New York, 1961), pp. 3–20, finds a resemblance be-

tween *Tamar* and Nietzsche's speech of Silenus in *The Birth of Tragedy*.
    Mercedes C. Monjian, *Robinson Jeffers: A Study in Inhumanism* (Pittsburgh, 1958), p. 2, says the poetry of Jeffers reveals "Nietzsche's sense of mission." Selden Rodman, "Transhuman Magnificence," *Saturday Review of Literature* 31 (31 July 1948): 14, calls Jeffers "the philosophical heir of Nietzsche and Spengler." Frajam Taylor, "The Enigma of Robinson Jeffers: II, The Hawk and the Stone," *Poetry* 55 (Oct. 1939): 39–44, compares Jeffers' hawk image to "the eagle of Nietzsche's Zarathustra," and sees Jeffers using Nietzsche's technique of denying "the joy of living ... merely ... to affirm more puissantly the thing he believes in...." and compares Tamar's speech to her father ("I'll show you our trouble, you sinned," etc.) to Nietzsche's "idea of a god who is willing not merely to bear the sins of mankind, but the guilt as well." H. H. Waggoner, *The Heel of Elohim: Science and Values in Modern American Poetry* (Norman, Okla., 1950), in the chapter "Robinson Jeffers: Here Is Reality," p. 126, sees *Margrave* as "the application of a philosophic theory, which seems to be a sort of Nietzschean nihilism." Eda Lou Walton, "Beauty of Storm Disproportionately," *Poetry* 51 (Jan. 1938): 210, says, "Freudian psychology and Nietzschean philosophy gave this poet the framework for his stories of man's tremendous revolt from mankind...." H. W. Wells, "A Philosophy of War: The Outlook of Robinson Jeffers," *College English* 6 (Nov. 1944): 86, assigns the poet "a belated place in the line of ultraromantic thought through Schopenhauer, Carlyle, Wagner, Nietzsche, D. H. Lawrence, and the Fascist Ezra Pound" and makes him "heir to a largely Germanic philosophy of violence...." A. N. Wilder, *The Spiritual Aspects of the New Poetry* (New York, 1940), in the chapter "Nihilism of Mr. Robinson Jeffers," p. 152, concludes, "If one must deprecate Mr. Jeffers one will say that he leans too much toward Nietzsche, rather than that he leans toward

the totemist!" Powell, *Robinson Jeffers,* refers to Nietzsche, p. 7, and to *Thus Spoke Zarathustra,* p. 152. Cf. G. G. Gates ("The Bread That Every Man Must Eat Alone," *College English* 4 [Dec. 1942]: 170–74) and H. H. Watts ("Robinson Jeffers and Eating the Serpent," *Sewanee Review* 49 [Jan. 1941]: 39–55), who analyze the Nietzschean characteristics of the poetry (e.g., theory of cycles, Eternal Recurrence, and Overcoming) without using specifically Nietzschean terminology.

2 C. I. Glicksberg, "The Poetry of Doom and Despair," *Humanist* 7 (Aug. 1947): 69–76, says, "Like Schopenhauer and Hartmann, Jeffers holds that existence is unalterably evil, but his conclusions are based on science and not on metaphysics." David B. Lutyens, *The Creative Encounter* (London, 1960), pp. 37–65, acknowledges his debt to Squires' *Loyalties,* and concurs that Jeffers' poetry represents "fusing the thought of Schopenhauer with the historicism of Oswald Spengler" (p. 38), yet he goes on to cite Jeffers' "doctrine . . . of self-transcendence" (p. 40).

3 Squires, *Loyalties,* p. 50.

4 Donnan Jeffers to Arthur B. Coffin, 24 March 1965.

5 See Jeffers, *Selected Letters,* ed. Ridgeway, no. 52 (16 Jan. 1926), pp. 57–58, where the poet speaks flatteringly of his Carmel barber and mentions talking with him "about Bergson and Schopenhauer."

6 Squires, *Loyalties,* p. 51.

7 Ibid., p. 50.

8 Ibid., p. 54.

9 See Walter Kaufmann, *Nietzsche: Philosopher, Psychologist, Antichrist,* 3d ed. (Princeton, N.J., 1968), pp. 152–53, 199.

10 Squires, *Loyalties,* p. 51.

11 Arthur Schopenhauer, *The World as Will and Idea,* trans. R. B. Haldane and J. Kemp, 3 vols. (London, 1883), vol. 1, p. 130. All subsequent quotes and references are to this edition, and citations indicated thus: 1:130, or 3:348–49.

12 Frederick Copleston, S.J., *Arthur Schopenhauer: Philosopher of Pessimism* (London, 1946), pp. 172–73. My example follows closely that in Fr. Copleston's text.

13 Patrick Gardiner, *Schopenhauer* (Baltimore: Penguin, 1963), p. 176 ff.

14 Quoted, ibid., p. 262.

15 Quoted, ibid., p. 263.

16 Waggoner, *Heel of Elohim*, pp. 105–32. See also John B. Watson, *The Battle of Behaviorism* (London, 1928), p. 27.

17 Cf. Gardiner, *Schopenhauer*, p. 294 ff.

18 Copleston, *Schopenhauer*, p. 122.

19 Arthur Schopenhauer, "A Few Words on Pantheism" from *Parerga und Parolipomena*, in *Religion: A Dialogue and Other Essays*, trans. T. Bailey Saunders. Schopenhauer Series, vol. 3. London, 1891.

20 Cf. Jeffers' foreword to Powell, *Robinson Jeffers*, p. xvi.

Chapter 3

1 Powell, *Robinson Jeffers*, p. 7.

2 In 1902, when Jeffers was fifteen, "according to one who knew him well . . . he was able to think in Italian, French, and German" (ibid., p. 7). Powell, *Books in My Baggage*, p. 142, also reports that Jeffers met his future wife in a class in Goethe's *Faust* at the University of Southern California graduate school, where she was "taking special work in German and philosophy." At first, Una resented Jeffers' joining the class because he, who had learned his German in Europe, replaced her as first in the class.

3 Alberts, *Bibliography*, p. xv. Cf. *Zarathustra*, pt. 4, chap. 4, "The Leech."

4 Friedrich Nietzsche, *The Birth of Tragedy*, in *Basic Writings of Nietzsche*, trans. and ed. Walter Kaufmann (New York, 1968), p. 35. Subsequent quotations from works in the *Basic Writings of Nietzsche* are indicated parenthetically in the text as *BWN*.

5 Kaufmann, *Nietzsche*, p. 102.

6 Ibid., p. 114.
7 Friedrich Nietzsche, *Thus Spoke Zarathustra,* in *The Portable Nietzsche,* trans. and ed. Walter Kaufmann (New York, 1954), p. 170. Subsequent quotations from works in *The Portable Nietzsche* are indicated parenthetically in the text as *PN.*
8 Quoted, Kaufmann, *Nietzsche,* p. 222.
9 Ibid., pp. 313–14. Cf. Nietzsche in *The Twilight of the Idols: "My conception of genius.* Great men, like great ages, are explosives in which a tremendous force is stored up; their precondition is always, historically and physiologically, that for a long time much has been gathered, stored up, saved up, and conserved for them—that there has been no explosion for a long time. . . . What does the environment matter then, or the age, or the 'spirit of the age,' or 'public opinion'! . . . The danger that lies in great men and ages is extraordinary; exhaustion of every kind, sterility, follow in their wake. The great human being is a finale; the great age—the Renaissance, for example—is a finale. The genius, in work and deed, is necessarily a squanderer: that he squanders himself, that is his greatness. The instinct of self-preservation is supended, as it were; the overpowering pressure of outflowing forces forbids him any such care or caution. People call this 'self-sacrifice' and praise his 'heroism,' his indifference to his own well-being, his devotion to an idea, a great cause, a fatherland: without exception, misunderstandings. He flows out, he overflows, he uses himself up, he does not spare himself—and this is a calamitous, involuntary fatality, no less than a river's flooding the land. Yet, because much is owed to such explosives, much has also been given them in return: for example, a kind of higher morality. After all, that is the way of human gratitude: It *misunderstands* its benefactors" (*PN,* pp. 547–48).
10 Donnan Jeffers to Arthur B. Coffin, 24 March 1965.
11 Quoted, Kaufmann, *Nietzsche,* p. 364.
12 Squires, *Loyalties,* p. 30.
13 Gates, "The Bread That Every Man Must Eat Alone," pp.

170–74, sees *Tamar* "flooded" with this atmosphere. In discussing *The Women at Point Sur* he also mentions cycles of events and patterns of behavior ("attitudes of humanity") without using Nietzschean terminology.

14 Gregory, "Poet without Critics: A Note on Robinson Jeffers," in his *The Dying Gladiators*, pp. 3–20, recognizes similarities between Nietzsche's speech of Silenus (*The Birth of Tragedy*), 2 Samuel, and Sade's *Justine*.

15 Jeffers, *Selected Letters,* ed. Ridgeway, no. 122 (5 Aug. 1927), pp. 115–16.

16 George Sterling, "Rhymes and Reactions," *Overland Monthly* 83 (Nov. 1925): 411, was obviously excited by Jeffers' "forbidden themes" (as Una called them) and exhorted his readers to get *Roan Stallion* and read it, although he had not yet seen it; cf. De Casseres, "Robinson Jeffers," pp. 262–66. In a review of *Roan Stallion, Tamar and Other Poems* in her magazine ("Power and Pomp," *Poetry* 28 [June 1926]: 160–64), Harriet Monroe wrote that *Roan Stallion* was " 'prentice work dug up and retouched . . . [and was] of a quality quite unworthy of the author of *Tamar.*" Percy Hutchison, referring to *Roan Stallion, Tamar and Other Poems,* wondered in print what Joseph Collins (author of *Taking the Literary Pulse: Psychological Studies of Life and Letters* [New York, 1924]) would think of these poems and the poet ("An Elder Poet and a Young One . . . ," *New York Times Book Review* [3 Jan. 1926], pp. 14, 24.

17 Monjian, *Robinson Jeffers*, p. 22.

18 Gilbert, *Shine, Perishing Republic*, p. 73. According to Gilbert's Note, Jeffers and his wife had read the manuscript.

19 Cestre, "Robinson Jeffers," pp. 491, 493.

20 Jeffers, *Selected Letters,* ed. Ridgeway, no. 122 (5 Aug. 1927), p. 116.

21 In the poem as it appears in *Roan Stallion, Tamar and Other Poems* (New York, 1925), other images of Clytemnestra's power occur on pp. 36, 37, 39, 42, 47, 48, 50, and 64.

22 Carpenter, *Robinson Jeffers*, p. 70.

23 Quoted, G. J. Nathan, "The Tower Beyond Tragedy," in *Theatre Book of the Year, 1950–1951* (New York, 1951), pp. 136–38. Production of the play began 26 Nov. 1950.

24 H. L. Davis, "Jeffers Denies Us Twice," *Poetry* 31 (Feb. 1928): 274.

25 Cargill, *Intellectual America*, p. 752.

26 Gilbert, *Shine, Perishing Republic*, p. 110.

27 Jeffers, *Selected Letters*, ed. Ridgeway, no. 22 (5 Aug. 1927), pp. 115–17. Cf. Mark Van Doren, "First Glance," *Nation* 125 (27 July 1927), p. 88.

28 Powell, *Robinson Jeffers*, p. 59. Before they yielded to their passions, Dante's Paolo and Francesca had read an amorous book by a "pander," i.e., "Galeotto," which is the Italian word for "pander" as well as the Italian rendering of the name of Gallehaut, the author of the French romance about Lancelot and Guinevere to which Dante refers.

29 Quoted, Powell, *Robinson Jeffers*, p. 46. Random House later published *Cawdor* in its own edition.

30 Cargill, *Intellectual America*, p. 753.

31 The Hippolytus theme is noted by both Donald W. Heiney (*Essentials of Contemporary Literature* [New York, 1954], p. 195) and Mark Van Doren ("Bits of Earth and Water," *Nation* 128 [9 Jan. 1929], p. 50). Morton D. Zabel, "The Problem of Tragedy," *Poetry* 33 (Mar. 1929): 336–40, compares the poem unfavorably with unspecified Greek predecessors. But none of them has explored this theme, as noted here and discussed in Chapter 7.

32 See Graham G. Hough, *The Dark Sun: A Study of D. H. Lawrence* (London, 1956) in the chapter "The Quarrel with Christianity," for a sympathetic discussion of *The Man Who Died* in the light of Lawrence's other works and of his main body of thought.

33 Jeffers, *Selected Letters*, ed. Ridgeway, no. 122 (5 Aug. 1927), p. 117, wrote to James Rorty that religions "whether we like it or not . . . derive from a 'private impurity' of some

kind in their originators." Vernon Loggins, *I Hear America* (New York, 1937), p. 69, in the chapter "Questioning Despair," accepts and repeats Powell's (*Robinson Jeffers*) argument in his own comment that *Dear Judas* is an "attempt to prove that the fundamental basis of Christianity is selfishness, a 'private impurity,' a thirst for power." I am aware of no other critic, however, who has indicated how Jeffers' approach reflects Nietzschean doctrine.

34 Cargill, *Intellectual America*, p. 755, calls it "one of the most beautiful of Jeffers' poems"; Percy Hutchison, "Robinson Jeffers Writes Two Passion Plays," *New York Times Book Review* (1 Dec. 1929), p. 12, prefers this poem over *Dear Judas,* apparently because "it is not classical but romantic." However, Rolfe Humphries, "Poet or Prophet?" *New Republic* 61 (15 Jan. 1930): 228–29, severely criticizes both the poet and poem; after printing a section of *The Loving Shepherdess* as if it were prose, he defies anyone to restore it to its original form on the basis of metrical analysis.

35 Wayland D. Hand, *A Dictionary of Words and Idioms Associated with Judas Iscariot: A Compilation Based Mainly on Material Found in the Germanic Languages* (Berkeley, 1942), pp. 322–23 and passim, adequately supports this contention.

36 Quoted, Hutchison, "Robinson Jeffers Writes Two Passion Plays," p. 12.

37 Louis Untermeyer, "Uneasy Death," *Saturday Review of Literature* 6 (19 Apr. 1930): 942.

38 Cf. W. S. Johnson, "The 'Savior' in the Poetry of Robinson Jeffers," *American Literature* 15 (May 1943): 159–68. Powell, *Robinson Jeffers,* p. 60n, gives the following information: Clare Walker "is taken, with a few changes and modern touches, from the character Feckless Fanny, whose history is given in full in a note to Scott's *The Heart of the Midlothian*"; cf. Jeffers, *Selected Poetry,* p. xvii. In Scott's version the strong father kills the lover.

39 Cf. F. I. Carpenter, "Robinson Jeffers and the Torches of

Violence," in *The Twenties: Poetry and Prose,* ed. Richard
E. Langford and William E. Taylor (De Land, Fla., 1966),
pp. 14–17.

40 The Jeffers family did have a daughter, Maev, born during
the first year of their marriage, but unfortunately the in-
fant lived only a few days. The twin sons, Donnan and
Garth, were born two years later.

41 Waggoner, "Science and the Poetry," pp. 275–88.

42 In 1938, Waggoner (ibid., p. 280) wrote that Jeffers' poetry
demonstrated a greater command of science than a hasty
reading of Sir James Jeans' *The Mysterious Universe* (New
York, 1930) could provide (if, indeed, Jeffers ever saw the
book). From the dates concerned (Waggoner refers to the
1933 edition) Jeans' book appeared too late to give Jeffers'
thinking of the twenties any of its impetus, but it could
have provided strong encouragement insofar as it supports
his conclusions and affirms the direction of his subsequent
thinking. Jeans, who has a strong Platonic bias, presents
some interesting conclusions in his final chapter, "Into the
Deep Waters." He argues that the stream of scientific thinking "is heading toward a non-mechanical reality." "The
old dualism of mind and matter," he predicts (pp. 158–
59), ". . . seems likely to disappear. . . . We discover that the
universe shows evidence of a designing or controlling power
that has something in common with our own individual
minds . . . the tendency to think in the way which . . . we
describe as mathematical [in the sense of pure mathemat-
ics]."

43 Jeffers, *Selected Letters,* ed. Ridgeway, no. 267 (21 Nov.
1937) p, 254.

44 Waggoner, "Science and the Poetry," pp. 275–88.

45 Jeffers' *Prescription of Painful Ends* (1940) in *Be Angry at
the Sun* is a more bitter statement of the position he takes
in the volume *Dear Judas:*

> Our own time . . .
> Has acids for honey, and for fine dreams

The immense vulgarities of misapplied science and decaying Christianity: therefore one christens each poem, in dutiful

Hope of burning off at least the top layer of the time's uncleanness, from the acid-bottles.

46 Sister M. J. Power, *Poets at Prayer* (New York, 1938), pp. 59–68, her chapter "Robinson Jeffers."

Chapter 4

1 Jeffers, *Themes,* p. 7.
2 Cargill, *Intellectual America,* pp. 756–57.
3 Granville Hicks, "A Transient Sickness," *Nation* 134 (13 Apr. 1932): 433–34.
4 Carpenter, *Robinson Jeffers,* p. 82.
5 James Rorty, "Symbolic Melodrama," *New Republic* 71 (18 May 1932): 24–25. See also William R. Benét, "Thurso's Landing," in *Designed for Reading,* ed. H. S. Canby, Amy Loveman, W. R. Benét, and others (New York, 1934), pp. 234–38, who notes that "Jeffers' philosophy has always been beyond good and evil." Walter Gierasch, "Robinson Jeffers," *English Journal* (college ed.) 28 (Apr. 1939): 284–95, notes instances of the futility of trying to maintain human ties of affection. Leon Howard, *Literature and the American Tradition* (New York, 1960), p. 293, writes that beginning with *Thurso's Landing* Jeffers "seems to be more concerned with violence as an error than with violence as an ideal." Rolfe Humphries, "Two Books by Jeffers" [i.e., *Thurso* and *Descent to the Dead*], *Poetry* 40 (June 1932): 154–58, writes that being "licked by modern life. . . . is what passes for the artist's tragedy with us; that, and paralysis of will so great that he can neither quit crying nor fight back." Percy Hutchison, "Robinson Jeffers' Dramatic Poem of Spiritual Tragedy," *New York Times Book Review* (3 Apr. 1932), p. 2, reveals in his review that he could not have read the complete poem, and he reasserts his preference for E. A. Robinson. Josephine Pinckney, "Jeffers and Mac-

Leish," *Virginia Quarterly Review* 8 (July 1932): 443–47, concludes that the three chief characters "are finely realized," but considers their thoughts too mature for young adults.

6 Alberts, *Bibliography*, p. 72.
7 Ibid.
8 Morton D. Zabel, "A Prophet in His Wilderness," *New Republic* 77 (3 Jan. 1934): 229–30.
9 Carpenter, *Robinson Jeffers*, p. 83, quotes Jeffers' opinion written to his publishers that "in poetry and dramatic value, and variety of character, it [*Give Your Heart*] seems to me rather better perhaps than Thurso. . . ."
10 Gilbert, *Shine, Perishing Republic*, p. 129, and Taylor, "Enigma of Robinson Jeffers," pp. 39–46, make more general observations about the influence of Nietzsche in this poem.
11 There have been several recent interpretations of Hagen's role in the *Nibelungenlied*. D. G. Mowatt, "Studies Towards an Interpretation of the 'Nibelungenlied,' " *German Life and Letters* 14 (1960–61): 257–70, sees Hagen as a man of "limited vision," who feels that Siegfried and Kriemhild "are foreign bodies in his world, and wants to get rid of them." H. B. Willson, "Blood and Wounds in the 'Nibelungenlied,' " *Modern Language Review* 55 (1960): 40–50, insists that "Kriemhilt and Hagen have both loved and hated 'without measure,' and no 'wordly' dialectic can solve the problem of their final destiny beyond the grave." J. K. Bostock, "The Message of the 'Nibelungenlied,' " *Modern Language Review* 55 (1960): 200–212, sees the poem as "a parade of the various types of egoist," which reveals that Hagen's "*triuwe* . . . is of a higher order than that of Sivrit," and concludes that the "*Nibelungenlied* is completely negative." W. T. H. Jackson, *The Literature of the Middle Ages* (New York, 1960), p. 210, says that loyalty "is the driving force behind all of Hagen's conduct . . . but it is loyalty to an idea rather than to a person."
12 Cf. Peter A. Munch, *Norse Mythology: Legends of Gods*

and Heroes, trans. S. B. Hustvedt (New York, 1926), pp. 192–203, 344–46. In the foreword of *Selected Poetry,* Jeffers adds to the confusion by saying that he thought "the Volsung Saga might serve for fable."

13 Watts, "Robinson Jeffers," p. 49. Watts' paper, pp. 39–55, contains a generally excellent discussion of what he calls Jeffers' "inverted mysticism."

14 For a comparison of the Greek tragedians and Jeffers' portrayal of emotion and passion, see P. B. Rice, "Jeffers and the Tragic Sense," *Nation* 141 (23 Oct. 1935): 480–82.

15 Cf. Walton, "Beauty of Storm," pp. 209–13, who writes, "Since the *Women of Point Sur [sic],* Jeffers has recognized the fact that his supermen usually fail to find their god of Nature, that they are crushed, ultimately, by their awareness of man-made laws."

16 Cargill, *Intellectual America,* p. 760.

17 Bernard DeVoto, *Minority Report* (Boston, 1940), p. 262.

18 Louise Bogan, "Landscape with Jeffers," in her *Selected Criticism* (New York, 1955), pp. 67–69.

Chapter 5

1 League of American Writers, *Writers Take Sides: Letters About the War in Spain from 418 American Authors,* ed. Millen Brand, Dorothy Brewster, Harry Carlisle, and Graff Conklin (New York, 1938). Donald Ogden Stewart, as president of the league, signed the letter of inquiry.

2 Ibid., pp. 73–74. Among the critics charging Fascism were Cargill, *Intellectual America,* p. 760; G. P. Meyer, *"Double Axe;* Reply to S. Rodman," *Saturday Review of Literature* 31 (11 Sept. 1948): 24; and Wells, "Philosophy of War," pp. 81–88, who reverses the opinion in the earlier "Grander Canyon," in his *American Way of Poetry* (New York, 1943), p. 160.

3 S. J. Kunitz, "Day Is a Poem," *Poetry,* 59 (Dec. 1941): 150.

4 See Squires' chapter "The Inhumanist" and passim in *Loyalties,* and Carpenter, *Robinson Jeffers,* p. 56. We may be

grateful to Squires for probing the problems of *The Double Axe,* whereas many critics have ignored the poem. Babette Deutsch, *Poetry in Our Time* (New York, 1956), in the chapter "A Look at the Worst," pp. 1–27, criticized Jeffers for writing a poem made of ideas instead of words. Rodman, "Transhuman Magnificence," pp. 13–14, wholeheartedly endorsed the political views of Jeffers (whom he saw as the "heir of Nietzsche"), and drew a hostile reply on the subject of totalitarian madness from Meyer, *"Double Axe,"* p. 24.

5 Quoted, G. S. Kirk and J. E. Raven, *The Presocratic Philosophers* (Cambridge, 1957), p. 212.

6 Ibid., p. 188.

7 Ibid., p. 209.

8 Carpenter, *Robinson Jeffers,* p. 91.

9 Kirk and Raven, *Presocratic Philosophers,* p. 191.

10 Cf. Powell, *Robinson Jeffers,* p. 106, and Alberts, *Bibliography,* p. 147.

11 Quoted, Kirk and Raven, *Presocratic Philosophers,* p. 193. Cf. also the old man's speech: "God does not judge: God *is.* Mine is the judgment" (p. 100).

12 Ibid., p. 195.

13 Cf. W. A. Smith, "Authors and Humanism," *Humanist* 11 (Oct. 1951): 193–204, who includes among questionnaire replies from several novelists and poets Jeffers' response, dated 25 March 1951:

> The word Humanism refers primarily to the Renaissance interest in art and literature rather than in theological doctrine; and personally I am content to leave it there. "Naturalistic Humanism"—in the modern sense—is no doubt a better philosophical attitude than many others; but the emphasis seems wrong; "human naturalism" would seem to me more satisfactory, with but little accent on the "human." Man is a part of nature, but a nearly infinitesimal part; the human race will cease after a while and leave no trace, but the great splendors of

nature will go on. Meanwhile most of our time and energy are necessarily spent on human affairs; that can't be prevented, though I think it should be minimized; but for philosophy, which is an endless research of truth, and for contemplation, which can be a sort of worship, I would suggest that the immense beauty of the earth and the outer universe, the divine "nature of things," is a more rewarding object. Certainly it is more pleasant to think of than the hopes and horrors of humanity, and more ennobling. It is a source of strength; the other of distraction.

14 The thirty-year-old promise, which Jeffers discusses in the introduction to the Modern Library edition (1935) of *Roan Stallion, Tamar and Other Poems,* is mentioned again in *But I Am Growing Old and Indolent* in the posthumous volume *The Beginning and the End and Other Poems,* p. 64, where it is described as the poet's promise to himself to "Make sacrifices once a year to magic / Horror away from the house," and Tamar, Cawdor, and Thurso's wife are cited as "imagined victims [to] be our redeemers."

15 See *Robinson Jeffers Newsletter,* ed. Melba B. Bennett, no. 2 (Nov. 1963) and no. 3 (Dec. 1963), for some of the details of the publication of the last volume. See also Robert J. Brophy, S.J., "A Textual Note on Robinson Jeffers' *The Beginning and the End,*" *Papers of the Bibliographical Society of America,* vol. 60 (1966), pp. 344–48.

Chapter 6

1 Jeffers, *Themes,* pp. 18–19.

2 H. Stuart Hughes, *Oswald Spengler: A Critical Estimate,* rev. ed. (New York, 1962), pp. 4, 167.

3 *The New Science of Giambattista Vico,* rev. trans. from 3d ed. (Naples, 1744) by T. G. Bergin and M. H. Fisch (Ithaca, N.Y., 1968), pp. xxvii–xxx, pars. 428–55 *passim.*

4 Jeffers, *Themes,* p. 18.

5 Vico, *New Science,* par. 31. *The Autobiography of Giam-*

battista Vico, trans. M. H. Fisch and T. G. Bergin (Ithaca, N.Y., 1963), pp. 50–52.

6 Fausto Nicolini, *La giovinezza di G. B. Vico,* 2d ed. (Bari, 1932), pp. 120–24, discusses Vico and Lucretius.

7 See Hughes, *Oswald Spengler,* pp. 62–63; Kaufmann, *Nietzsche,* pp. 123, 149–50, 296–97, 305–6, 328–29, 415 (n. 2), 421–22.

8 Oswald Spengler, *The Decline of the West,* trans. C. F. Atkinson, 2 vols. (New York, 1926–28), vol. 1, p. 113. The volumes were originally published in German 1918–22.

9 Spengler, *Decline,* vol. 1, p. xiv. See also vol. 1, pp. 24, 315, 346, 363.

10 Spengler's "morphological" method and theory of waves and decay are present in: *The Broken Balance, The Humanist's Tragedy, Hands, The Tower Beyond Tragedy* (Cassandra's speech, p. 55), *Shine, Perishing Republic, Practical People, Point Pinos and Point Lobos, The Cycle,* prelude to *The Women at Point Sur, Cawdor* (pp. 114–16), *Ghosts in England, I Shall Laugh Purely, Battle, The Double Axe* (p. 95), and *Diagram.*

11 Oswald Spengler, *Politische Schriften* (Munich, 1933), pp. x, xiii. Oswald Spengler, *Hour of Decision,* trans. C. F. Atkinson (New York, 1934), pp. x–xii.

12 Watts, "Robinson Jeffers," pp. 39–55, makes the same distinction between Spengler's and Jeffers' use of the cyclical theory, but ascribes the difference to Jeffers' mysticism.

13 Cf. Bernard DeVoto, "They Turned Their Backs on America," *Saturday Review of Literature* 27 (8 Apr. 1944): 5–8; Martha Hackman, "Whitman, Jeffers, and Freedom," *Prairie Schooner* 20 (Fall, 1946): 182–84; Kunitz, "Day is a Poem," pp. 148–54; R. E. Roberts, "Lonely Eminence," *Saturday Review of Literature* 25 (25 Apr. 1942): 8.

14 *Encyclopaedia Britannica,* 14th ed., s. v. Petrie, William Matthew Flinders; *Dictionary of National Biography; Times* (London) *Literary Supplement* (8 Aug. 1942), p. 388; Flinders Petrie, *Seventy Years in Archaeology* (New York, 1932).

15 Spengler, *Decline,* 1: 427n.

16 Flinders Petrie, *The Revolutions of Civilization* (London and New York, 1911), p. 11.
17 Robinson Jeffers, *An Artist* (Austin, 1928), unpaged, includes this letter.
18 Donnan Jeffers to Arthur B. Coffin, 24 Mar. 1965. Of Ellis' books once to be found at Tor House, an inventory of the poet's library in 1966 revealed only one volume of *Studies in the Psychology of Sex.*
19 Havelock Ellis, *The Dance of Life* (Boston, 1923).
20 Havelock Ellis, *Fountain of Life; Being the Impressions and Comments of Havelock Ellis* (Boston, 1930), p. 133.
21 Havelock Ellis, *The New Spirit* (New York, 1921), p. 2.
22 See Ellis, *Dance,* chap. 5: "The Art of Religion."
23 Cf. Jeffers to H. H. Waggoner, in *Selected Letters,* ed. Ridgeway, no. 267 (21 Nov. 1937), pp. 254–55, no. 271 (1 Feb. 1938), pp. 261–62.

Chapter 7

1 Mark Van Doren, "First Glance," *Nation* 120 (11 Mar. 1925): 268.
2 In addition to the instances mentioned, see *Meditation on Saviors* and *Cawdor* (references to Oedipus), *The Broken Balance* (Plutarch's "Life of Sulla"), *Shine, Republic* (Tacitus and Aeschylus), *Hellenistics, Prescription of Painful Ends* (Lucretius and Plato), *Faith* (Lucretius), *The Double Axe* (Heraclitus, Plutarch), *De Rerum Virtute* (note of debt to Lucretius and Heraclitus), *The Epic Stars* (Homer), *Eager to Be Praised* (Lucretius, Pindar, Archilochus, Virgil), *The Silent Shepherds* (Petronius' *Satyricon*), *At the Fall of an Age* (Pausanias).
3 Alberts, *Bibliography,* p. 150, and Powell, *Robinson Jeffers,* p. 118. Cf. the evaluations of Dudley Fitts, "The Hellenism of Robinson Jeffers," *Kenyon Review* (Autumn, 1946): 678–83; G. J. Nathan, "Medea," *Theatre Book of the Year, 1947–1948* (New York, 1948), pp. 104–12; Kenneth Rexroth, review of Squires, *Loyalties, Saturday Review of Literature,* 40 (10 Aug. 1957): 30.

4 Aristophanes, *The Frogs,* trans. Gilbert Murray, in *Seven Famous Greek Plays,* ed. Whitney J. Oates and Eugene O'Neill, Jr. (New York, 1954), p. 402.

5 Robinson Jeffers, "Robinson Jeffers Writes a New Preface to His Tale of Fury, Tragedy and Medea," *San Francisco Chronicle* (5 Sept. 1948), pp. 9, 11, is included in Bennett, *Stone Mason,* pp. 216–20.

6 Cargill, *Intellectual America,* p. 757.

7 Philip W. Harsh, *A Handbook of Classical Drama* (Stanford, Calif., 1944), p. 83.

8 Ibid., p. 183.

9 Cf. Jeffers, *Selected Letters,* ed. Ridgeway, no. 84 (13 Sept. 1926), pp. 83–84, who asked George Sterling if he remembered the story in which Catullus' Attis castrates himself.

10 Euripides, *Hippolytus,* trans. Gilbert Murray, in *Greek Literature,* ed. Whitney J. Oates and Charles T. Murphy (New York, 1944), lines 317, 612.

11 Bennett, *Stone Mason,* p. 154, writes: "Jeffers had predicted that *Give Your Heart to the Hawks* would be 'more human than usual, without the mysticism of scandal, though I hope rather interesting. The story is the Greek story of Phaedra, transferred to this coast. *Desire Under the Elms* but a variant of it; but in mine the young man is inseducible, as in the Greek.' " As Mrs. Bennett notes, Jeffers' remark is taken from a collection of the poet's personal notes at Tor House, but quite clearly his observation applies to *Cawdor,* not to *Give Your Heart to the Hawks,* as Mrs. Bennett assigns it.

12 Douglas Bush, *Mythology and the Romantic Tradition in English Poetry* (Cambridge, Mass., 1957), p. 519.

13 See Jeffers' article on his *Medea,* in Bennett, *Stone Mason,* pp. 216–20.

14 Cf. Fitts, "Hellenism of Jeffers," p. 681, "The Euripidean energy . . . has been transformed into as coarse a ranting as ever fluttered the nickelodeons."

15 C. R. Haines, *Sappho: The Poems and Fragments* (New York, 1926), no. 129, p. 157.

16 See Bennett, *Stone Mason,* p. 227.

17 Cf. the indications of homosexuality in Hippolytus, *Hungerfield and Other Poems,* pp. 40–41, 42, 49, 54, 69, 73.

18 In his review of the play, "Medea," pp. 104–12, Nathan felt that where Jeffers sought sensationalism in order to appeal to modern appetites the original Euripides play would have failed. See Jeffers, *Selected Letters,* ed. Ridgeway, no. 381 (1954), p. 356.

19 Gilbert, *Shine, Perishing Republic,* p. 97.

Chapter 8

1 Jeffers developed his Inhumanism from the ideas in Lucretius' *De Rerum Natura.* I do not, however, contradict my earlier explication of Hoult Gore ("Love and Hate" section of *The Double Axe*) as a Heraclitean hero because, even though Lucretius (bk. 1) refutes the Heraclitean theory that everything is constituted of fire or some other single element, the Roman's theory of the nature of things is not inimical to the Greek's logos.

In the late poem *The Beginning and the End,* Jeffers tells us that man's mission is to find and feel life, for all animal experience is a part of God's life. Except for the Christian note here, Jeffers echoes Epicurus' theory that all knowledge is derived from the senses and that things are exactly as they appear to be to our senses. Material objects are perceived; therefore they exist. Lucretius, whom Jeffers quoted earlier in this poem, used the same Epicurean argument in *De Rerum Natura* (1: 422–25).

2 Lucretius, *De Rerum Natura,* trans. Cyril Bailey (Oxford, 1947). All quotations from Lucretius are from this translation.

The following poems refer explicitly to Lucretius: *Prescription of Painful Ends, Faith, The Beginning and the End, Eager to Be Praised,* and *De Rerum Virtute.*

Jeffers, "A Few Memories," pp. 329, 351, called George Sterling an Epicurean after the style of Lucretius; and see

Jeffers' statement in Alberts, *Bibliography,* p. 136, and his letter to Theodore Lilienthal (*Selected Letters,* ed. Ridgeway, no. 378 [2 Feb. 1953], pp. 354–55), which acknowledges the debt of his poem *De Rerum Virtute* to Lucretius. Squires, *Loyalties,* pp. 180–90, has a generally useful discussion of Lucretius and Jeffers.

See also Powell, *Robinson Jeffers,* pp. xx, 4, 112; Powell, "Double Marriage," pp. 278–82; Carpenter, *Robinson Jeffers,* p. 109; Carpenter, "Death Comes," pp. 97–104; Gilbert, *Shine, Perishing Republic,* p. 147; Roberts, "Lonely Eminence," p. 8; and Wells, *American Way,* pp. 148–60.

3 Jeffers, *Selected Letters,* ed. Ridegway, no. 122 (5 Aug. 1927), p. 116.

4 Lucretius, *De Rerum Natura,* lines 72–73.

5 George Santayana, *Three Philosophical Poets* (Cambridge, Mass., 1910), pp. 32–34.

6 Schopenhauer, "A Few Words on Pantheism," in his *Parerga und Paralipomena.* In *The World as Will and Idea,* trans. Haldane and Kemp, vol. 1, p. 412, Schopenhauer quotes the opening paragraph of Book 2 of *De Rerum Natura.*

7 Cf. Jeffers, *Selected Letters,* ed. Ridgeway, no. 348 (Oct. 1950), p. 327, who, writing to a close friend about Una Jeffers' death a month earlier, said "that her awareness and beauty are dissolved into the world, and make it more beautiful. But an old superstition keeps me praying silently."

8 See Benedict de Spinoza, *The Chief Works of Benedict de Spinoza,* trans. R. H. M. Elwes, 2 vols. (New York, 1955).

9 Stuart Hampshire, *Spinoza* (New York, 1956), p. 121.

10 Jeffers, *Selected Letters,* ed. Ridgeway, no. 194 (11 July, 1931), p. 182.

11 Ibid., no. 195 (Sept. 1931), p. 184.

12 Cf. Spinoza's attack on anthropocentrism which is developed in the appendix to Book 1 of the *Ethics.*

13 Jeffers, *Selected Letters,* ed. Ridgeway, no. 122 (5 Aug.
   1927), p. 116.
14 Cf. *Ethics,* pt. 5, prop. 20.

bibliography

Works by Robinson Jeffers

Apology for Bad Dreams. Paris: privately printed by Harry Ward Ritchie, 1930. A limited edition of 30 copies.

An Artist. Austin, Texas: privately printed by J. S. Mayfield, 1928. A limited edition of 200 copies.

Be Angry at the Sun. New York: Random House, 1941.

The Beginning and the End and Other Poems. New York: Random House, 1963.

Californians. New York: Macmillan, 1916.

Cawdor and Other Poems. New York: H. Liveright, 1928; London: Hogarth, 1930.

Dear Judas and Other Poems. New York: H. Liveright, 1929; London: Hogarth, 1930.

De Rerum Virtute. San Francisco: Grabhorn, 1953. A limited edition.

Descent to the Dead. New York: Random House, 1931. Limited to 500 signed copies. The sixteen poems of this edition were later included in *Give Your Heart to the Hawks and Other Poems*.

The Double Axe and Other Poems. New York: Random House, 1948.

"A Few Memories," *Overland Monthly* 85 (Nov. 1927): 329, 351.

"First Book," *Colophon*, 10, pt. 10 (26 May 1932):1–8. Reprinted in *Breaking into Print*, edited by Elmer Adler, pp. 85–91. New York: Simon and Schuster, 1937.

Flagons and Apples. Los Angeles: Grafton, 1912.

Foreword to D. H. Lawrence, *Fire and Other Poems*. San Francisco: Grabhorn Press, 1940.

Foreword to Lawrence C. Powell, *Robinson Jeffers: The Man and His Work*. Rev. ed. Pasadena, Calif.: San Pasqual Press, 1940.

Give Your Heart to the Hawks and Other Poems. New York: Random House, 1933.

Hungerfield and Other Poems. New York: Random House, 1954.

Medea: Freely Adapted from the "Medea" of Euripides. New York: Random House, 1946.

Poetry, Gongorism and a Thousand Years. Los Angeles: Ward Ritchie, 1949. Reprinted from *New York Times Book Review*, 18 Jan. 1948.

Reply in *Writers Take Sides: Letters About the War in Spain from 418 American Authors*. Edited by Millen Brand, Dorothy Brewster, Harry Carlisle, and Graff Conklin. New York: League of American Writers, 1938.

Roan Stallion, Tamar and Other Poems. New York: Boni & Liveright, 1925; London: Hogarth, 1928; New York: Modern Library, 1935.

Robinson Jeffers, Selected Poems. New York: Random House, Vintage Books, 1965.

"Robinson Jeffers Writes a New Preface to His Tale of Fury, Tragedy and Medea," *San Francisco Chronicle* (5 Sept. 1948), pp. 9, 11.

The Selected Letters of Robinson Jeffers. Edited by Ann N. Ridgeway. Baltimore: Johns Hopkins Press, 1968.

The Selected Poetry of Robinson Jeffers. New York: Random House, 1938.

Solstice and Other Poems. New York: Random House, 1935.

"Statement on Humanism," *Humanist* 11 (Oct. 1951):200–201.

Such Counsels You Gave to Me and Other Poems. New York: Random House, 1937.

Tamar and Other Poems. New York: Peter G. Boyle, 1924.

Themes in My Poems. San Francisco: Book Club of California, 1956.

Thurso's Landing and Other Poems. New York: Liveright, 1932.

The Women at Point Sur. New York: Boni & Liveright, 1927.

Secondary Sources

Alberts, S. S. *A Bibliography of the Works of Robinson Jeffers.* New York: Random House, 1933.

Antoninus, Brother [Everson, William]. *Robinson Jeffers: Fragments of an Older Fury.* Berkeley: Oyez, 1968.

Aristophanes. *The Frogs.* Translated by Gilbert Murray. In *Seven Famous Greek Plays,* edited by Whitney J. Oates and Eugene O'Neill, Jr. New York: Random House, 1954.

Benét, William R. "Thurso's Landing." In *Designed for Reading,* edited by H. S. Canby, Amy Loveman, W. R. Benét, et al., pp. 234–38. New York: Macmillan, 1934.

Bennett, Melba Berry. *The Stone Mason of Tor House: The Life and Work of Robinson Jeffers.* Los Angeles: Ward Ritchie Press, 1966.

Bogan, Louise. "Landscape with Jeffers." In her *Selected Criticism: Poetry and Prose,* pp. 67–69. New York: Noonday Press, 1955.

Bostock, J. K. "The Message of the 'Nibelungenlied,' " *Modern Language Review* 55 (1960):200–212.

Brophy, Robert J., S.J. "A Textual Note on Robinson Jeffers' *The Beginning and the End,*" *Papers of the Bibliographical Society of America* 60 (1966):344–48.

Busch, Niven. "Duel on a Headland," *Saturday Review of Literature* 11 (9 Mar. 1935):533.

Bush, Douglas. *Mythology and the Romantic Tradition in English Poetry*, pp. 481–525. Cambridge: Harvard University Press, 1957.

Cargill, Oscar. *Intellectual America: Ideas on the March*, pp. 741–61. New York: Macmillan, 1941.

Carpenter, Frederic I. "Death Comes for Robinson Jeffers," *University Review* 7 (Dec. 1940):97–104. Reprinted in Frederic I. Carpenter, *American Literature and the Dream*, pp. 144–54 (New York: Philosophical Library, 1955).

——. *Robinson Jeffers*. New York: Twayne, 1962.

——. "Robinson Jeffers and the Torches of Violence." In *The Twenties: Poetry and Prose*, edited by Richard E. Langford and William E. Taylor. De Land, Fla.: E. Edwards Press, 1966.

——. "The Values of Robinson Jeffers," *American Literature* 11 (Jan. 1940):353–66.

Cestre, Charles. "Robinson Jeffers," *Revue Anglo-Américaine* 4 (Aug. 1927):489–502.

Copleston, Frederick, S.J. *Arthur Schopenhauer: Philosopher of Pessimism*. London: Burns, Oates and Washbourne, 1946.

Cunningham, C. C. "The Rhythm of Robinson Jeffers' Poetry as Revealed by Oral Reading," *Quarterly Journal of Speech* 32 (Oct. 1946):351–57.

Davis, Harold L. "Jeffers Denies Us Twice," *Poetry* 31 (Feb. 1928):274–79. Review of *The Women at Point Sur*.

De Casseres, Benjamin. "Robinson Jeffers: Tragic Terror," *Bookman* 66 (Nov. 1927):262–66.

Deutsch, Babette. "A Look at the Worst." In her *Poetry in Our Time*. New York: Columbia University Press, 1956.

DeVoto, Bernard. "Lycanthropy." In his *Minority Report*, pp. 257–64. Boston: Little, Brown, 1940.

——. "They Turned Their Backs on America," *Saturday Review of Literature* 27 (8 Apr. 1944):5–8.

Ellis, Havelock. *The Dance of Life*. Boston: Houghton Mifflin, 1923.

————. *Fountain of Life: Being the Impressions and Comments of Havelock Ellis.* Boston: Houghton Mifflin, 1930.

————. *The New Spirit.* New York: Boni and Liveright, 1921.

Euripides. *Hippolytus.* Translated by Gilbert Murray. In *Greek Literature in Translation,* edited by Whitney J. Oates and Charles T. Murphy. New York: Longmans, Green, 1944.

Fitts, Dudley. "The Hellenism of Robinson Jeffers," *Kenyon Review* 8 (Autumn 1946):678–83.

Fletcher, James G. "The Dilemma of Robinson Jeffers," *Poetry* 43 (Mar. 1934):338–42.

Gardiner, Patrick. *Schopenhauer.* Baltimore: Penguin, 1963.

Gates, G. G. "The Bread That Every Man Must Eat Alone," *College English* 4 (Dec. 1942):170–74

Gierasch, Walter. "Robinson Jeffers," *English Journal* (college edition), 28 (Apr. 1939):284–95.

Gilbert, Rudolph. *Shine, Perishing Republic: Robinson Jeffers and the Tragic Sense in Modern Poetry.* Boston: Bruce Humphries, 1936.

Glicksberg, Charles I. "The Poetry of Doom and Despair," *Humanist* 7 (Aug. 1947):69–76.

Gregory, Horace. "Poet Without Critics: A Note on Robinson Jeffers." In his *The Dying Gladiators and Other Essays,* pp. 3–20. New York: Grove Press, 1961.

————. "Suicide in the Jungle," *New Masses* 10 (13 Feb. 1934): 18–19.

————, and Zaturenska, Marya. "Robinson Jeffers and the Birth of Tragedy." In their *History of American Poetry, 1900–1940,* pp. 398–412. New York: Harcourt, Brace, 1946.

Hackman, Martha. "Whitman, Jeffers, and Freedom," *Prairie Schooner* 20 (Fall 1946):182–84.

Haines, C. R. *Sappho: The Poems and Fragments.* New York: E. P. Dutton, 1926.

Hampshire, Stuart. *Spinoza.* New York: Barnes & Noble, 1956.

Hand, Wayland D. *A Dictionary of Words and Idioms Associated with Judas Iscariot.* Berkeley: University of California Press, 1942.

"Harrowed Marrow," *Time* 19 (4 Apr. 1932):63–64. Review of *Thurso's Landing and Other Poems.*

Harsh, Philip W. *A Handbook of Classical Drama.* Stanford, Calif.: Stanford University Press, 1944.

Heiney, Donald W. *Essentials of Contemporary Literature.* New York: Barron's Educational Series, 1954.

Hicks, Granville. "A Transient Sickness," *Nation* 134 (13 Apr. 1932):433–34.

Hough, Graham G. *The Dark Sun: A Study of D. H. Lawrence.* London: Duckworth, 1956.

Howard, Leon. *Literature and the American Tradition.* New York: Doubleday, Anchor Books, 1960.

Hughes, H. Stuart. *Oswald Spengler.* Rev. ed. New York: Charles Scribner's, 1962.

Humphries, Rolfe. "Poet or Prophet?" *New Republic* 61 (15 Jan. 1930):228–29. Review of *Dear Judas and Other Poems.*

———. "Two Books by Jeffers," *Poetry* 40 (June 1932):154–58. Review of *Thurso's Landing and Other Poems* and *Descent to the Dead.*

Hutchison, Percy. "An Elder Poet and a Young One ...," *New York Times Book Review* (3 Jan. 1926), pp. 14, 24.

———. "Robinson Jeffers' Dramatic Poem of Spiritual Tragedy," *New York Times Book Review* (3 Apr. 1932), p. 2. Review of *Thurso's Landing and Other Poems.*

———. "Robinson Jeffers Writes Two Passion Plays," *New York Times Book Review* (1 Dec. 1929), p. 12. Review of *Dear Judas and Other Poems.*

Jackson, W. T. H. *The Literature of the Middle Ages.* New York: Columbia University Press, 1960.

Jeans, Sir James. *The Mysterious Universe.* New York: Macmillan, 1930.

Jeffers, Donnan. Letter to Arthur B. Coffin, 24 Mar. 1965.

Johnson, William S. "The 'Savior' in the Poetry of Robinson Jeffers," *American Literature* 15 (May 1943):159–68.

Kaufmann, Walter. *Nietzsche: Philosopher, Psychologist, Antichrist.* 3d ed. Princeton: Princeton University Press, 1968.

Kirk, G. S., and Raven, J. E. *The Presocratic Philosophers.* Cambridge University Press, 1957.

Klein, Herbert. "The Prosody of Robinson Jeffers." M.A. thesis, Occidental College, 1930.

Kunitz, Stanley J. "Day Is a Poem," *Poetry* 59 (Dec. 1941): 148–54.

League of American Writers. *Writers Take Sides: Letters About the War in Spain from 418 American Authors.* Edited by Millen Brand, Dorothy Brewster, Harry Carlisle, and Graff Conklin. New York, 1938.

Loggins, Vernon. "Questioning Despair." In his *I Hear America.* New York: Thomas Y. Crowell, 1937.

Lucretius. *De Rerum Natura.* Translated by Cyril Bailey. 3 vols. Oxford University Press, Clarendon Press, 1947.

Lutyens, David B. *The Creative Encounter.* London: Secker and Warburg, 1960.

Meyer, G. P. *"Double Axe;* Reply to Selden Rodman," *Saturday Review of Literature* 31 (11 Sept. 1948):24.

Miller, Benjamin. "Toward a Religious Philosophy of the Theatre," *Personalist* 20 (Oct. 1939):361–76.

Monjian, Mercedes C. *Robinson Jeffers: A Study in Inhumanism.* Pittsburgh: University of Pittsburgh Press, 1958.

Monroe, Harriet. "Power and Pomp," *Poetry* 28 (June 1926): 160–64.

Mowatt, D. G. "Studies Towards an Interpretation of the 'Nibelungenlied,'" *German Life and Letters* 14 (1960–61): 257–70.

Munch, Peter A. *Norse Mythology: Legends of Gods and Heroes.* Translated by S. B. Hustvedt. New York: American-Scandinavian Foundation, 1926.

Nathan, G. J. "Medea." In *Theatre Book of the Year, 1947–1948,* pp. 104–12. New York: Knopf, 1948.

———. "The Tower Beyond Tragedy." in *Theatre Book of the Year, 1950–1951,* pp. 136–38. New York: Knopf, 1951.

Nicolini, Fausto. *La giovinezza di G. B. Vico.* 2d ed. Bari: Laterza e figli, 1932.

Nietzsche, Friedrich. *Basic Writings of Nietzsche.* Translated and edited by Walter Kaufmann. New York: Modern Library, 1968.

———. *The Portable Nietzsche.* Translated and edited by Walter Kaufmann. New York: Viking Press, 1954.

Petrie, Flinders. *The Revolutions of Civilization.* New York and London: Harper, 1911.

———. *Seventy Years in Archaeology.* New York: H. Holt, 1932.

Pinckney, Josephine. "Jeffers and MacLeish," *Virginia Quarterly Review* 8 (July 1932):443–47.

Powell, L. C. "The Double Marriage of Robinson Jeffers," *Southwest Review* 41 (Summer, 1956):278–82.

———. "The Making of a Poet." In his *Books in My Baggage: Adventures in Reading and Collecting,* pp. 139–47. Cleveland: World Publishing Co., 1960.

———. *Robinson Jeffers: The Man and His Work.* Pasadena, Calif.: San Pasqual Press, 1940.

Power, Sister M. J. "Robinson Jeffers." In her *Poets at Prayer,* pp. 59–68. New York: Sheed & Ward, 1938.

Rexroth, Kenneth. Review of Squires, *The Loyalties of Robinson Jeffers. Saturday Review of Literature* 40 (10 Aug. 1957): 30.

Rice, P. B. "Jeffers and the Tragic Sense," *Nation* 141 (23 Oct. 1935):480–82.

Roberts, R. E. "Lonely Eminence," *Saturday Review of Literature* 25 (25 Apr. 1942):8.

Robinson Jeffers Newsletter. Edited by Melba B. Bennett (nos. 1–22) and Robert J. Brophy (nos. 23–). Los Angeles: Robinson Jeffers Committee, Occidental College, 1962–.

Rodman, Selden. "Transhuman Magnificence," *Saturday Review of Literature* 31 (31 July 1948):13–14. Review of *The Double Axe and Other Poems.*

Rorty, James. "Symbolic Melodrama," *New Republic* 71 (18 May 1932):24–25. Review of *Descent to the Dead* and *Thurso's Landing and Other Poems.*

Santayana, George. *Three Philosophical Poets.* Cambridge, Mass.: Harvard University Press, 1910.

Schopenhauer, Arthur. "A Few Words on Pantheism" from *Parerga und Paralipomena.* In *Religion: A Dialogue and Other Essays,* translated by T. Bailey Saunders. Schopenhauer Series, vol. 3. London: S. Sonnenschein, 1891.

———. *The World as Will and Idea.* Translated by R. B. Haldane and J. Kemp. 3 vols. London: Trübner, 1883.

Shelley, Percy B. *A Defence of Poetry.*

Short, R. W. "The Tower Beyond Tragedy," *Southern Review* 7 (Summer, 1941):132–44.

Smith, Warren Allen. "Authors and Humanism," *Humanist* 11 (Oct. 1951):193–204.

Spengler, Oswald. *The Decline of the West.* Translated by C. F. Atkinson. 2 vols. New York: Knopf, 1926–28.

———. *The Hour of Decision.* Translated by C. F. Atkinson. New York: Knopf, 1934.

———. *Politische Schriften.* Munich: Beck, 1932.

Spinoza, Benedict de. *The Chief Works of Benedict de Spinoza.* Translated by R. H. M. Elwes. 2 vols. New York: Dover Publications, 1955.

Squires, Radcliffe J. *The Loyalties of Robinson Jeffers.* Ann Arbor: University of Michigan Press, 1956.

Sterling, George. "Rhymes and Reactions," *Overland Monthly* 83 (Nov. 1925):411. Review of *Tamar and Other Poems.*

———. *Robinson Jeffers: The Man and the Artist.* New York: Boni and Liveright, 1926.

Taylor, Frajam. "The Enigma of Robinson Jeffers: II. The Hawk and the Stone," *Poetry* 55 (Oct. 1939):39–46.

Untermeyer, Louis. "Uneasy Death," *Saturday Review of Literature* 6 (19 Apr. 1930):942.

Van Doren, Mark. "Bits of Earth and Water," *Nation* 128 (9 Jan. 1929):50. Review of *Cawdor and Other Poems.*

———. "First Glance," *Nation* 120 (11 Mar. 1925):268. Review of *Tamar and Other Poems.*

———. "First Glance," *Nation* 125 (27 July 1927):88. Review

of *The Women at Point Sur.*

Vico, Giambattista. *The Autobiography of Giambattista Vico.* Translated by M. H. Fisch and T. G. Bergin. Ithaca, N.Y.: Cornell University Press, 1963.

———. *The New Science of Giambattista Vico.* Translated from 3d ed. (1744) by T. G. Bergin and M. H. Fisch. Rev. ed. Ithaca, N.Y.: Cornell University Press, 1968.

Waggoner, H. H. "Robinson Jeffers: Here is Reality." In his *The Heel of Elohim: Science and Values in Modern American Poetry,* pp. 105–32. Norman, Okla. University of Oklahoma Press, 1950.

———. "Science and the Poetry of Robinson Jeffers," *American Literature* 10 (Nov. 1938):275–88.

Walton, Eda Lou. "Beauty of Storm Disproportionately," *Poetry* 51 (Jan. 1938):209–13.

Watson, John B. *The Battle of Behaviorism.* London: K. Paul, Trench, Trübner, 1928.

Watts, Harold H. "Robinson Jeffers and Eating the Serpent," *Sewanee Review* 49 (Jan. 1941):39–55.

Wells, Henry W. *American Way of Poetry.* New York: Russell & Russell, 1943.

———. "A Philosophy of War: The Outlook of Robinson Jeffers," *College English* 6 (Nov. 1944):81–88.

Wilder, Amos N. "Nihilism of Mr. Robinson Jeffers." In his *The Spiritual Aspects of the New Poetry,* pp. 141–52. New York: Harper, 1940.

Willson, H. B. "Blood and Wounds in the 'Nibelungenlied,' " *Modern Language Review* 55 (1960):40–50.

Zabel, Morton D. "The Problem of Tragedy," *Poetry* 33 (Mar. 1929):336–40.

———. "A Prophet in His Wilderness," *New Republic* 77 (3 Jan. 1934):229–30. Review of *Give Your Heart to the Hawks and Other Poems.*

index